FALL*I*NG

DANCE IN DIALOGUE

Series Editors: Anita Gonzalez, Katerina Paramana and Victoria Thoms

The interdisciplinary books series *Dance in Dialogue* critically examines the relations between Performance, Dance, and other disciplines. It fosters interdisciplinary approaches, cross-disciplinary exchanges, and conversation as a mode of knowledge production. The series aims to offer new ways of interrogating the relation of performance and dance, in its broadest conception to include the body, embodiment, and the choreographic, to other disciplines and to political, cultural, social, and economic issues and contexts in and in relation to how it is created, presented, and theorised.

We seek to challenge the ways in which scholarship has been traditionally represented and disseminated, critically explore the dialogical relationship between theory and practice, and foster the ethos of collaboration, dialogue, and political engagement that is needed for vibrant knowledge production within and outside of academia. We encourage experimentation in publication format and research developed through innovative forms of collaborative and collective working across different modes of disciplinary and interdisciplinary inquiry and dissemination.

To realise this vision, the series offers two distinct publication formats via its two strands:

- *In Conversation*: A collection of short books that present radical thinking emerging from curated conversations between the body(ies)/performance/dance/choreography and another discipline, area of research, field of knowledge or practice on topical artistic, cultural, and political issues. Written by leading thinkers (artists and scholars) who critically explore the insights the different areas of knowledge and practice offer into one another, as well as the affordances, potentials, and implications of these insights for the contemporary world, these approximately 40,000-word books typically develop out of international conversation events and are published within approximately a year after them.
- *Moving Forward*: A collection of cutting-edge and forward-thinking, full-length monographs and edited collections that challenge understandings of the body(ies)/performance/dance/choreography and their relation to political, cultural, and socioeconomic issues and contexts, foster dialogue and interdisciplinarity, and critically explore the relationship between theory and practice.

Other titles in the series

Moving Forward titles:

The Choreopolitics of Alain Platel's les ballets C de la B:
Emotions, Gestures, Politics
Edited by Christel Stalpaert, Guy Cools and Hildegard De Vuyst

FALL*I*NG
through dance and life

Emilyn Claid

BLOOMSBURY ACADEMIC
LONDON • NEW YORK • OXFORD • NEW DELHI • SYDNEY

BLOOMSBURY ACADEMIC
Bloomsbury Publishing Plc
50 Bedford Square, London, WC1B 3DP, UK
1385 Broadway, New York, NY 10018, USA
29 Earlsfort Terrace, Dublin 2, Ireland

BLOOMSBURY, BLOOMSBURY ACADEMIC and the Diana logo are trademarks of Bloomsbury Publishing Plc

First published in Great Britain 2021
This paperback edition published 2022

Copyright © Emilyn Claid, 2021

Emilyn Claid has asserted her right under the Copyright,
Designs and Patents Act, 1988, to be identified as Author of this work.

For legal purposes the Acknowledgements on p. xii constitute an extension of this copyright page.

Series design by Charlotte Daniels
Cover image: Screenprint by silkeschelenzstudio.uk

All rights reserved. No part of this publication may be reproduced or transmitted in any form or by any means, electronic or mechanical, including photocopying, recording, or any information storage or retrieval system, without prior permission in writing from the publishers.

Bloomsbury Publishing Plc does not have any control over, or responsibility for, any third-party websites referred to or in this book. All internet addresses given in this book were correct at the time of going to press. The author and publisher regret any inconvenience caused if addresses have changed or sites have ceased to exist, but can accept no responsibility for any such changes.

A catalogue record for this book is available from the British Library.

Library of Congress Cataloging-in-Publication Data
Names: Claid, Emilyn, author.
Title: Falling through dance and life / Emilyn Claid.
Description: London ; New York : Bloomsbury Academic, 2021. | Series: Dance in dialogue | Includes bibliographical references. | Summary: "This is a book about falling as a means of reconfiguring our relationship with living and dying. Dancer, choreographer, educator and therapist, Emilyn Claid, draws inspiration from her personal and professional experiences to explore alternative approaches to being present in the world. Contemporary movement based performers ground their practices in understanding the interplay of gravity and the body. Somatic intentional falling provides them a creative resource for developing both self and environmental support. The physical, metaphorical and psychological impact of these practices informs the theories and perspectives presented in this book. As falling can be dangerous and painful, encouraging people to do so willingly might be considered a provocative premise. Western culture generally resists falling because it provokes fear and represents failure. Out of this tension a paradox emerges: falling, we are both powerless subjects and agents of change, a dynamic distinction that enlivens discussions throughout the writing. Emilyn engages with different dance genres, live performance and therapeutic interactions to form her ideas and interlaces her arguments with issues of gender and race. She describes how surrender to gravity can transform our perceptions and facilitate ways of being that are relational and life enhancing. Woven throughout, autobiographical, poetic, philosophical, descriptive and theoretical voices combine to question the fixation of Western culture on uprightness and supremacy. A simple act of falling builds momentum through eclectic discussions, uncovering connections to shame, laughter, trauma, ageing and the thrill of release"– Provided by publisher.
Identifiers: LCCN 2020045175 (print) | LCCN 2020045176 (ebook) | ISBN 9781350075719 (hardback) | ISBN 9781350075726 (ebook) | ISBN 9781350075733 (epub)
Subjects: LCSH: Dance–Pyschological aspects. | Dance–Physiological aspects. | Gravity in art. | Movement, Aesthetics of. | Claid, Emilyn. | Dancers–Biography.
Classification: LCC GV1588.5 .C53 2021 (print) | LCC GV1588.5 (ebook) | DDC 152.3—dc23
LC record available at https://lccn.loc.gov/2020045175
LC ebook record available at https://lccn.loc.gov/2020045176

ISBN: HB: 978-1-3500-7571-9
PB: 978-1-3502-0264-1
ePDF: 978-1-3500-7572-6
eBook: 978-1-3500-7573-3

Series: Dance in Dialogue

Typeset by RefineCatch Limited, Bungay, Suffolk

To find out more about our authors and books, visit www.bloomsbury.com and sign up for our newsletters.

For Lech

CONTENTS

List of Illustrations xi
Acknowledgements xii

Introduction 1
    Structure and content 3
    Falling through dance 4
    A practice of falling 7
    Conceptual falls 9
    A contextual fabric 11
    Back stories 14

1 Falling Apart 18
    A remedy 18
    Up is good 19
    Supreme feats 21
    Standing bones 23
    Rolling 26
    Stiff and brave 27
    Iconic heroine 29
    Earth's grief 31
    About dying 33
    Recalling ground 35
    Infant wisdom 37
    Under side 38
    Contact high 39
    The ladder scene 42
    Releasing dance 43
    A disgrace 44
    Constructing risk 45
    Bridge 46

Teeter totter 48
A still point 51
Packaging 51
Dying for love 52
Sublime banality 54
Endurance 56
Death dives 57
The buck stops here 59

2 Falling Out 62
A lumbering tilt 62
About shame 63
Dust 65
Pulling up 66
Grand slam 68
A dead black 69
Stiff upper lip 73
Not a black problem 75
Keeping face 78
A good white 79
Wrong bodies 80
A cool walk 82
Humiliate the boy 84
Cinderella in drag 87
Transaction 89
Yes to trash 90
Basiphobia 92
Grieving together 93
Meltdown 95
My son and me 95
April 2020 96
Optimistic deception 98
Stripped 101
Excessive slips 103

3 Falling Away 105
Sholiba 105
Forgetting 105

Vert leaps 107
Not going gently 108
Willing transition 111
Rigged flesh 111
Caught on the blink 113
A cold stage 116
Defiance 117
Angel wings 120
Thrills 121
Out of circus 123
Evoked companions 124
Sex in crisis 127
Failing success 132
Moro Reflex 133
Arête 133
A thump 135
Neutral buoyancy 136
A cliff edge 137
Lean On Me 140
Barefoot 141
Sand walking 142
Torturous delight 144

4 Falling About 148
Pratfalls 148
Star stumbles 151
About laughter 152
Nihilistic optimism 154
It's not funny 155
Gravestone laughs 157
Pen pals 163
Flattening the corpse 164
Feisty decay 165
Flip-flops and tunics 167
Gibberish 168
Represented real 170
Curiosity refreshed 172
What now 173

A void a day 176
Off your knees 177
Can I Let You Go? 179
Nothing in our way 180
Body stories 183
A cruel spring 186
Dance with me 187

Bibliography 188
Index 198

ILLUSTRATIONS

1.1	Jane Dudley in *Dancing Inside* (dir. Lacey, 1999).	36
1.2	Antonia Baehr in *Rire/Laugh/Lachen* (2008).	55
2.1	Colin Poole and Simon Ellis in *A Separation* (2014).	72
2.2	Joseph Mercier in *Giselle, or I'm too Horny to be a Prince* (2014).	85
2.3	*Arrangement* by Joe Moran (2014, 2019).	102
3.1	Lindsey Butcher in *Rites of War* (Gravity & Levity, 2013).	118
3.2	Lloyd Newson and Nigel Charnock in *My Sex, Our Dance* (1986).	130
3.3	*Keeping Up (butter shoes)*, Amy Sharrocks (2013 still).	142
3.4	Celeste Dandeker in a swivel walker (1984).	145
4.1	TC Howard in *Stupid Women* (Houstoun, 2015).	161
4.2	*Staging Ages* (H2Dance, 2015).	170
4.3	Mette Edvardsen in *No Title* (2014).	182

ACKNOWLEDGEMENTS

My thanks go to the following people for their encouragement, assistance, expertise, editorial skills and critical feedback: Chris Dukes, Rachael Gomme, Martin Hargreaves, Chris Jones, Joe Kelleher, Joseph Mercier, Lynda Osborne, Luke Pell, Timothy Spain and Fiona Williams. Thanks also to my colleagues at Falmouth University, University of Roehampton, the Dance in Dialogue series editors, Bloomsbury editors and to all the artists who have contributed to the ideas and practices in this book.

Introduction

An autumn afternoon in 2018. I am at my allotment in south-east London picking apples. My three-year-old grandson is with me. He keeps himself busy searching on the ground for windfalls. As he stands up, a breeze sweeps through the branches and an apple falls on his head. We look at each other in surprise and laugh.

Release your eyes from gazing at this page. Let the muscles of your face and jaw relax and drop your head forward. Notice the weight of your feet in contact with the ground. Focus on breathing out. Rest here for a while, sensing your body subject to gravity and supported by the ground . . . If you would like to continue reading, I welcome you to a discussion that draws inspiration from the gestures you have just embodied.

Why a book on falling? Why not flying or jumping? Anxious curiosity crosses people's faces, or jokes are cracked to ward off the gravity of the subject. Yes, falling is a dangerous topic on which to devote an entire book. The consequences of falling can be devastating – falling destroys lives, communities and infrastructures. Yet, with every moment of our time on Earth, with every breath and walking stride, we human beings are either falling or avoiding falling as a consequence of gravity – the consistent force that so profoundly affects all living things, all of the time. For the most part, certainly in Western culture, associations with falling are infused with fear and usually linked to injury, disfigurement, pain or death. But falling can also be a creative resource. It can nurture vitality and presence. I invite readers to engage with gravity with a sense of intent, to be curious about its productive potential, while respecting its danger and risk.

Advancing alternative perspectives on such a freighted theme stems from my life in dance and, in later years, from my practice as a psychotherapist. As a dancer, I learned to fall. Exploring ways to accept the uncertainty, loss of control and disorientation entailed in dropping towards the ground comprises a significant part of most dancers' experience. Later, training as a psychotherapist, I faced existential fears of desolation, loss and the inevitability of death, that can often resemble falling, into darkness, and sometimes make life feel unbearable. My familiarity through dance with intentional falling has provided me with embodied support and practical tools that I can now use with clients experiencing these psychological fears. As mind and body interrelate so vibrantly, a practice of intentional falling – surrendering to gravity to be supported by the ground – releases fluidity of thought and provides physical resources for living with psychological uncertainty. Intentional falling enhances capacity to manage fear, anxiety and panic. It helps loosen the tensions that petrify actions and hinder our ability to initiate change.

The danger of gravity is always present. Thinking differently about falling in this particular project does not mean disregarding gravity's propensity for wreaking damage throughout our lives and all around the globe. During earthquakes, people are crushed in collapsing buildings. Landfalls change both topography and the psychologies of entire communities. People falling to their deaths highlight the stark realities of gravity. It is a merciless force we take lightly at our peril. It demands we be careful, protect ourselves and reflect on our relationship with the environment. Falling is painful, scary, bruising and bloody. As a victim of gravity, I gasp and shiver at its unforgiving power. In addition, the fear of physical falling has infiltrated the English language through negative conceptual metaphors that are culturally defined, inflicting powerful psychological impact on how we function and feel in the world. The damaging consequences of living with gravitational force appear frequently in this book; some are shadows I can neither dismiss nor forget, commanding my attention, wrenching me away from my flights of fantasy on the subject of falling.

With no small amount of terror and uncertainty in the front of my mind, writing on gravity as a reassuring, creative and life-enhancing force confronts me with a paradox: how to embrace falling as a source of support and vitality when, ethically, conceptually and physically, falling evokes fear of death and the possibility of shame. Surely, we should hold on tight and shore up, to help mitigate uncertainty. Well ... falling is both dangerous *and* a source of vitality. Falling, we are powerless subjects *and* agents of change. This paradoxical tension remains ever present. When I propose an alternative imaginary about falling and enthuse about ways to sense and be present with gravity, I am also aware of the perils that have affected me personally and profoundly. Remembering when my son fell still sends tremors through my flesh and bones. My friend, Celeste Dandeker, suffered a catastrophic fall while dancing on stage, an accident that left her disabled, radically transforming her life and her community. And, how can I write about falling without confronting 9/11, an event that released radical and sustained uncertainty into the world? This tragedy, and many more, impact my body and inform my thinking throughout this project.

Maintaining a paradoxical tension between vitality and danger is crucial in this book and to this project. I am not campaigning for a resolution of the fear of falling. As long as the ground is hard, falling will hurt. Sensing fear is an important safety mechanism that helps us avoid the trauma of falling. I am wondering, though – in the light of my own experiences and those of the Euro-American community of movement-based performers – whether our negative, fear-based responses to gravity and falling, which have informed our concepts and influenced our language, might be eased and loosened through the practice of intentional falling. Without gravitational support to be with uncertainty and the precarities shaking Western life, we dampen both vivacity and presence, and diminish our openness to novel experiences, fresh perspectives and creative new ways of being in the world.

Structure and content

This book follows three interlacing thematic threads: falling through dance, a practice of falling, and conceptual falls. They weave through a contextual fabric of performance practices, theoretical frames, political ramblings, therapeutic considerations, traumatic events, death-defying thrills, hypothetical wanderings, descriptive narratives and personal stories. The writings are not grouped according to the three themes, ideas are woven into an assortment of scenes and arrayed throughout the book, interrupting linearity and inviting imaginative associations. I introduce the threads here to provide a framework through which to view the scenes.

The first thread, falling through dance, highlights the wealth of relationships that Western dancers and choreographers have explored with gravity since the mid-twentieth century: American modern dance, somatic movement practices, physical theatre, dance theatre, live art and the current era of post-dance. I draw on my own experience – and reflect on the work of performers and performance-makers – to describe many instances where falling becomes a signature gesture of artistic and cultural politics.

The second thread consists of intentional falling practices, an accumulation of activities exploring gravity and ground, developed through my life-long commitment to dance. These practices have matured over years of teaching and of facilitating workshops with dancers and non-dancers – particularly psychotherapists. The book offers a series of tasks with which readers might experiment. Some are as simple as breathing out, dropping the head, or rethinking ways to get down to the ground; others are suggestions for standing and walking that work with gravity, rather than fighting against it. These experimental exercises include falling alone, supported falling and ways of being around others who fall. They induce subtle shifts in our approach to gravity and encourage the development of self-support strategies for co-existing with this inexorable force. As a result, they facilitate fluidity of thought, and loosen the rigidity of our fears around falling.

The third thematic thread – conceptual falls – winds through considerations of shame, laughter and dying, along with a range of involuntary sensations kindled by falling. As life experiences, shame, laughter and dying are transformational processes, they happen to and between us. As concepts, they are framed and informed by linguistic metaphors, which link fear and negativity to physical acts of falling, affecting the way we experience gravity and how we process the involuntary sensations incurred. Gravitational forces and the physicality of falling (or not falling) shape Western culture socially, politically and racially through the linguistic synthesis of physical experience, metaphor and psychology. My aim in this book is to give particular focus to artists who – reversing negative cultural associations – are finding ways to *be with* shame, laughter and dying, and to explore the creative potential of these phenomena in life and performance.

I have structured the contents of this book as I would choreography. Ideas comprising the three threads within their contextual fabric are presented as standalone writings – images in a tapestry – grouped into four sections. The book presents a collage of scenes arranged to texture their dynamics and rhythms. Much like performers, topics enter and exit; ideas are juxtaposed, contrasted, echoed and allowed to dissolve. Descriptive, theoretical, historical, analytical, poetic, performative and personal writings, together with artists' interviews, are placed next to one another often for their differences rather than similarities. I have used a choreographic structure of fragmentation to avoid linear narratives or definitive logic. I hope fresh thoughts develop with the help of readers' associative and imaginative capacities, rather than piling up incrementally. Falling – as a theme – calls for such a structure, where the writing can undo, unfix, drop and let go into liminal areas with uncertain outcomes.

There is no specific order in which to read the material and no beginning, middle or end, other than the unavoidable delineation of page numbers. There is no conclusion to sum up the themes or to provide an ending to seal ideas in place. There is no goal to rush towards. I encourage readers to open this volume at any page, slow down to engage with different passages, allow multiple understandings to tumble about simultaneously and make spontaneous connections between disparate slivers of things. No scene is more important than any other, and each scene falls into a gap between two other pieces. The gaps between fragments, which interrupt a through-line, are intended to give pause, to allow for impact, and, like falling, to ruffle the flow of making meaning.

Falling through dance

The following helter-skelter ride to introduce falling through dance is intended to provide a broad narrative thread about practices and ideas that will be unravelled and argued more fully throughout the book. The choice of events is based on my lived experiences as a dance artist and as a white woman, inevitably bound by my culture, race, gender and age. This is a personal rather than a general dance history about dance and falling, an experiential perspective that provides a basis for practice-led research, allowing me to stretch outwards from my own body to engage with a wide range of movement-based performance, with artistic and theoretical deliberations.

The field of somatic studies undoubtedly lends itself to a philosophy of falling as a creative resource. Somatic movement practices are grounded in sensation – feeling in every sense – as experienced by body and mind in response to internal and external environments. The term *somatic* was coined by Thomas Hanna in 1970; for Hanna, *soma* refers to an experiencing body, rather than a body objectified. An understanding of somatic movement practices grows from bodily perceived sensations, rather than from external objective goals, whereby behaviour, emotions, the senses, movements and psychology are all integrated as psycho-physical or mind-body wholeness. Hyper-awareness of the body in relation to gravity and ground is the throbbing pulse of somatic movement practices.

Mabel Elsworth Todd and Barbara Clark were somatic movement pioneers who researched human movement development through two overlapping practices of movement-thought: body mechanics (working with anatomical structures) and ideokinesis (sensorial imagery).[1] These practices encourage an undoing of habitual, fixed patterns of movement, incorporating core principles deeply connected to an interdependent relationship between body, gravity and environment (ground). The impact of a somatic approach on dance as a performing art was, and is, immense, particularly through the practice of Release Technique. Current contemporary dance practices such as Flying Low and Passing Through – developed by David Zambrano – are enlivened by a somatic, released-based understanding of gravity. Dancers are liberated from the tensions of upwardly orientated alignment to explore a wealth of gravity-embracing possibilities which vastly enrich their choreographic and improvisational adventures.

In the 1930s, as Mabel Elsworth Todd was teaching in New York and the dance marathons of the Great Depression were in full swing, Martha Graham was in her element. Acclaimed choreographer of American Modern Dance,[2] Martha created a technique of falling that became a signature component of her choreographic vocabulary. Her falls emphasized an individual's rise out of darkness into light, a movement philosophy rejected by somatic practitioners, both in practice and in politics.

The heroic dynamics of modern dance provided a backdrop against which American post-modern dance artists in the 1960s and 1970s moved

---

[1]Somatic pioneers include: Frederick Alexander, Lulu Sweigard, Joan Skinner, Bonnie Bainbridge Cohen, Elsa Gindler, Ida Rolf, Irmgard Bartenieff, Charlotte Selver and Moshé Feldenkrais.
[2]Doris Humphrey, another modern dance choreographer at the time, also integrated falling, working with an ideology of up and down as 'two polar extremes of balance and unbalance' (McDonagh 1990: 17), physicalized through use of breath and rhythmic swing. Yet falls were not essential to Doris's training. She was influenced by Todd's work on body mechanics when they both taught at the New School of Social Research in 1931 (Huxley 2012).

in stark relief, while exploring a novel relationship to gravity. Steve Paxton, founder of Contact Improvisation (CI), emerged as a seminal figure in this movement. Falling constitutes a key component in CI practice and philosophy. Since the 1960s, CI's influence on the dynamic space of falling has inspired both choreographic and improvisational innovation in the dancing of duets, shifting not only the gender fixation on men lifting women – familiar in most conventional dance forms – but transforming as well the traditional aesthetics of upward linearity. Freed from fixed expectations about lifting, duet dancing could now be about partnered falling.

By the late 1970s, Europe was afire with innovations in dance theatre, primarily sparked by Pina Bausch in Germany and Jan Fabre in Belgium. These artists pushed against boundaries constructed by a different dance history than that of America. While US dance innovators were resisting the heroic ideals of modern dance, European dance theatre artists were rejecting the traditions of ballet and German expressionist dance. They initiated a violent break – not only with the movement vocabularies previously in place – but also with the hierarchical, choreographic structures that promoted those traditions (Laermans and Gielen 2000; Servos 2008).

This break began in the studio, between dance-makers and performers. Whereas post-modern artists, somatic practitioners and contact improvisers looked to internally discovered impulses for motivation, European dance and physical theatre performers brought the entire human mess into the studio, exposing the realities of relations of desire. Following Pina Bausch, dance and physical theatre directors such as Lloyd Newson and Wim Vandekeybus devised work *with* performers; their personal lives and their relations with one another became potential material, unleashing in performance the energy of loss, abandonment, love, power, sexuality and aggression. Falling – as a commitment to descent and not as a prelude to upward recovery – became a principal trope defining dance and physical theatre, inhibiting the harmonious flow of movement through time and space.

During this period, conservatoire dance training incorporated CI and Release Technique into the curriculum to provide an additional layer of technical skill – muscular fitness with somatic intelligence. As a consequence, dancers' physical abilities to perform risk-taking falls became extraordinarily inventive. Just as ballet is renowned for its dazzling transcendent linearity, so falling in dance theatre became spectacular, with lightning-fast, highly skilled, gravity-relishing splats. Dance theatre and ballet, though far apart aesthetically, were now fused as opposite sides of the same theatrical coin, as commodities in a market valuing spectacle above all (Debord 1967; Lepecki 2006). As with most innovative dance practices, dance theatre falls became packaged and codified in the lexicon of contemporary dance movement, and by end of the 1990s was known as Eurocrash (Brennan 1997).

Following on from the innovations of dance and physical theatre, European dance artists engendered another vital paradigm shift in the late 1980s and 1990s. Dance artists such as Jerome Bel, Xavier Le Roy,

Jonathan Burrows and Boris Charmatz, influenced by the multi-dimensional connections of contemporary culture, began drawing on an eclectic mix of visual art, live art, conceptual art, minimalism and theatre to make inter-disciplinary dance performance, working in galleries and site specific spaces, rather than, only, proscenium stages (Heathfield 2006). As dance artists' practices became inter-disciplinary, the lines between live art and dance became blurred. Scattered throughout this book are references to live art performers, such as Bas Jan Ader and Kira O'Reilly, who also expose (or have exposed) their human vulnerability through physical acts of falling.

The current exhaustion in dance is partly a result of perpetual efforts to meet demands for innovation and the disappointment of seeing innovation repackaged in a neo-liberal capitalist market. Paradoxically, current funding for dance innovation, certainly in the UK, continues to be a low priority for arts funding bodies. At the time of writing, dance performance finds itself at an intriguing impasse, falling away from the production of capitalist spectacle, while exploring ways to exist with the economic uncertainty of foregoing conventional production values. 'At the end of this 50 year period we find ourselves unsure whether we want any more to dance at all. Which doesn't mean we don't like to dance, but that we're not quite sure where to go with it' (Burrows 2017: 94). Fatigued by dance spectacle, independent dance artists such as Mette Edvardsen and Mårten Spångberg are questioning the purpose of dance performance, echoing the post-modern agendas of New York City's Judson Church movement in the 1960s and new dance politics in the UK in the 1970s (Claid 2006).

Encounters with falling in modern dance, somatic processes, physical theatre, contact improvisation, performance art, and dance theatre – and throughout this period of post-dance exhaustion – have all contributed to my current view of falling as a potentially creative resource. The history of these experiments informs the practice of falling as a way to live with and embrace the *potency* of gravity as vital presence. Experiences with these practices have informed my research and today inspire the rituals with gravity that influence the flow of ideas in this project.

A practice of falling

The intentional acts of falling giving ballast to this project aim to increase vitality and a sense of immediacy, by developing environmental and self-support that appear when we loosen physical fears and our rigid thinking around falling. A second goal in advocating intentional falling is to examine the ways in which negative associations with falling permeate language and culture. The impact of gravity on the human body resonates through language in the form of metaphors defining spatial and emotional concepts (Lakoff and Johnson 1980). As body, psychology, language and culture are all interdependent, these metaphors influence psychological states and inform physical gestures. Separating this circuitry would be an impossible task, like trying to separate body from mind. The idea, then, with a practice of falling is that interacting with gravity in alternative ways can initiate psychological and conceptual shifts.

The practice is presented as a series of activities that, within a workshop context, provide multi-layered experiences. Honed through dance and psychotherapy practice, these activities invite readers into their bodies, providing physical immediacy with the ideas in the writing. The activities are offered as safely structured suggestions with which to explore our being. Importantly, they require no dance skills.

The diverse communities of practitioners in dance and psychotherapy approach falling differently. I mention these differences because working in both fields has helped me develop falling tasks that – while eminently physical – depend on the holistic instincts and subjective conviction that people bring to the process, rather than on codified dance techniques.[3] Trained contemporary dancers fall gracefully and quietly. They are muscularly assured, physically co-ordinated and often familiar with such forms as Aikido, Release Technique, CI and Flying Low. Training of this kind facilitates easy descent to the ground. Contemporary dancers *trust* the ground. They are familiar with coded movements on different levels in all directions and with a somatic understanding of the restorative function of interacting with gravity through physical training. The price of this facility – this access to physical grace – is that dancers tend to leave their emotions and humanity outside the studio, and rely instead on their disciplined bodies and codified skills. In the studio, repetitive engagement with movement prevails, and movement sequences happen so fast there is little time to *sense* the impact of falling or even of witnessing falling.

Furthermore, dancers often feel shame when the slightest gesture slips out of conformity with the aesthetic code to which they ascribe. To add salt to the wound – or sugar to the pie – when a dancer slips out of code, others will compensate with understanding and sweetness – anything to avoid shaming. Confluence is essential. Hugs abound, ruptures are rare, differences ignored. The more skilful the fall, the less sensation is felt. When I facilitate falling workshops with professional dancers, my purpose is to encourage human-ness in the studio, building trust between dancers as different *people*, rather than as dancers.

Facilitating workshops with non-dancers is different. Psychotherapists generally have no difficulty bringing their whole selves into the room and making themselves available to interact with one another. Their fears of falling, though, are often close to the surface, together with traumatic

---

[3]These observations are derived from my workshops on falling at psychotherapy conferences in Asilomar, Brisbane, Taormina, Toronto and the UK and dance workshops in Auckland, Brisbane, Melbourne, London, Leeds, Falmouth and Dartington since 2013.

responses of flight or freeze. They can be emotionally affected by seeing each other falling. Very small gestures of falling are enough to evoke powerful relational and empathic responses. Acts of intentional falling are challenging for non-dancers. Focusing attention on the intimate sensations of gravity's effects on their bodies can provoke fearful and shameful moments. So, tasks begin with lying on the ground – the safest place to sense the body in gravity (grounding) – and through slow and careful trust-building procedures culminate in dancing together, where participants feel the impact of letting their partners fall (Osborne and Claid 2015).

I invite readers who are dancers to bring their human selves, cultural differences and their gendered emotional bodies into the practice of falling, as well as their codified skills. For readers who are not dancers, I suggest approaching the falling activities as safely constructed experiments in challenging preconceived expectations. I trust disabled readers to adjust acts of falling to suit their individual bodies.

Conceptual falls

Shame, laughter and dying are not necessarily physical falls, but their conceptualization in language and metaphor emphasizes downward trajectories. Metaphor pervades everyday life as everyday life pervades metaphor. Language used to define emotion depends on orientational metaphors, which in turn use imagery from the motor-function system, further embedding the connections of motion and emotion through language. Many parents in the West experience a feeling of pride when their child first stands up, and conversely, a feeling of shame when their child falls behind other children in learning to walk. Emotions develop through physical experiences and are shaped by language. Bodily states influence language, just as language conditions bodily states. When metaphors are negatively framed, negativity feeds back into bodies and informs emotions and movement.

Shame draws its conceptual clarity from orientational metaphors, persistently reflected as downward sinking. As linguistic theorist Zoltán Kövecses confirms in his study of emotion and metaphor, language 'is not only a reflection of the experiences but it also creates them. Simply put, we say what we feel and we feel what we say' (2000: 192). The metaphorical conceptualization of shame includes phrases such as 'bury my head in the sand', 'weighing him down' and 'shattered' (Kövecses 2000: 33). My own experiences of shame fuse the sinking sensation of *being* shamed as a woman and a dancer with – as a white woman of privilege – an inherited potential to shame others.

In the West, racism has thrived on the persistent, toxic shaming of black people by whites. The field of dance is no exception, a reality I know well from my familiarity with the institutional racism in Eurocentric ballet. The white shame of racism (Eddo-Lodge 2017; Irving 2014) shadowed the work of post-modern and new dance artists in the 1960s and 1970s. It helped drive the artistic agendas of white artists toward a rejection of spectacle through somatic engagement, to relinquish the quest for heroic identity. Yet for many black artist/researchers such as Thomas de Frantz, establishing black identity has been a primary aim, pursued within the same artistic and economic frames where white artists work to undo identity (Claid 2006). As the current post-dance era encourages conceptual questioning of, and writing about – while barely doing – dance, I find myself wondering if this is yet another white artists' agenda. Black dance artists, meanwhile, have embodied falling gestures of shame as sources of pride, featured prominently in break dance, hip hop and voguing.[4] Black performance artists, such as Colin Poole and Pope L., have seized derogatory terms and creatively put them to use in performance, and – by physically and figuratively 'getting down' – embracing gravity's artistic possibilities (King 2004).

Laughter's associations with orientational metaphors also come into focus. A pleasurable release, laughter destabilizes and renders us helpless in desirable ways, as language reflects with metaphors like dissolving, creasing up, cracking up, collapsing, gagging, convulsing, bursting, flailing, losing it, doubled over and falling about laughing. In performance, laughter physically undoes an audience. When laughter is unleashed by performers falling, as in Wendy Houstoun's work, then a delicious double act of falling-about-laughing-about-falling occurs between performers and spectators. With the notoriously ignoble pratfall, humour is sparked with physical rather than verbal skills; spectators laugh, performers do not. I am intrigued as well by a contrasting scenario, where inter-disciplinary artists such as La Ribot and Antonia Baehr – who employ significant, yet different, approaches to falling – use laughter as a choreographic tool, or as abstract material. Spectators do not laugh. Or rather, spectators *might* laugh in response to relational infectious affect, but the works themselves do not aim to amuse. The performers' laughter is presented in ways other than as triggers of humour for spectators.

Ageing is a process of falling and failing. Flesh falls, face falls, skin falls; as skeletons accommodate gravity's constant pull, joints may stiffen with the effort of keeping bodies upright. In Western culture and language, metaphors for ageing reinforce the process: over the hill, craggy, frail, fragile, rickety, one foot in the grave, running out of gas and falling like porcelain figures (Buta et al. 2018). Yet, for many ageing people, thinking enters its richest phase, which seems to suggest that dying is a time when body and mind no longer synchronize (Nakajima 2017). As with shame and laughter, I am

---

[4]In the UK, *Breakin' Convention – International Festival of Hip Hop Dance Theatre* provides a performance platform for innovative contemporary dance practices by black artists.

attempting to *be with* ageing as a source of vibrant presence. Rather than replacing stereotypes around ageing with new, chipper, positive messages (Gullette 2004; Martin 2017), I am asking myself, what is emerging – now – in this falling towards death? Two films – *Dancing Inside* (Lacey 1999), featuring teacher and dancer Jane Dudley just before she died, and *Returning Home* (Abrahams 2003) about Anna Halprin – show ageing dancers embracing dying with curiosity for what the process reveals.

Shame, laughter and dying are three different kinds of falling, often framed with metaphors based on physical falls, which inform in turn the embodied experience of these concepts. As the aim of this project is to embrace the relationship of body, gravity and ground, I address the ways performers are rethinking laughter, dying and shame through artistic and imaginative engagement with falling. When falling is reconsidered – is reappraised as a source of vitality, presence and immediacy – then language may evolve, and laughter, shame and dying can be seen through a different lens.

A contextual fabric

Without a doubt, this is a practice-led research project. It might begin with the simplest of movement practices – a release of a smile, an exhalation of breath – but these embodied gestures are, even in their micro realization, already deeply interconnected to wider contextual fields of socio-cultural politics, philosophies and artistic endeavours. 'Nobody works in a vacuum; all creative work operates within – or reacts against – established discourses' (Nelson 2006: 113–14). Culturally and politically, I have been writing this book throughout the UK's drawn-out departure from the European Union (2016–20), a withdrawal supported, marginally, by over half the population and spurred in part by government promises of returning productivity and wealth – without foreign intrusion. The period leading up to separation has been one of sadness for many, including myself. The British government seemed intent – even belligerent – about selling a dream that sailing alone into the world at large will take us somewhere better. Time will tell, but I look for ways of supporting myself through instability and isolation – baldly emphasized as Covid-19 overtook the Brexit process, increasing the sense of precarity in the minds and bodies of our global community.

I am writing, as well, at a time when a majority of citizens in the United States are influenced by promises from President Trump that the country can once again be *great*. As the West falls further into economic decline, Western powers have been clawing at the shirt tails of their histories in attempts to recover pride through nationalism, protectionism and isolation. One way to explain the effects of capitalist decline is through the changes taking place in production. The meaning of life-long work has changed (Berlant 2011;

Weeks 2011; Kleinman 2019). Mass production for capitalist markets promised security, pride and unassailable identity at the end of a long working life, along with the widespread employment of both skilled and unskilled labour. In postmodern capitalism, mass production has been replaced by diversity and flexibility in both production and workforce. Technology and automation are driving these shifts and require specialized skills to meet and service specific market demands. Post-Fordist capitalism stimulates and consumes innovation and creativity, but working opportunities are uneven, uncertain, globally competitive, and unavailable to increasing numbers of workers. In these rapidly changing circumstances – often characterized as a knowledge-based economy – there are no promises of long-term employment and no hierarchical ladders to climb.

Most independent dance artists are familiar with precarious conditions and know these declining capitalist production values well; we move between freelance employments around the globe with frequent uncertainty and little economic stability. Mass production brought repetition and boredom, yet stability for working people. The knowledge-based economy inspires flexibility and innovation, yet widespread precarity and, for many, loss of purpose, lack of direction, poverty and feelings of shame. Many dance and performance artists bolster their ability to function in uncertainty with an embodied intimacy with gravity and ground, fostering agile relations with an unreliable, neo-liberal capitalist frame.

I am not proposing falling as a solution to capitalist decline and radical uncertainty – nor as a return to what was – but as a way to co-exist with decline, precarity and the challenge of not knowing. Western leaders' attempts to preserve capitalist progress and all it represents – pride in individualism, an exclusive sense of rightness and the privileges of whiteness – are becoming increasingly unconvincing. For many people, dreams of a capitalist good life have collapsed and there is no alternative to reach for. A practice of being with gravity, falling to ground, may seem insignificant, minuscule in the global context, yet I propose it here as a kind of sustenance, a means of co-existing with capitalist decline and the shame and uncertainty that follows. My thinking is enriched by André Lepecki's writings on dance and exhaustion (2006), and the writings of Ann Cooper Albright (2013, 2017), including her latest book *How to Land: Finding Ground in an Unstable World* (2019) which was published just as I was completing the final draft of this book. Albright explores falling through her teaching practice, CI, and her writings on the political, social and economic unpredictability in Western current affairs align with my ideas.

Another contextual frame hovering above the arena of falls is the co-dependent coupling of fear and thrills. For many, playing with gravity is a life-enhancing prospect. Enthusiasts seek out increasingly spectacular and risky extreme sports – vertiginous interfaces with the adrenalin, excitement and terror of almost falling. Some dance and circus artists, such as John-Paul Zaccarini, Elizabeth Streb, Lindsey Butcher and Kate Lawrence, are drawn irresistibly to heights and near-death falling experiences, gambling their bodies – their primary means of livelihood – on the spectacular rewards of gravity-defying productions. Working at great heights compels performers to override their fears of falling, while simultaneously testing those fears. Training for aerial work drives these artists daily beyond the limits of physical pain. As their bodies become desensitized, the need for increasing risks to achieve similar levels of fear and reward intensifies. For the same reasons, enthusiasts are drawn to see increasingly dangerous high-flying stunts, queue for hours for ever-more elaborate roller coaster thrills, or stand at the edge of precipitous drops for intimate encounters with vertigo. The catalyst sparking fascination with heights is the adrenalin-charged terror of what could happen and sometimes does – the prospect of falling to one's death.

The entire falling project draws inspiration from queer sensibilities and perspectives. The underlying philosophy of falling reflects the undoing by queer performers of monolithic, normative identities. This falling, as a movement of unmoored transition, reflects a queering of desire, an embodied process of desiring – without fixed objects – and devoid of predetermined goals (Probyn 1995; Grosz 1995). Falling itself becomes an act of submission, an invigorating acquiescence which queer theorists Halperin and Traub (2009) describe as queer shame, itself a site of creativity and of resistance to the normalizing principles of both heteronormativity and gay pride. I consider the work of performers Nigel Charnock, Joseph Mercier and Joe Moran through a similar lens, with attention to the tactics these queer artists use to undo fixed identities. I look as well to the work of Lauren Berlant (2011), Jack Halberstam (2011) and Judith Butler (2004), who characterize queer attitudes to shame, falling and failure as creative strategies for surviving political uncertainty.

An important contextual frame for rethinking body, gravity and ground, is the interwoven network of dance with humanistic pyschotherapies, which draws extensively from somatic principles. Mabel Elsworth Todd, Thomas Hanna and Barbara Clark were intensely aware of how the cultural, psychological and physical aspects of being human are inseparable. In the 1960s, when Gestalt therapy founder Fritz Perls worked closely with dancer Anna Halprin, they significantly influenced each other's work (Ross and Schechner 2007). Psychotherapists Ruella Frank and Frances La Barre (2011) draw on Bonnie Bainbridge Cohen's Body–Mind Centering and the developmental movement patterns of yield, push, reach, pull, grasp and release that occur between infant and carer, and which continue to affect adult relationships. Psychotherapists Peter Levine (1997), Babette Rothschild (2000), Pat Ogden and Janine Fisher (2015) integrate somatic awareness into their work with trauma clients. *The Oxford Handbook of Dance and Wellbeing* (Karkov, Oliver and Lycouris 2017) makes continual reference to the interrelationship of therapy and somatic studies. Existential psychotherapy's intersubjective leanings – where 'I' does not exist apart from 'you' – have deeply informed the perception of psychological falling as a relational experience, rather than individually isolating, and therefore as less fearful or painful. This intermingling of somatics with psychotherapy permeates this book as a strategy for mitigating traumatic fears of falling.

Back stories

Ever since I dropped out of ballet as a young person, this project has been waiting to emerge in writing. The impetus that first set my thoughts whirling around the notion of falling as a productive resource comes from my own experiences. Like smouldering coals warming ideas from within, lived experience reminds me that the best theories and concepts quickly grow cold without an experiential glow. My story has a typical beginning for a middle-class white girl growing up in the UK. I was a child star, destined to shine amongst other stars in a transcendent universe of bejewelled ballerinas. A dedicated stage-school student, I was swept up in a constant whirl of performances, rehearsals, exams and competitions. With medals and silver cups galore, I rose up and up, with praise and rewards just barely outweighing the daily doses of criticism. I was going to be first a soloist, then a principal dancer. I would be famous. I would eventually have a school of my own – and then get married, of course. That was my dream, and I went blindly forward, flying to Toronto at age sixteen to join the National Ballet of Canada.

The tipping point came fast. A nagging, debilitating pain in my foot was diagnosed as osteoarthritis, to which I refused to admit. Eating disorders engulfed me, casting shadows over my days and every waking hour. With my forbidden indulgences, I quickly put on weight. I was too tall to be partnered and my tits – for a ballet dancer – were of impressive size. Wherever I congregated with other dancers, I was placed at the end of the line, at the back of the stage, as the tallest swan, an oversized snowflake or some forlorn flower wheeled on to waltz on a creaking, shuddering trolley. Despite some interesting acting roles during my second year in the ballet company, like Mercutio's gypsy galpal in *Romeo and Juliet* (Cranko 1962) and the Black Queen in Erik Bruhn's *Swan Lake* (1966), I was rented out most of the time to carry a spear – well upstage – in Canadian Opera Company productions. Toward the end of my second year, French choreographer Roland Petit arrived in Toronto to stage *Kraanerg* (1969). The cast lists went up and my name was *not* there, not even as understudy. I left the company soon after. The shame of failure was an overwhelming sensation of falling with no supportive ground.

Looking back, this shaming was the start of some riotously creative encounters with uncertainty – about life and dance – uncertainty shaped by continual questioning and falling out of normativity, out of established codes. I fell from the height of my pink *pointe* shoe tips to the cultural depths of stomping around in Doc Martens; from high leg extensions to somatic body work; from holding-on-breathing-in to letting-go-breathing-out; from my expectations of a white wedding dress to the delicious ambiguities of queer life; from the formal hierarchies of institutional structures to messy failures of collective work; from muscular youth to the worn reality of wrinkled skin; from theatrical narratives of hope and love to existential acceptance of nothingness. A continuous slope downward of unexpected riches, my life turns out to be an ever-changing, always surprising, inventive process, transmuting between dance artist, writer, choreographer, teacher, lesbian, mother, queer, psychotherapist and academic researcher. I see my life as a long, slow pratfall, a seriously exhilarating laugh towards dying. My story begins with the shame of failure; yet *being with* that failure, working through that shame, with no attempts to find redemption, has taught me failure's potential to inspire creative change. Since failure in Western culture is characterized using metaphors based on falling, my experiences have prepared me to engage with the physicality of falling as a stimulating resource for reframing apparent flops.

Writing about falling, as a practice-led research project, began when I broached PhD studies in the 1990s. Notions of falling ran through my thoughts as an ever-present undercurrent while I was teasing out a queer perspective on androgyny in dance, exploring the seductive qualities of performers who, in movement language and aesthetics, were sliding on a spectrum, playing between the performative traits of masculinity and femininity. In 2004, *Women in Performance: A Journal of Feminist Theory* produced a volume of writings called 'Falling'. Published five years after 9/11, when the Western world was still reeling with trauma, this volume focuses bravely on an array of falling in dance, while remaining sensitive to the potential triggering effects such discussions might unleash. Ellen Graff gives detailed descriptions of the choreographic falls of Martha Graham. André Lepecki reflects on issues of racism and colonialism, citing Heidegger's notion of instability as integral to being and presence. Jennifer Fisher writes about falling in love in the ballet *Romeo and Juliet*, with vivid descriptions of the physicality of balletic swooning. Particularly useful in this volume is Jason King's account of the creative strategies black artists use to effectively refigure white stereotypes of black failure.

In 2013, I co-edited an issue of *Performance Research* called 'On Falling', with theatre writer Ric Allsopp, containing contributions from across performance disciplines. We grouped the writings under three rubrics: falling as physical risk; artistic promise; and metaphor. Catherine James writes about vertigo, the construction of New York skyscrapers and the risky stunts of comic silent film actor Harold Lloyd. Amy Sharrocks lays out an overview of falling in live art, while writers Charlie Fox and Francisco Sousa Lobo examine the work of Jas Ban Ader and his live-art enactments of falling. Hari Marini writes of the slow weathering of the brutalist architecture of London's National Theatre. Ann Cooper Albright's writing on contact improvisation draws parallels to Denis Darzacq's photographs of young hip-hop dancers caught falling in mid-air.

While providing useful insights and parallels, the two issues of these journals do not articulate a practice of falling which, for this project, remains central to the subsequent lines of inquiry and forms a crucible where ideas take shape and evolve. To address this lack I facilitated the *Falling About* research lab in 2013, designed to allow practitioners from various disciplines to share practices, reflections and experiences of falling.[5] Sixty artists, academics, students and teachers met for a weekend at London's Siobhan Davies Dance Studios to engage in a welter of activities and discussions on the theme of falling. Performances, interventions and installations were shared by practitioners from the fields of live art, theology, architecture, music, physical theatre and circus.

The first morning was devoted to the falling practices embedded within a range of disciplines. Susan Sentler led participants through the intricacies of Graham falls, and explained that the most direct access to Martha's sense of falling was through the experience of 'laughing or crying'. Erica Stanton taught us a swing from choreographer José Limón, who incorporated falling into his movement philosophy of breath, weight, suspension, fall and recovery. Working with contact improviser Lalitaraja, we closed our eyes while he took us through an experience of the Small Dance as initiated in the 1970s by Steve Paxton. Stefanie Sachsenmaier demonstrated dropping and sinking, practised in the basic stance and initial gestures of a t'ai chi sequence. With Peri Mackintosh, we learned how to support a partner down to the floor in an aikido fall: 'Welcome your partner into your own sinking verticality. Invite them into your own drop' (Mackintosh 2013). Each of these falls illustrates core elements of its host technique and style. Each intentional surrender to gravity follows a set of rules within a codified system and, to achieve mastery, requires habitual repetition and the development of skills.

The lab moved on to contributions from practitioners in fields other than dance. Theologist Johanne Hoff talked about The Fall in Christianity; architect Frances Hollis presented images of falling buildings; musician Simon Limbrick explored the ways the lower registers create sensations of weight in music; circus performer Peta Lily led a session on clowning skills; live artist/sculptor Amy Sharrocks set up an installation of shoes that invite acts of falling – such as high heels and stilts – and encouraged participants to experiment. Each presenter was asked to address the ways acts of falling in their own field – rather than recovery from falling – might be considered creative resources.

---

[5] Quotes from participants at the lab can be found at https://roehamptondance.com/falling/writings/

The second day we walked, ran, fell about and supported each other falling without reliance on specific technical codes. We experimented with relational falling and took note of the emotional impact of witnessing someone else falling. These activities drew our attention to the inseparable nature of the physical, metaphorical and psychological impacts of falling. Reflecting on the lab inspired me in ways that have informed the ideas for this book: to practise physical falling requires environmental safety; due to their reliance on technical codes, dancers have less fear of falling than non-dancers; laughter – like falling – is a sensation of uncontrollable imbalance between one familiar state and another; spectacular, fast or physically dangerous falls are not necessary for experiencing the effects of falling; the release of a smile, or the drop of a head have relational impact; falling itself is relational and happens when humans encounter one another; a gap of silence and stillness can provoke feelings of shame, absurdity, uncertainty and nothingness.

These back stories highlight important characteristics found throughout this venture. Lived experience entwines with contextual theories. The physical, psychological and metaphorical aspects of falling are synchronized in Western culture to define failure. A simple micro-gesture alluding to falling can evoke macro-global concerns. Fundamentally, thinking and moving through a framework of falling unleashes creative reworkings of fixed hierarchies of knowledge.

In the early months of 2020, the coronavirus pandemic swept around the globe. I completed this book's final draft as the virus took hold of Europe. By the time this book is published, perspectives will have changed, and the ideas discussed will resonate differently. This collection of writings on falling moves towards publication at a time when many of our theories, practices and institutions are themselves in free fall. We are letting go of much of what we have taken for granted and reconsidering our approach to everything. While the tone of the writing reflects life before Covid-19, the ideas and practices discussed in this book are even more relevant now. The aim of this project is always to offer support in the face of uncertainty, to suggest ways of rethinking our dependence on verticality and to provide physical and psychological strategies for re-valuing our relations to gravity during times of chaos.

Note: I intentionally use different systems for referencing names. When writing about artists, dancers, choreographers, teachers and performers, I use their first names. Their contributions are intersubjective, relational processes where respectful informality facilitates fluid, creative dialogue. Following academic protocols, I reference the *writings* of theorists and artists by citing their last names. With this method, I hope to highlight the contrasting qualities of live practices and written texts, and invite readers to engage with the source materials from a range of embodied and intellectual perspectives.

1

Falling Apart

A REMEDY

I dedicated a week to intentional falling, in a dance studio, in 2013. For three hours each day, I fell down: slowly at first, then gradually getting faster, then tumbling, crashing and sliding, my body finding its confidence and becoming looser and freer as the week progressed. I fell while standing still, from chairs and from walking, running and rolling down stairs. I felt tired, bruised but exhilarated. After five days I stood still in the studio and imagined myself falling, remembering in my body the distance, energy, impact and sensations of dropping to the ground. I did not need to keep falling to know I could fall. I was standing up, but with the sensations of letting go always present. My body, gravity and the ground were interconnected. I experienced a state of continuously dropping while standing still. Falling was now 'imprinted and distilled as a *sense* and remembered on my body as potency' (Claid 2018).

'Potency' is a term I appropriate from homeopathy and homeopathic remedies. The British Homeopathic Association describes homeopathy as 'a form of holistic medicine ... based on the principle of "like cures like" – in other words, a substance taken in small amounts will cure the same symptoms it causes if it was taken in large amounts' (Hahnemann [1842] 2001). The amounts are, in fact, minuscule. The remedies are diluted and vigorously shaken until the original substance has all but disappeared, a process called 'potentization'. A homeopathic remedy is a form of potency.

My week in the studio led me through a similar process of potentization. As the week continued and I fell less, I was diluting falling until I was left with an infinitesimal sense of surrendering my weight to the force of gravity. I was forming a potency – diluted from extensive repetitions – as a remedy for my fears of falling. Living with the potency of gravity as an embodied experience mitigates my psychological fears, especially as I get older, and helps me reconsider the top-down polarity of values enshrined in many linguistic metaphors.

UP IS GOOD

'Falling', as a verb, adjective and noun, infuses the English language, conceptually, metaphorically and psychologically. The addition of another word creates meaning other than literal, physical falling: falling apart, falling asleep, falling ill, falling over yourself, falling pregnant, falling about laughing and falling in – and out of – line. Falling in love conjures the notion of swooning: passing out, fainting or being overcome with emotion.

Through a metaphorical, conceptual medium – such as the English language – 'we understand things in terms of other things. Concepts are metaphorically structured ... *Every* experience takes place within a vast background of cultural presuppositions' (Lakoff and Johnson 1980: 56–7). In English, the conceptual understanding of space is often framed by human motor functions. Perhaps the most basic example is that standing is *up* and falling is *down*. Emotions are also often processed through metaphor, especially those where motor functions serve as vehicles for conveying meaning. Because falls are considered by definition dangerous and painful, falling is both metaphorically and conceptually associated with negative emotions. In Western culture, as a result, standing up is happy, falling down is sad (Lakoff and Johnson 1980). These spatial orientations structure other sets of binary values: good is up, bad is down, brightness up, gloom down, rationality both up and good, emotional behaviour both down and bad. Linguistic theorist Zoltán Kövecses develops the theme: 'Control is up, lack of control is down: I'm *on top* of the situation. He is *under* my control. That was a *low-down* thing to do. She's an *upstanding* citizen, the discussion *fell* to an emotional level. He couldn't *rise* above his emotions' (2000: 36).

Synchronized with language, Western culture persists in an endeavour to rise, to resist falling, to strive towards institutional control, upwardly focused verticality, linearity and steadfast uprightness, pinned up by morality, spirituality, propriety and virtue. The metaphorical binary from rising to falling infiltrates aesthetics, religion, psychology, economics and race relations. Being bigger, stronger, more knowledgeable, and moving forward in time are associated with growing up and considered to be life-giving and positive. Upward-ness is structured through social hierarchies; getting to the top is the goal, associated with pride, class, economic success. Rise to new heights, aspire to lofty status within halls of academia, achieve flights of excellence, become high flyers. Western culture is immersed in positive rising. Heights of wealth and happiness are measured in rising pop charts, commodity sales, wealth registers, interest rates, careers and each country's economic status.

Contrarily, sinking to the lowest of the low, feeling down in the dumps, being down-and-out or dirt-poor, plumbing new depths, being labelled as a fallen woman, falling from grace – these phrases appropriate falling as a metaphor for failure and shame. Economic depression is inundated with falling metaphors: crash, deflation, downturn, plunge, collapse, slump, plummeting demand. Social, political and economic success depends on rising, not falling, and a persistent binary of positive/negative flourishes between the two terms.[1]

Within the confines of Western civilization, there is universal agreement, a world view, a cosmology, that up is good and down is bad. This cosmology is deeply embedded in religious mythology and metaphor. Christianity abounds with falling myths – Adam and Eve, Satan – and narratives that foster a notion of a *good* self as pre-existent, divinely created, an essence given by God. Across the world, East and West, goodness – god-ness – has been associated with sun, sky, moon and stars. Most readers will agree that religions have developed underworld narratives, where evil, dark and hellish events occur. In religious art, failing goodness is depicted as falling, affirming goodness as transcendent.

These values are consistently reinforced through linguistic repetition and in turn influence people's daily lives and outlook, movements and social interactions. Embodying upward-ness as a life well led, means falling is smeared with fear, failure, vulnerability, uncertainty and shame. Minds and bodies are trained *not* to fall, producing fixed resistance in human bodies to their otherwise fluidly kinaesthetic responses to gravity and the environment. Through the entwining of body and language, movement and metaphor, Western culture has developed an attachment to physical and psychological upward-ness that denies the potential of falling and failure as creative sources for being present in the world.

An acknowledgement of the perpetually interwoven relations between language, metaphor and human movements, and a reconsideration of ways of moving, can potentially both influence language and reconfigure the values given to up and down. Change is happening. For instance, the North American phrases 'getting down', a metaphor for enthusiastic engagement with something, and 'I'm down with that', meaning positive agreement, have now entered the English lexicon. Both emerge from black American culture and demonstrate not only the relationship between movement and metaphor but also the importance of creative interdependence of cultural differences, as ways of changing the values given to linguistic metaphors.

> The earth is indifferent to falling and rising. It doesn't care to rise and fall. It rises and falls all the time – mountains, cliffs, coastal paths – but it doesn't have a feeling about this. That's what we bring to the equation.
>
> HALLETT and SMITH 2017: 30

---

[1] In old English *feallen* means to fall, fail, decay or die. To *fail* draws from the Latin *fallere* – to beguile, deceive, elude, pass – and from the German *fallan* – to fall (Soden 2003). Several European languages have etymological connections between the two words, emphasizing the metaphorical and linguistic links between falling and failing.

SUPREME FEATS

I arrive in Manhattan in 1969, plunging into a marijuana-flowering, hippie-wandering, bedraggled, hot, multi-cultural Lower East Side. I lodge in a nineteenth-century tenement block. Six heavy locks decorate the front door; the kitchen sideboard hinges upwards to reveal a bath; dark sweltering rooms are divided with bead curtains. Cockroaches chatter incessantly every dawn and dusk, tut-tutting about sharing space with humans. I had been offered a scholarship at the Martha Graham School: free dance classes in return for looking after Martha's garden – the school backyard. Apparently, English girls know about gardens. I had mentioned something about tying daffodil stalks together when they finish flowering so that the plants grow straight up the following year. That had been enough to award me the scholarship.

In the daily class, I am wearing leotard and footless tights, sitting on the floor in a studio – with pieces of Noguchi furniture stacked in the corners. Martha is teaching. We begin with our feet drawn in, knees dropped outwards, hands clasping ankles, furiously contracting our torsos, spines curved over, eyes focused on the pelvis. Martha speaks. 'As you release, you call out I AM.' We all obligingly release our spines upwards, stretch our legs out wide to the side, feet pointed, knees locked, buttocks clenched. We open our arms out the side, palms up, backs arched, chests to the ceiling. In high release, pushing off the floor with all our earnest might, we murmur 'I AM'. We repeat the gesture again and again until the room resounds with voices proclaiming 'I AM' in coordination with movements of ecstatic physical release. The idea that I can take up space in this way is an adrenalin-filled and seductive scenario after years of classical ballet. I am struck by how muscular tension and gestural power inspire me with a sense of agency.

Embodying daily imposed ritualistic movements of individual hedonism is how I learnt Martha's falls, which she worked on for fifty years: 'refining complex ways to descend and ascend . . . they grew astonishingly beautiful, varied and complex' (de Mille 1991: 101). To execute Martha's classic fall requires momentous effort, technical rigour and an ability to retain complex choreography, as the following description suggests.

Begin standing with feet in balletic first position. Take a deep plié (knee bend), arms lifting sideways to overhead. In plié, contract your pelvis, and as you contract, your left knee turns inwards to meet the right knee and your hands clasp overhead. Turn your left foot over so that the instep meets the floor and reach high into your clasped hands. Remain in contraction and lower your body onto the left hip and thigh, but do not let your knees touch the floor. Deepen your contraction while folding your upper body over your folded legs, arms sweeping down to complete the curve. Release by lengthening your torso flat like a plank on its side, knees bent, arms down, one under your body, one above. Contract again, curving your back onto the floor, knees still bent, arms stretched out parallel to your body with hands cupped. Your head is arched back onto the floor so that you are looking to the ceiling. This is the lowest point of the fall. From here a further series of complex movements bring you back up to standing. The final movement is a lunge forward onto your left leg on a diagonal, foot parallel, weight shifted into left hip. Your body turns to face front, twisted in opposition to your left leg and you look backward towards your right foot.

Graham technique has standing, sitting and travelling falls, as well as forward, back, side and split falls, all requiring different physical requirements (Graff 2004). There are attack falls, which hit the floor, and dramatic falls where narratives affect their quality. There are knee falls and 'dead man' falls – four stilted zombie-like walking steps before a split fall – and the spiral fall. Even though Martha writes that 'no real dancer I know learns counts' (Graham 1991: 243), in class these falls were practised on counts, each count dictating a shift in gesture towards, and away from, the ground, emphasizing the control required to accomplish a successful fall.

No movements in the Graham technique yield to gravity without excessive resistance in the opposite direction. 'The body's energies are never (or rarely) allowed to seep into the floor, but remain gathered, mobilized for a quick recovery, a renewal of the power of the dancer. In Graham technique, the fall is rarely a true surrender' (Graff 2004: 3). By 1969, when I was there, falls had been incorporated into training, practised in isolation, set apart from other phrases of movement, usually at the end of each class. Just as the ballerina's task of thirty-two fouettés at the end of a ballet class is a test of skill, stamina, control and balance, so Martha's falls are the ultimate challenge of the Graham technique, a supreme feat to be accomplished.

The 'height' of the fall is just before landing, a tussle between will and submission. 'The element of excitement was supplied by the fraction of a second during which the body was totally off balance and falling' (de Mille 1991: 89). I could resist, I could use extreme effort, but I would eventually have to submit to the ground. In this tightly controlled choreography, I can almost time my surrender, relish my own dramatic submission to a performance of death on the floor.

Falling outside of Martha's codified choreographic design represents a failure of will, just like the inability to stay on *pointe* in ballet. So, the falls are contradictory. The trajectory of falling is comprised of choreographed, complex, physically effortful phrases of movement designed to demonstrate strength. As a spatial element, movements towards and away from the floor were integrated into her technique and language as a play between balance, off-balance and resistance. Martha's falls were never 'a literal representation of reality, but instead an embodiment of inner experience; not a reductive language, but a poetic language that derives its meaning from the layering of the physical and psychic' (Graff 2004: 108).[2]

I do not forget the vibrant contradictions that her training held on my body in the late 1960s. I experienced a sense of singular, independent, physical power as a woman and a dancer. As I recovered from each fall, I was reaching for *my* potential, *my* uniqueness, *my* dance, *my* expression, with a sense of agency that had been missing for me as a ballet dancer. I felt physically strong and expressively powerful. At the same time, that individualistic pride-full sense of I AM was unsustainable outside the confines of Martha's studio. Down in the East Village, mingling with hippies, artists and queers, I shed that performance for an iconoclastic, left-wing, social-political scene of joint-rolling and Bob Dylan.

STANDING BONES

Mabel Elsworth Todd was a pioneer in the fields of physical education, medical science and physiotherapy. After studying physics, mechanics, anatomy and physiology, Mabel initiated and developed ideokinesis, a field of somatic movement knowledge that radically influenced dance training and performance. Ideokinesis aims to improve physical posture through focus on imagery and imagined actions (Todd [1937] 1977b). Rejecting physical education's often mindlessly repetitive drills based on Cartesian notions of a mind-body split, Mabel researched the mechanics of posture to discover what she called a 'bodily economy' (Todd [1937] 1977b: xiii). For Mabel, the notion of upright posture based on resisting gravity through tensing/strengthening muscles was a fundamental cause of human suffering – both physical and psychological – and could lead to many disabilities associated with ageing, as well as muscular and skeletal dysfunction.

Mabel investigated ways for human bodies to remove unnecessary strain and energy from functional movement through an understanding of how the mechanics of the body – spine, muscles and neuro-physical systems – balance themselves in relation to gravity, inertia and momentum. Investigating weaknesses that occurred through evolutionary development toward upright posture, Mabel asked some basic questions:

> How does the pull of gravity act upon the spinal curves, and upon the flat body walls, which balance at front and back, upon this curved, supporting

---

[2]Graff describes Jocasta's final fall in *Night Journey* (Graham, 1947), when she hangs herself. Her fall is final. 'She does not land in a position. She lands in a figureless sprawl, a blot on the ground, like one of those Rorschach blots. She lies there in nothingness' (Graham 1991: 216 cited in Graff 2004: 114).

> upright? How do these function to meet the pull of gravity and to keep the skeletal structure supporting its mass of weight? What are the lines of force operating continuously upon the skeleton? These questions and more we must ask ourselves if we wish to solve the mechanical problem of posture and movement of man in the upright position.
>
> TODD [1937] 1977b: 8

Mabel's research informed her teaching, and in 1929, she published a syllabus that underpinned the central concerns of her book, *The Thinking Body* (1937), a revolutionary text for many dance artists in the 1970s, myself included. Her teaching focused on how bodies find balance through anatomical alignment and economic use of muscular tension. Mabel's core principle was to allow the bones and skeletal structure to do the work of resisting gravity – not the muscles. Skeletal structure, like architecture, is capable of balancing upwardly; it does not need to be *held* up.

> When standing, if the three bulks of weight – head, chest and pelvis – are held in alignment at their own spinal levels and balanced at their bony joinings, the muscles do not have to work nearly so hard to keep them there as when they are held out of alignment. Gravity itself is harnessed when we keep our weights balanced.
>
> TODD [1937] 1977b: 38

The kinaesthetic study and understanding of the human skeleton as a structure designed to bear and move weight provides an avenue toward reducing stress. 'Why hold the bony parts of our body when we can let them hang or sit?' (Todd [1937] 1977b: 33). The bones are engineered and mechanically constructed to balance gravitational pull; it is not the job of the muscles to do the work of the bones. Following her explorations into balancing the alignment of pelvis, chest and head, she advocated the avoidance of fixing positions for any body part, thus allowing freedom of movement, reduction of strain and the nurturing of a body ready for action.

> There is a natural alignment of all the bones to each other. If this natural relationship is disturbed it produces an unequal pull upon muscles and ligaments. Hence, any attempt to hold bones out of their natural alignment involves an unnecessary strain and a waste of energy.
>
> TODD 1977a: 5

Crucial to her approach of allowing muscles to release so that bones could do their work was her recognition of the dangers of how new ways of moving can become fixed. Mabel's work emphasized process rather than technique, a path toward responsiveness and fluidity.

With its infinite branches throughout the structure, the nervous system forms a network of highly vibrant fibres stimulating advantageously or otherwise the delicately organized materials of the body. Constant stimuli are producing constant reactions. There can be no such thing as fixity in such a fluctuating mass. Every thought, every sensation causes a change somewhere in the structure.

TODD 1977a: 9

Mabel's pioneering work allowed dancers to understand in body and mind how to let go of fixed and coded habits, first through using anatomical imagery and second through fostering responsiveness and fluidity by sensing the body in relation to its environment – particularly gravity and ground. 'In order that the movements of our body shall be adjustable to the forces about us, the substance of our structure must be response' (Todd 1977a: 8). In saying this, Mabel was also stressing the link between fixed patterns of physical uprightness and habitual psychological processes; her research into principles of posture inevitably lay emphasis on the psycho-physical mechanisms involved in a body's organic reaction to the problem of resisting gravity in an upright position.[3]

Mabel laid a fundamental pathway for the somatic movement practitioners who followed, in particular Barbara Clark. As a teacher, Barbara also emphasized the unpatterning of fixed uprightness, considering muscular tension to be 'misplaced attempts to defy the force of gravity' (Matt 1993: 65). Barbara accentuated the development of deeper muscles, closest to the bones, so that surface muscles could let go of tension.

Engrossed in Todd's imagery, Barbara rebuilt her body, from the inside, socket by socket. She said it was simply a matter of 'learning to center,' finding balance through the centers of the joints and using muscles at the center of the body. In the process she began to 'let go of the old' – old habits of moving, old ways of thinking and old emotions.

MATT 1993: 22

Mabel taught Barbara, who in turn taught Nancy Topf, Mary Fulkerson, Marsha Paludan and John Rolland. John also worked with Joan Skinner, founder of Release Technique. Through the work of these movement researchers, somatic practices spread throughout the Western world, exerting formidable influence on dance training and performance.

Giving body–mind attention to how humans stand up refines understanding of anatomical balance, economy of movement, gravitational

---

[3]In New York, Mabel worked in parallel with Frederick Alexander, founder of Alexander Technique, another fundamental influence on the development of somatic movement practices for dancers (Huxley 2012).

awareness and the perception of self as interacting with the environment. Body mechanics and ideokinesis provide sources of discovery for ways of standing, without fighting the environment or gravity. Mabel was instrumental as a somatic pioneer in encouraging the economic use of effort and the release of unnecessary muscular tension to allow the skeleton – the infrastructure of bones evolved through thousands of years and shared across races and cultures in diverse environments and habitus – to do its work of standing.

ROLLING

As Director of Dance, I am browsing in the library at Dartington College of Arts in 2005, and a VHS cassette catches my eye, unassumingly stacked among well-worn items of defunct technology. What first hooks my attention is the date, 1978, along with one of the credited venues – X6 Dance Space. Dartington College of Arts was part of the Dartington Estate, nestled in the lush green hills of Devon in south-west England. In contrast, X6 Dance Space was situated on the sixth floor of a defunct industrial warehouse near Tower Bridge in London. Both venues, rural and urban, were hotbeds of innovative new dance practices in the 1970s. As a founder member of the X6 Dance Collective, I'm intrigued, and so slide the VHS from its dark, silent berth and venture in search of a VHS player.[4]

Dance without Steps (1978) was created for the BBC Open University course 'Arts & Environment' and includes material contributed by dance artist Miranda Tufnell and visual artist Chris Crickmay. The film documents an emerging awareness in the UK that dancing can embrace pedestrian non-codified action, an awareness informed by somatic movement practices. Curious to discover what was filmed at X6 Dance Space, I speed the tape forward to Miranda Tufnell as she lies on the floor in a pool of sunlight. I remember how morning sun would flood through the doors at one end of the warehouse and shine out through the doors thrown open at the opposite end, infusing the maple floor boards with summer warmth. The camera is positioned to take in the length of the space, suggesting an infinite perspective under an expanse of sky, obscuring the sheer drop down to the ground six floors below. Health and safety regulations were barely considered back then.

Miranda, dressed in brown T-shirt and tracksuit bottoms, lies on her back, with her knees up, feet flat on the floor. Slowly, she lets her knees fall

---

[4]X6 Dance Collective: Maedee Dupres, Jacky Lansley, Fergus Early, Mary Prestidge and myself (Claid 2006).

to her right side, the weight of which peels her left hip from the floor. As she continues responding to the momentum of gravity, her torso and arms are drawn into the action and, thus, she begins rolling. Or rather, she is *being* rolled as gravity dictates her direction and speed. She is internally sensing how the weight of her body is generating motion, how she's falling in a circle around her own axis, how she's rolling through falling. She provides a commentary:

> When does an everyday movement become dance movement? When you become aware of yourself in the space. Lying on the floor, simply letting the weight of the body direct the movement over the floor. Almost like following yourself as you roll . . . The roll happens through the body, not to do with making this position or that. Allowing the body to move, with its own momentum, allowing a repertory of movement to evolve. How does rolling and following the weight of the body lead to dance? For me that *is* dance, dance is movement, if I can convey that sensation to you through the clarity with which I perform those movements. That *is* dance. The technique is to do with the ability to coordinate mind and body, ideas and movement. Not to look specialised, or give a virtuoso performance, but to try and give back to an audience very simple movement.
>
> TUFNELL 1978

Miranda's experience of rolling marks a seminal moment in the UK, highlighting a time when dance artists engaged in a radical inquiry about *how* moving affects *what* is moving – listening, internally, to how bodies move with gravity, rather than paying homage to external images. Miranda's rolling marks a moment when somatic awareness infused the synapses of contemporary dance, influencing movement languages, choreography and improvisational performance. Incorporating a somatic approach into dance training incited profound challenges to the aesthetics of dance performance, offering gravity-drawn poetics as an alternative to the conventions of upward linearity. The practice of rolling allows for a slow and careful study of how bodies move, how they interact with momentum and inertia – with the laws of mechanics. In the 1970s, I rolled both on the X6 floor and in the beams of a brilliant Devonshire sun at Dartington. And I witnessed dancers rolling in performance for hours . . . and hours.

STIFF AND BRAVE

'I' stands tall, proud, straight, alone, thin, stiff and brave – an upstanding citizen. English is the only language in which the first person pronoun is composed of a single letter. 'We', on the other hand, is a word with buckets to drop into, crossings and touching of lines, a curve that turns in on itself, a broken circle. 'We' is two letters making something more than themselves, not like the individual 'I'. Imagine if the letter 'I' were to fall. As neither character nor symbol is 'I' disposed to bend, fold or adapt. When 'I' falls, it does so with a hollow clatter, like a deposed bronze figure, exposing the fallacies of its former status. So 'I' does whatever it can to continue standing erect.

The upward centrality of the individualistic 'I' has been hailed as a great achievement of modern culture – signifying and promoting human dignity, pride, human rights, autonomy, self-sufficiency, self-development and self-motivation. Emerging at a crucial time in the Victorian period, with its legacy of industrialization, nationalism, colonialism, white supremacy, patriarchal phallocentrism and corporate capitalism, individualism promoted a notion of a unique yet universal sense of self as subject. The 'Enlightenment view of human nature placed such an overbearing emphasis on universal characteristics that it relegated the differential effects of culture to secondary status ... Stripped of its social contexts, human nature is ineluctably individualistic' (Walls 2004: 606).

The quote above from psychoanalyst Gary Walls underscores his critical questioning of the individualistic nature of early Freudian psychoanalysis, whereby each person's unique being was nurtured as the centre of his or her distinctive universe and the exclusive feelings that needed to unfold. Walls' post-humanist view is corroborated by psychoanalyst Jeffrey Rubin, who also questions the 'I-ness' (1998: 127) of psychoanalytic traditions, focusing on the 'blindness of the seeing I' (1998: 13) and the censorship and one-sided subjective interpretation of Freudian psychoanalysis. 'While every person may be at the centre of his or her own world, no one is the centre of the whole world. Thinking that we are – which individualism encourages – may compromise empathy and tolerance, foster disconnect from others, and engender self-alienation' (Rubin 1998: 13). Psychoanalysis was a product of Western Enlightenment just as much as it was Freud's invention, promoting 'affirmation of paternalistic gender roles, individual achievement, personal responsibility, and a strongly bounded self' (Walls 2004: 606). Early psychoanalysis nurtured a focus on ego, self-centredness and self-consciousness, diverting patients' suffering from social, political, economic and racial causes for that suffering. Classism and patriarchy as 'the values of Western individualism are so implicitly contained within the structure of analytic therapy as to render it useless as a therapeutic resource for anyone outside the cultural mainstream' (Walls 2004: 611). Freudian psychoanalysis was then inflated by Social Darwinism – a philosophy that developed towards the end of the nineteenth century – extending Darwin's notion of the survival of the fittest. This theory that some individuals are superior to others feeds the idea that certain social classes, cultures and races are also superior.

The rampaging, individualistic notion of 'I' as universal subject, has proved a disaster, provoking materialistic greed, racism, fundamentalism and bigotry, a cause and result of suffering and disharmony. In today's culturally pluralistic world, and led by feminist, race, queer and environmental politics, individualism as an ideal is being deconstructed and revised, its monuments toppled, unravelling what Freud had promoted as 'the basic imperatives of the individual: aggression, destruction, predatory sexuality, and an asocial selfishness' (Wheeler 1997: 24). The writings of Rubin and Walls – which follow in the footprints of profound, critical, feminist writings on psychoanalysis by authors such as Kristeva (1980), Irigaray (1985), Benjamin (1988) and Grosz (1989) – support a contemporary re-shaping of psychoanalysis away from its phallocentric history towards a relational practice (Stolorow and Atwood 1992). I persist in discussing these antiquated viewpoints because institutionalized ideologies of individualism magnify, politically and culturally, what is happening on human bodies. Because individualism promotes physical upward verticality as a signifier of virtue, pride, morality and fitness of flesh. Because failure to stand upright is associated with shame.

Bodies and culture are a Mobius strip, intertwined and forever at each other's beckoning. The more individualism promotes a stiff brave 'I', the more physical and psychological falling become equated with fear and failure. It is but a small wobble from here to link body and politics, to link white supremacy's striving for ascendency with a physical resistance to gravity. Western dance has certainly had a historical role in upholding individualism. Yet since the mid twentieth century, methods of production and ways of moving have ceased to promote the 'I' of enlightened verticality. Dancers, and therapists, have learnt to fall and in so doing, offer the Mobius strip of body and culture an alternative 'I', based in I-You: collaboration, connection and environmental partnership.

ICONIC HEROINE

Martha Graham's falls were performed solo, as statements of struggle against the dark underside of humanity, symbolizing a heroic challenge and fight for individual freedom in the face of evil. *Down* symbolized dark and *up* symbolized light. A dancer's task was to practise strength of will while executing a fall, to fight against weakness and resist submission, while recovery was always a rise towards artistic freedom. 'You never go down and up, but from lightness to darkness and back to light again. For a moment the earth and gravity conquer the body, but it fights back and wins!' (Graham quoted in de Mille 1991: 216).

Martha's preoccupation with dark and light reflected her enthusiasm for the theories of Jung and Freud and particularly, those underworld spaces that conjure archetypal images of shadows, mystery, and the unknown. Many of Martha's choreographies represented 'a prime example of psychoanalytic modernism' (Franko 2014: 6), steeped in notions of the unconscious. Works such as *Deaths and Entrances* (1943), *Appalachian Spring* (1944), *Cave of the Heart* (1946) and *Night Journey* (1947) bear hidden messages and sublimated meanings in their interweavings of psychology and myth of both a personal and political nature.

Martha's falls reflect an era of Enlightenment, when the prideful 'I' stood unique and alone. She worked on her falls during the Great Depression and the rise of fascism before the Second World War. At the time, there were two flourishing and interweaving strands of American modern dance. One was led by third- and fourth-generation immigrants, mostly white northern Europeans who recognized themselves as established Americans. This strand of modern dance was comparatively bourgeois, led by the 'Big Four': Martha Graham, Doris Humphrey, Charles Weidman and Hanya Holm (Graff 1997; McDonagh [1970] 1990). The second was led by new arrivals, particularly the children of mostly poor Russian Jewish immigrants who embraced communism (Graff 1997). Strongly associated with socialism and anti-fascism, these dancers identified with and supported workers' struggles and working-class causes (Prickett 1990). Collectively organized as a 'New Dance' movement, this revolutionary strand included Sophie Maslow, Anna Sokolow and Helen Tamiris.

Martha, as one of the Big Four, dominated American modern dance history as a leading canonical figure. She was the figurehead, the new world ambassador for modern dance. Martha did not have to identify herself as American; she *was* America. 'Graham's choreography proposed a country that encompassed all races and creeds in its past, in its present, and in the future. It was, after all, her America' (Graff 1997: 21). Her liberal attitudes gathered Other-ness into One-ness, a familiar characteristic of the dominant white middle class anywhere in the Western world. Alternatively, the revolutionary new dancers could not assimilate themselves easily into the vision of America proposed by Graham. They could, however, identify with others who were displaced: 'every other person who lacked a place in American mythology: Negroes, workers, immigrants, Okies ... Class ties brought all of these groups together' (Graff 1997: 21).

To paint Martha as a tragic figure of individualism, standing alone against the 'unsympathetic, brutal, and above all ignorant' masses (Graff 1997: 109), might appear somewhat harsh, given her inspirational contribution to modern dance. Yet even in the late 1930s when Martha did take a strong stand against fascism,[5] even when the two strands of modern dance – revolutionary and bourgeois – came together in the face of what was

---

[5]In 1936, Martha Graham refused to take up the Nazi Culture Ministry's invitation to participate in the Berlin Olympic Games as they were fascistically motivated (Graff 1997; Franko 2014).

happening in Europe, even then her standing and her falling were a solo act. *Heretic* (1929), which culminates in Graham's iconic spiral fall, showcases *her* as the central figure, as a heroic example of the triumphant 'I'. Martha dedicated her solo pieces *Immediate Tragedy* (1937) and *Deep Song* (1937) to the plight of those affected by the Spanish Civil War. In his review of these two pieces, Henry Gilfond wrote: 'It is not Spain that we see in her clean impassioned movement ... The dedication is not a Spaniard's; it is an American's' (Gilfond 1938: 8 cited in Graff 1997: 121). A critique that hints at Martha's political view as one that assimilates cultural differences into a white, American, universal embrace.

Socially aware and politically active dancers who came to learn her falls faced a contradiction in beliefs. The physical stamina, muscular control and co-ordination of the Graham technique could be put to use by dancers to express revolutionary concerns, but this meant entering an elitist training establishment built around a hierarchy of teachers and students. For dancers who supported leftist politics and class struggle, Martha's falls evoked a much sought-after physical articulation of power, yet provoked a heroism that needed to be overcome through collective action. For Martha, fall and recovery were statements of individual struggle. For revolutionary dancers, the physical control required to perform her falls became a collective embodiment of power and freedom.

Martha fell alone and rose alone. Her falls represented independence and enterprise. They dramatized her personal strength, her ability to dance without reliance on others. She did not need partners to support her falls, or to help her recover, but demonstrated instead her – a woman's – individualistic capability for mastery.

EARTH'S GRIEF

Find yourself a warm floor and lower yourself down until your body is resting on the ground, on your back. Yes, I am inviting you to lie down. This sounds simple, and it is, but it can lead to – be a portal into – surprisingly rewarding results. For the safest place to experience gravity is on the ground. As you lie there, listen to your breathing and how every breath out embodies a slight fall. Sense your skin, flesh and bones in contact with the ground. Let go with your head, neck, torso, limbs. Imagine sinking further, melting, seeping downwards as a continual process of falling, while taking support from the ground. Take time to sense a constant interactive relationship between your body, gravity and ground. A process that somatic practitioner Andrea Olsen calls a 'pre-movement of the body-mind' that 'informs what will happen' (2017: 181). In Bonnie Bainbridge Cohen's somatic practice of Body–Mind Centering, lying down and letting go create a place of rest, a necessary function of the parasympathetic nervous system to save energy, slow the heart rate, and increase intestinal and gland activity.[6] The practice is a one directional flow towards gravity, 'a resting, recuperative, regenerative state' (Cohen 2012: 181).

While you are lying down, letting go, sensing gravity, breathing, you might find yourself feeling emotional. This is not unusual. When your nervous system is at rest from the fear of falling, no longer busy resisting gravity, there is space for underlying emotions to surface. The imagery of melting into the ground releases our fears of falling and simultaneously, can evoke emotional darkness. Talking of a time of illness, Cohen describes how:

> Part of my process was sinking like a whale in a storm. You just sink and sink and sink, and maybe there's a fire, maybe there's flames, maybe there's pain, whatever it is, you just sink under it. You get below the form and you get below the pathways, you get back to the emptiness of the blackened void.
>
> COHEN 2012: 182

Be curious if this happens – you are supported by the ground. It is through the darkness, safely supported by the ground, that the potential for change takes place. I encourage you not to be afraid of the empty void that might occur as you lie still, breathing. Therapeutically, the void can be an invigorating therapeutic experience. 'We find when we accept and enter this nothingness, the void ... becomes alive, is being filled. The sterile void becomes the fertile void' (Perls 1969: 57).[7] The void space of falling into ground – while safely lying down – is a place where change is seeded. This existential psychotherapeutic perspective is followed through by Emmy van Deurzen, who writes of accepting nothingness as a challenging opportunity, an 'experience of being confronted with the abyss ... It is a feeling of disappearing ... It is possibility of impossibility' (van Deurzen and Arnold-Baker 2005: 6).

Lying on the ground, sometimes I feel so sad. Sometimes I have a feeling of existential emptiness. Yet I know I am safe here sinking into the ground, and these feelings that arise are offering me a necessary polarity to the endless stresses of speedy living. Sometimes I wonder, if it is Earth's sadness that I sense, now I have slowed down to be in contact and to listen.

---

[6]The parasympathetic nervous system is a division of the autonomic nervous system (Cohen 2012). If the parasympathetic nervous system is ignored, or resisted, the sympathetic and somatic systems are overworked, stress occurs and sleep becomes difficult.
[7]Fritz Perls, founder of Gestalt psychotherapy.

ABOUT DYING

Growing old is both a physical and metaphorical process of falling and is, of course, inevitable. As human bodies age, flesh sags, muscles drop, skin wrinkles and folds. Yet at the same time, in contradiction – and, perhaps, opposition – to the gradual collapse of flesh, ageing bodies resist gravity. Fear and stress stiffen joints and muscles, which causes tension and rigidity, along with efforts to hold the body away from the ground. How ironic then, that even when the body has weathered gravity's pull, and formerly toned muscles are now collapsing downwards, getting down *to* the ground becomes such a challenging and fearful process, where the ground forever seems further away. In Western culture, actual falling as an old person ('So-and-so had *a fall*') signifies a physical, metaphorical and psychological turning point where a person is considered too old, fragile, senile or weak to manage on her own. She needs assistance. Growing old has taken a turn away from its etymological roots. In fact, *growing* and *old* are terms that are now mismatched, an issue Thomas Hanna addresses in his somatic research into ageing processes.

> 'Old' in its Latin root, *alo*, and in its ancient Germanic form, *alt*, means – quite surprisingly – 'to nourish' and 'to bring up'. More generally, *alo* means to strengthen, increase, and advance. It means to become taller and to become deeper . . . In view of the etymology of 'old', it is fascinating to note that 'growing old' has come to mean exactly the opposite of the original meaning of 'old'.
>
> HANNA 1988: 88

In the West ageing conjures thoughts of retirement, resignation and terminal decline; these terms evoke significantly negative, metaphorical associations with falling, quite apart from concerns about actual physical falls. Since language and metaphor exert powerful effects on the way people see the world, these terms influence perceptions of ageing in both the young and the old. What's more, ageism in the West is stereotyped and catalogued using social, cultural, statistical, chronological, psychological and biological metrics to describe expectations for its progressive stages (Woodward 2006). These categories provide methods with which to avoid the underlying theme – death. Old people are dying, and living while doing so.

As an ageing dancer, I am impacted daily by culturally defined stereotypes which measure and prescribe my abilities. These stereotypes exert significant influence on ways of thinking and of being old. Two particular models appear to dominate Western thinking around ageing. The first follows a progress-peak-and-decline narrative, while the second ascribes to the 'wisdom of old age' scenario (Martin 2017). The former presumes a peak age of around thirty-five years, after which people gradually decline in productivity. Many older dancers – myself included – certainly feel the weight of this assumption (Schweiger 2012), yet nonetheless persist in performing. Maverick independent dance performer Wendy Houstoun, for instance, now in her sixties, has no intention of 'retiring' and nor should she. I did not consider myself much of a performer until, at forty-three, I opened my solo show *Virginia Minx at Play* (1992). According to most expectations, I was well past my sell-by date, and so was surprised by the reviews: 'Claid is the Che Guevara of British dance, revolutionising its institutions, its techniques and even its audiences' (Sacks 1993). The second stereotype – generally considered positive – reveres the serenity, grace, poignancy and elegance of maturity, along with the supposed wisdom, transcendence and philosophical perspectives of the latter years. This scenario, though, neglects to acknowledge the fear, rage, sense of loss, bitterness and ongoing sexual appetites experienced by older people – like me.

I embrace falling – physical, metaphorical and psychological – as a valuable source of vitality and presence. It is no surprise then that, especially as a dancer, I am seeking an alternative philosophy of ageing, one that encourages curiosity about the process and a willingness both to *be with* dying, and to mine the later phases of life for their inventive potential. This does not mean redoubling efforts to perform as though young, or to maintain youthful energy. Nor does it mean accepting – or giving in to – the ageing stereotypes proliferating throughout Western culture. Rather, it is a philosophy that questions what the process of ageing reveals in dancing, rather than dancing to escape the ageing process. Susanne Martin, in her study of ageing in dance (2017), cites the work of dance improvisers Andrew Morrish, Kirstie Simson and Julyen Hamilton, now in their sixties. These older performers are investigating the process of dying as it plays out in their own bodies, not to recapture any aspect of their younger selves, nor necessarily as a path towards increased well-being, but with intense interest in what is forever emerging during the course of ageing into dying.

> I can remember when my ageing process first started. There were some very clear moments when I felt … something has gone. And then you start saying: I've turned a corner. And then you realise … what an interesting new street I'm in. The one where I cannot do these things.
>
> MORRISH quoted in MARTIN 2017: 103–04

Improvisation facilitates dancing into dying because the form encourages ever-changing engagement with perception; it requires participants to respond to whatever is happening moment by moment and in any given environment. In Hanna's (1988) account of the etymology of 'old', the term 'increase' – or in*crease* – teases my attention, with its suggestion of wrinkling embedded in a word meaning growth. With this ironic double entendre in mind, I'm advocating for a new approach to gravity – that frightening force we confront in old age. Rather than representing fearful prospects, gravity can be exploited as a way of releasing bodies from the physical conditions of stiffness and tension and of resisting the external stereotypes that govern the ageing process. Through acceptance and surrender, a dying process becomes not a loss, but a way to gain agency and a wealth of inspiration. Accepting dying as a way to live.

RECALLING GROUND

American modern dancer Jane Dudley joined the staff at the London Contemporary Dance School in 1970. She had danced with Martha Graham, with the New Dance Group and had been artistic director of Batsheva Dance Company in Israel before arriving in London. Two years before her death in 2001, she featured in the film *Dancing Inside* (Lacey 1999). The film presents Jane, at the age of eighty-five, performing choreographed dances and reflecting on her life. With her voice-over accompanying much of the action, she also speaks at times directly to camera, a layering of words for Jocelyn Pook's haunting, ambient score. A particularly poignant moment occurs when she recalls her choice to give up being a mother to pursue a career in dance. Leaving her son is delicately portrayed through a choreographed duet with dancer/psychotherapist Frank Bock, who knew Jane during her later years. In the film she also talks openly about coming to terms with death, about wanting to adopt an attitude of preparation rather than of worry, acceptance of the end rather than belief in an afterlife. While contemplating bequests, though, while wondering to whom she might leave a delicate object or beautiful piece of furniture, she admits with a smile that she is not yet ready to embrace this attitude entirely.

At one point, director Gillian Lacey asks Jane, now severely disabled by arthritis, if she is still able to get down to the ground. As a young contemporary dancer Jane would have included this ritual as a part of her daily practice. Dressed in a raincoat and carrying a cane, Jane has been discussing the complicated process of sitting down and getting up, particularly in public spaces and around other people. She tells Gillian how 'chilling' this can be as it demonstrates 'one's timidities' (Lacey 1999). But she embraces Lacey's challenge with whimsical humour, saying: 'I could try . . . gosh, I may not get up again. I have not done this in years. It's a lot to do with courage, when you get older – how much you're interested in life. Because it's very easy just to shut yourself in and spend the time in bed' (Lacey 1999).

Jane clears a space at the foot of her bed and, standing facing the bed, places her hands firmly on the mattress and lowers her knees to the floor.

She executes this task with strategic effort, working around arthritic pains in hips, knees and ankles. She takes on the task as a choreographic puzzle, carefully considering the placement of her body each moment of the way. She reaches her right hand to the floor as an exploratory prelude and then slowly, slowly, shifts her weight downwards in incremental stages, with her knees and feet held stiffly to one side, until she drops the final distance with a thump. She lands on the small of her back, her knees bent up, her torso propped up on her elbows. She rests there in a pose similar to the iconic 'pleading' position, a key moment in Martha Graham's falling routines. 'Is that all right?' She laughs and says, 'I'm not sure I want this embarrassing material to go out on air'. Gillian moves in to help her up, but Jane says, 'I can do it on my own' and manoeuvres herself back up to sit on the bed. Having completed this ordeal of recovery, she laughs again. There is a childish joy in her eyes. Sitting, she falls sideways onto the bed – easily, without tension – and buries her head in a cushion.

I am moved to write about this episode, knowing Jane as a teacher and advocate for the Martha Graham technique (Claid 2006). Following in the Modern Dance tradition, Jane taught the Graham falls as choreographed phrases that emphasize an ascent towards the light rather than a drop to the ground. Yet, here is Jane, in Lacey's film, negotiating with gravity, stripping away the mythical connotations, learning to face the stark realities of falling towards death.

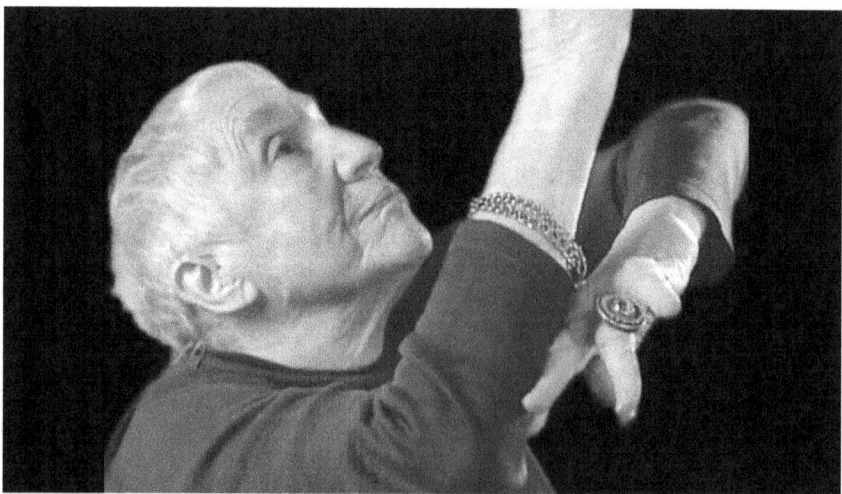

FIGURE 1.1 *Jane Dudley in* Dancing Inside *(dir. Lacey, 1999). APT Film & TV for BBC2..*

INFANT WISDOM

Falling Together, Falling About, Falling Apart (2014) was a two-day workshop performance artist/academic Mark Harvey and I facilitated in Auckland, New Zealand. We began the first day lying on the ground, experimenting with the following exercise.

While you lie down, delving, sinking, into your personal deep, consider the volume of space your body will pass through to get from where you are lying to standing up. Imagine how you might begin to move from down to up, but don't yet act on the thought. What path could you take? Imagine how you might get there. Rather than picking yourself up, bracing your muscles and straining your neck, imagine gentle shifts you could make to give further into the ground, with an aim to push away from it. Ponder the idea for a while, while sensing your body's responses. Then begin to experiment.

For every giving into the ground, allow a push away. Begin with minuscule movements – rocking, rolling, arching, stretching. Use your limbs and torso to yield towards and then push away from the ground through the progressive stages of sitting, crawling, crouching and those in between. Wend your way gradually towards upright posture – without emphasizing or privileging the act of standing any more than falling – while simultaneously releasing the hierarchical binary between the two. Let them have equal value.

Fundamental, developmental movements – yielding, pushing, reaching, grasping, pulling and releasing (Cohen 2012; Frank and La Barre 2011) – will all come into play in the passage from lying prone to standing. In Western culture we see physical growth and physical abilities, from infancy to adulthood, through a particular lens, and focus primarily on a goal-orientated hierarchy of movements, where push, reach, grasp and pull take precedence over yield and release. Enjoy improvising here with yield and release, allowing the other four developmental movements to come into play as a consequence. Allow progress upwards to become a downward process.

One participant at the workshop in Auckland brought her nine-month baby to the studio. As the infant had not yet learnt to walk, she spent a morning crawling about the space and sitting amongst us. She watched intently as adult participants practised falling towards standing. After a while, the baby began to experiment. She worked her way up to standing and then purposefully sat down again. She did this again and again with a particular rhythm that seemed to favour dropping over standing. As I watched, I imagined how this little person might be learning about her body in gravity, by interacting with the adults around her. She seemed to be searching for a balance – when standing – that did not depend on resistance to gravity or achieving an erect posture. She also seemed to be prepared to fall as many times as necessary until she could find a balance in her bones that allowed her to stand. Standing up was a consequence of her experimenting with, rather than against, gravity. Actually, I will go further and say that she stood up *in order* to experience falling down. Standing was not her goal.

Rather than focusing on standing as a primary progression into the world, this exercise encourages a physical and psychological shift towards equalizing perceptions of up and down. Yielding towards the ground while pushing away from it reframes the experience of standing; it recalibrates the transition from lying down such that the goal of standing is no longer upright-ness. Standing is simply a pause before falling.

UNDER SIDE

Steve Paxton was introduced to the martial art form of aikido in 1964 while performing in Tokyo with Merce Cunningham's company. Aikido provided Steve with both skills and a philosophy of falling, enabling the founding of Contact Improvisation (CI). The following text is an edited version of an email discussion between Steve and myself.

> What awakened my curiosity about aikido was [being able] to study a movement form not shaped by Western Dance. Or by Art at all. That study illuminated my dance studies as well as teaching me this new form.
> Aikido demos are lively, magical, formally improvised events, from slow motion attacks one on one, to real-time multiple adversary attacks of one person. There is a clear geometry and physics between the attacker and the aikidoist, available choreographies are initiated by the style of attack and the options taken in response.
> The overall stance of the aikidoist is erect on demi-plié with extended arms. The movements of this role are swivels, deflections, extended grips, with which the attacker is either flipped into the air or taken to the ground. I was struck with the technical aspect; the extended arms reminded me of Western dance, the division of the body into extended upper body and compressed lower body was intriguing.
> Artistically, as a dancer, I found the new technique expanded my sense of personal space. Dance had mainly taught moving about upright, on foot or feet, extending into space, and changing arrangements of limbs for artistic reasons. Aikido taught extension much more precisely, for survival reasons, and emphasized extending in an arc.
> An aikido fall involves imagining a line of flowing energy from the centre of mass in the pelvis through the lower scapula, down the underside of the arm, and out the last two fingers into space. The arm is bowed and inverted, so that the underside is top. The little finger touches the mat first, the bowed arm keeps contact with the mat onto the shoulder. The

path across the back is diagonal. The full weight of the body doesn't land until the shoulder or back is in contact with the mat. The forward foot is the same as the arm, the body rolls onto the knee/shin of the back leg, the fore leg can then step up to a stand.

A roll transmutes falling toward the ground into rolling along the surface, which in turn transmutes fear of falling into a manageable incident. Study of a martial art involves facing many 'fearable' elements. Aikido is taught so that typical fears are quieted. The student knows what technique to apply, and what the result should be. If the attacker is sent into the air, the aikido roll is utilized. No one need be injured, and gradually the techniques become second nature, and the attacks become faster and even unpredictable. Further, it is part of the ethos of aikido that the attacker not be injured. The psychology here is that most conflicts will only be heightened if the aim is to disable the attacker by injury. Some aikido techniques would not be teachable without safe falling. If one learns that falling is not injurious or painful, fear evaporates.

I learned that specific body shapes and energies could render falling safe. Falling is not always salvageable, as happens sometimes on ice, for example. In these falls, I seem to revert to a pre-training state of contraction, clinching, making injury all the more likely. Extension into the fall is the critical safety feature, and contracting provides no cushion, no helpful guidance, no incremental allowance of mass onto the surface.

Aikido is a martial art, meaning that there is an attack/defence dynamic. CI works because the partners are following each other. CI has no goal, so it is not exactly a game or a sport. With aikido, body and senses are trained to operate in any relation to gravity (the earth) and as a result of this, Contact Improvisation became thinkable. CI needed to become thinkable before I could propose it.

PAXTON, email conversation with author, 2017

CONTACT HIGH

A vast body of texts define, describe, evaluate, critique, politicize, socialize and analyse the collaborative intelligence, innovation and life-changing properties of CI (Paxton 1977, 1979; Novack 1990; Koteen and Smith 2008; Albright 2013, 2017, 2019). Two bodies share their weight through a tactile connection, both bodies equally grounded and off balance to each other and themselves. Listening, sensing and following this dynamic point of contact provides dancers with the impulse to move. The weighted touch of contact rolls across their moving bodies offering an assured yet uncertain, ever-changing sense of space/time gravitational awareness. CI duet dancing can be inspirational, dangerous, surprising, fluid, abrupt, risk-taking, confluent, playful, dull and funny in equal measure – both to perform and witness. In CI nothing is fixed; it is just 'an evolving system of movement . . . between two moving bodies and their combined relationship to the physical laws that govern their motion – gravity, momentum, inertia' (Koteen and Smith 2008: xii).

Contact improvisor Nancy Stark Smith describes a 'contact high' as:

> Every part of me feels very alive – turned on, awake, present, ready, both comfortable and on my edge, sharpened and softened, deepened and extended, challenged and soothed – physically and energetically tuned to myself and others, I'm directly in dialogue with my environment. Moved – body, mind, spirit, imagination, humour, heart – and in motion. Inspired.
>
> KOTEEN and SMITH 2008: 20

Since momentum of *falling* unleashes the 'high' of CI, Smith's response outlines a delicious paradox. That acts of falling down can result in a high. Requiring alertness and nurturing spontaneity and sensory precision, the practice of falling forms the heart of CI and is fundamental to its poetics. Dancing with gravity induces a physically charged quality of hyper-presence, of being 'present in the mass/matter' (Koteen and Smith 2008: 49). To imagine CI without falling would be like a hurricane without a vortex, an ocean without waves.[8]

> The body, in order to open to the sensations of momentum, weight, and balance, must learn to release excess muscular tension and abandon a certain amount of wilful volition to the natural flow of movement at hand. Skills such as rolling, falling, and being upside down are explored . . . supporting or taking someone's body weight, giving your own weight . . . Organic body movement is motion manifest in activity directly dealing with the physical forces of the environment, gravity being the major influence.
>
> LEPKOFF 1976: 16

> Accepting gravity, falling, following momentum . . . flipping horizons, torquing pathways and unexpected chutes.
>
> SMITH 1983–4: 91

In contact improvisation we can depend on only three things: (1) one's self, (2) that the force of gravity works continually in one direction,

---

[8] CI also engages with throwing, catching, leaping, lifting and turning – yet all actions are practised with an aware, sensed response to the physical laws of gravity and momentum.

down, and (3) that the floor supports our weight. It is a difficult task to say goodbye to that level line that we are unconsciously oriented to twenty-four hours of the day, the horizon.

SIDDALL 1976–7: 12

In Contact Improvisation we fall alone and together . . . Releasing, folding and activating weight flow through the joints, opens and softens participants to each other and the floor. In this softened and receptive state we are able to adapt quickly and quietly to the most charged of falling encounters.

PETRONIO 1979–80: 53

These descriptions could very well apply to some of the wilder parties of one's youth. There is indeed something celebratory, even bacchanalian, in the abandonment to gravity and the spirit of play. In their documentary *Chute* (1979), Nelson, Christiansen and Paxton (1981–2) edited together falls filmed during a 1972 contact jam at the John Weber Gallery, New York City. Paxton's voiceover begins: 'I am examining the passage from up to down. I look at the range of the passage, from the Small Dance of standing, to the linked falls of walking, to swoops and dives from high points on other bodies.'[9]

Grainy black-and-white footage shows dancers clambering, twisting, teetering, sliding, rough-and-tumbling off and around each other, exploring partnered falling. Relishing physical disorientation, dancers roll, flip upside down and surrender their weight to partners and to the ground, sometimes clumsy, often surprising. They test unpredictable pathways between each other and towards the floor through the shared but unspoken risks of playing with gravity, applying physical intelligence and instantly questioning each kinetic development. This was indeed a party, the film captures a moment of revelling – a high point perhaps – in the dance community's re-engineering of its relationship to gravity.

Gravity's effect on all our tissues, on the very water in our cells, suggests to me that it can be thought of as a complex array of events, which in combination produce a general sense of 'me', moving or still. Alter a few of those events, even mentally or emotionally, and the qualities of the relationship to gravity will change as well.

PAXTON 2018: 33

---

[9] For *Chute*, Nelson, Christiansen and Paxton edited fifteen minutes of material into ten minutes of falling: 'Considering the perception that even a walk is a series of falls, we found that our definition was so inclusive that logging was unwieldy, and classification became inevitable: sloughed falls, horizontal falls, accidents, falling up, falling down, controlled falls, freefalls, "splats" et al' (Nelson, Christiansen and Paxton 1981–2: 86–7). *Chute* was followed by *Fall After Newton* (dir. Weis, Christiansen, Kraus, 1987), edited from the same 1972 material.

THE LADDER SCENE

The obsessive murder of young, gay, single men by Dennis Nilsen spurred Lloyd Newson, Nigel Charnock, Russell Maliphant and Douglas Wright to develop their work *Dead Dreams of Monochrome Men* (*DDMM*, directed by Newson for DV8 in 1988). David Hinton's black-and-white film version (1990) adds a grainy murkiness to the seething underworld of fantasy and violence infusing the stage piece. Lloyd explains:

> It was as much about Dennis Nilsen as it was about us. Making *Dead Dreams* was hard and very bleak. Three of us ended up going to see therapists, as a result of making the piece. My therapist said, 'You're dealing with very negative energy, about a man who took the lives of other people and you are deeply inhabiting the story. It's not surprising you feel bleak'. *Dead Dreams* has a lot of falling, people being knocked over, people collapsing, bodies going limp and people falling from great heights. During the creation of the work we shared personal stories and this forged bonds between the four of us on stage.
>
> NEWSON interview with author 2018

One of *DDMM's* emblematic falling sequences begins when Nigel and Russell stand facing each other. Russell repeatedly lifts a hand to stroke Nigel's face, but Nigel flinches from his touch each time. When Nigel, in turn, gestures towards him, Russell shoves him to the ground. A relentless testing of trust is established. Nigel runs to a ladder fixed to a wall and climbs a few steps. He swivels to face Russell, pauses, then drops like a plank. Russell catches him full-bodied against his chest and pushes him back up. Nigel climbs a few steps higher, pivots and – with one arm hooked around a rung – hangs precariously out over Russell. A moment of suspension occurs, with Russell looking up with his arms outstretched and Nigel peering down from above. He falls, Russell catches him, and they both hit the ground with the impact. Nigel disentangles himself and scrambles even higher. In the film version, the camera frames his perspective looking down on Russell, always gazing expectantly up. Nigel once again drops his full weight onto the now struggling Russell, knocking him backwards. Nigel climbs higher once more – this time *too* high. Russell looks up, slumps and turns away. Nigel plummets, but saves himself on a bar attached to an adjacent wall.

Lloyd describes how they created this moment:

> We were struggling to find physical forms to express our ideas – we had no role model. At one point we were sitting and talking about relationships between men, and Nigel said, 'I always set people up to fail'. 'What do you mean?' 'I mean, I set them tasks where they will fail, but if they

achieve that, I set another task'. Nigel said he does this in relationships both emotionally and physically. An idea popped into my head and I said, 'OK, let's set up exactly that. Tasks so that people fail or fall'. So, we created a situation where he climbed a ladder and someone had to catch him when he fell. And he got higher and higher. He made sure, because that's Nigel's DNA, that finally Russell couldn't catch him.

NEWSON interview 2018

The ladder scene sweeps away fairy tales, happy endings and idealized unions with significant others. Fuck it. Let go of fear. Let go of hope. There's nothing to lose, nothing to keep. Expect nothing, there *is* nothing, nowhere else to go but down. Nigel's falls conjure dark, nihilistic perspectives, as did the impact of HIV and of Nilsen's murders across gay communities.

RELEASING DANCE

Of all the dance techniques in Western white professional contemporary dance training, Release Technique most fully incorporates a somatic understanding of gravity and falling. In Release Technique, gravity and momentum initiate movement. 'There is so much falling in ... Release. Falling is incredibly rich in both practice and philosophy' (Moran interview with author 2019). Release incorporates ideokinesis, breath and anatomical structure – components that trace back to Mabel Elsworth Todd's body mechanics, Barbara Clark's plumb-line imagery and Frederick Alexander's re-alignment of the body around a lengthening spine.

Joan Skinner is credited as the principal initiator of Release Technique. She had been a dancer with Martha Graham and Merce Cunningham where 'all she heard was "grip, hold, pull up, grip, pull up"... She wondered how it was possible to "grip, hold on, pull up" ... and breathe' (Agis and Moran 2002: 21). Joan went on to study with Cora Belle Hunter (a graduate student of Todd) and also trained in Alexander Technique. In the late 1960s, when Joan was researching her technique in the context of modern dance, four post-modern dancers, Nancy Topf, Mary Fulkerson, John Rolland and Marsha Paludan, studied with her. They went on to develop their own versions of Release (Buckwalter 2012). Joan's work became known as Skinner Releasing Technique, while Nancy called her work Anatomical Release Technique and Mary termed hers simply Release. Marsha, who had studied with Anna Halprin, introduced improvisation to the field of Release. 'These two elements – imagery used to affect the body, and improvised movement exploration – remain basic principles of both Skinner's work and the work of the four friends' (Buckwalter 2012: 4). In the 1970s and 1980s, Mary taught at Dartington College of Arts in the UK, and her version of

Release spread throughout Europe, influencing the work of British somatic movement dancers such as Miranda Tufnell, Laurie Booth, Julyen Hamilton and Kirstie Simson. Joan and her quartet of colleagues bequeathed to dance training a rich genealogy of internally placed somatic imagery, body mechanics and improvisation.

British artists Gaby Agis and Joe Moran, who trained with Joan, explain that 'in the releasing class, poetic guided imagery leads the student into a state just below conscious control. It is in this state that the dancer can move and blend with the image. The dancer can be taken by the image' (Agis and Moran 2002: 21). Importantly, the term 'release' does not mean 'relax'. The imagery facilitates a release from fixed tensions so that dancers attain a dynamic freedom, 'releasing blocks . . . releasing power and releasing energy' (Agis and Moran 2002: 21). Joan often gave students the image of 'marionette strings', whereby a body is held up internally by imaginary rigging so that muscles and joints are free to fall and enabled to flow. Release Technique entails a perpetual search for 'an underlying body – a naked body of raw reflex without layers of conditioning' (Buckwalter 2012: 36). It functions through pedestrian, sensory-based movements grounded in internally perceived images of the body welcoming gravity.

A DISGRACE

Central to our collective work at X6 Dance Space (1975–80) was a refiguration of aspects of professional dance practice – training, performing and making. Alongside submersion into feminist politics, we explored somatic movement practices, which became integral to unwrapping traditional dance histories that had left such psychological and physical damage on many dancers' bodies, including my own. To survive financially during this time of discovery, I accepted a part-time teaching job at the Laban Centre for Movement and Dance, which had moved to London in 1975 from Kent in south-east England. The Laban Centre was seeking to establish itself as a professional training conservatoire. I was invited to teach ballet and contemporary dance. Inevitably, I could not resist introducing somatic principles into my teaching practice, particularly as I was obsessed at the time with Mabel Elsworth Todd's philosophical, psycho-somatic approach to human movement development.

One morning, teaching a ballet class, I explained Mabel's principles of anatomical alignment to support students' understanding of how to stand without fixing uprightness. We were sitting on the floor, discussing how to drop our tailbones to lengthen our spines. I had invited the students to remove their ballet slippers. Rather than wearing ballet's uniform of tights and leotards, some students were dressed in baggy tracksuit bottoms and

I was wearing a flowered skirt and footless tights, which, I must admit, were somewhat well worn. Interrupting our research, five school inspectors entered the studio to observe the class. As I envisage that moment now, I can understand why the inspectors might have been unnerved. After all, this was a ballet class and these officials were visiting the Centre to approve educational funding for Laban's conservatoire status. Soon after, the director at the time declined to renew my contract, suggesting that perhaps my work might be better suited to postgraduate students – post training.[10]

On reflection, I am not sure whether it was the holes in my tights or the fact that we had slumped to the ground in a ballet class that got me fired. What I do know is that what we were brewing at X6 – rethinking ballet training through somatic principles, working with rather than resisting gravity – was ahead of its time. My class fell short of meeting requirements for ballet training and was inappropriate for an institution with up-and-coming conservatoire status. My class, focusing on downward drop rather than upward lift, was an act of physical and metaphorical disgrace. It would be another twenty years before performer and teacher Gill Clarke was invited to incorporate somatic knowledges into professional dance training at the Laban Centre, in her role as Head of Performance Studies.

CONSTRUCTING RISK

Performance artist Bas Jan Ader constructed one-off situations in which he dared himself to fall and put his body at significant risk. Contemporary dancers are proficient at falling – as dancing. Their training builds strength and muscular coordination to increase the safety of their falls. For the most part, contemporary dancers fall from reasonable heights, in choreographies that are precisely timed and repeatable. When live/performance artists fall, they spotlight physical risk – as a critical condition of their work. Although Bas's live-art falls were only a promise of falling (Harvey 2013), he *confronted* gravity in ways that unsettled assumptions of spectators concerning his and their safety in the world (Verwoert 2006; Wolfs 2006; Dumbadze 2013; Brezavšček 2013; Sousa Lobo 2013).

---

[10]Dance academic Ann Cooper Albright had a similar experience when she began teaching somatic work at university, although she was not actually fired. Observing her class from outside the studio, looking in through a small window, her colleagues made an assumption that her class – where students were lying about on the floor seemingly doing nothing – was 'frankly useless', concluding that Albright was 'taking the lazy way out of teaching a technical, rigorous and dynamic dance class' (Albright 2017: 63).

Bas shot a series of short, black-and-white videos (1967–75) composed of constructed events in which he has no choice but to fall.[11] *Fall 1 Los Angeles* (1970) sees him sitting on a chair on the roof of a house. He rocks the chair – tipping and losing balance – until he and the chair tumble off the roof. In *I'm Too Sad to Tell You* (1971), he sits crying for the entirety of the film. *Fall 2* (1970) finds him peddling a bike downhill at top speed and without hesitation plunging straight into an Amsterdam canal, bike and all. In *Broken Fall, Organic* (1971) he hangs by his arms from a branch of a tree over a stretch of water until gravity overcomes him and he drops. No spectators appear in these films, and the performances are one-time events, filmed in order to be witnessed through time.

Bas was familiar with failures and falls in his life outside his artistic practice. He was two years old when his father was killed by Nazis for protecting Jews. He performed at his own wedding by leaning on crutches and in 1975, he died – somewhere in the Atlantic Ocean – while attempting to cross in a small sailing boat from the UK to America. His performances reveal him testing, then succumbing to, the force of gravity, which he neither fought nor mastered, instead devising situations where he was entirely vulnerable, had no control, and during which he remained passive. With this approach he rejected – with obvious conviction – the role of the artist as dominant subject; gravity was always in charge. As a post-Second World War artist, his falls were anti-spectacle and non-romantic; they deconstructed the association of war with victory and the expectations of heroism. By submitting to gravity, Bas rejected notions of immortality, offering 'extraordinary affirmations of existence in the brief but telling rehearsals for death, in the very banality of a miraculous gravity' (Fox 2013: 68). Bas revealed the absurdity of manly adventures, and with his crumbling but effortful performances of falling, he tipped spectacular performance into a bin where hope and glory lie discarded.

BRIDGE

All you have to do is stand up and relax ... and at a certain point you realize that you've relaxed everything that you can relax but you're still standing and in that standing is quite a lot of minute movement ... finding that limit to which you could no further relax without falling down, you're put in touch with a basic sustaining effort that goes on constantly in the body ... background movement static ... We're trying

---

[11]See Jan Ader's official website: www.basjanader.com.

to get in touch with these kinds of primal forces in the body and make them readily apparent. Call it the 'small dance'.

PAXTON 1977: 23

I was introduced to Steve's Small Dance in the 1970s at X6 Dance Space in London and I recall it as a practice of letting go of all but minimal effort to remain standing. Releasing external, muscular control turned my attention to minute details of my body in relation to gravity, animating a sense of the enormity of sensation that flows within apparent stillness. 'You've been swimming in gravity since the day you were born. Every cell knows where down is. Easily forgotten. Your mass and earth's mass calling to each other' (Paxton 1986: 50). The meditative practices of Small Dance facilitated experimentation with minuscule shifts of weight between one foot and another, which in turn allowed me to notice the complexity of nerves, senses, thoughts and feelings that are present in any preparation for action. Attending to smallness of doing evokes an expansion of stillness to include a multiplicity of possibilities towards action. The smaller the dance, the more information becomes available about how movement might happen. The tiniest shifts of weight between one foot and the other magnify and widen as an arc through time and space. With each shift, there is a sense of falling down rather than standing up. 'In exploring the small dance of skeletal alignment while standing, I am sensing subtle falls of parts of the skeleton' (Paxton 1979: 26).

In New York in the early 1970s, the Small Dance acted as a pollinating force, between Release and CI practitioners, providing a bridge between internally sensed somatic attention and externally focused contact partnering. Through practice of the Small Dance at experimental movement gatherings, somatic pioneers such as Mary Fulkerson, Nancy Topf and Barbara Dilly, who were working with body mechanics, ideokinesis and Release techniques, found common ground with CI dancers such as Nancy Stark Smith and Steve Paxton. 'This rigorous contemplative practice tuned us to the subtlety and intelligence of the reflexes of the body, which in turn became the foundation for the more overtly disorienting flinging and flying of bodies in space' (Koteen and Smith 2008: 21–2). Through the Small Dance, both forms recognized a shared 'interest in a new functional aesthetic of movement' and a similarity in embodiment of imagery (Buckwalter 2012: 4–5). Following on, Mary found that Release provided a conceptual framework with which to engage with CI (Buckwalter 2012). Similarly, Steve, curious as to what Release practitioners might do with the anatomical knowledge and the movement vocabulary they were sensing, suggested CI as a developing pathway, 'moving from the interior of one's functioning anatomy, to functioning with another' (Paxton 1975–6: 4).

I mention this meeting of forms because now, in 2020, Release and CI are rarely taught apart in Higher Education dance training. For me, this fusing is grounded in the practice of the Small Dance, highly significant for its stillness, smallness and attention to falling while standing. 'Stillness promotes a kind of play in the mind, it is highly inventive and real. To examine a thought in stillness is to face it on its own terms. There is no pretense to thoughts that arise from stillness' (Fulkerson 1981: 6).

TEETER TOTTER

Pina Bausch's *Café Müller* (1978) marks her creative transition from *Ausdruckstanz* to *Tanztheater* and the beginning of a revolution in post-war European dance aesthetics. In this dance theatre work, falling is a dominant figure (Heathfield 2006).

Ausdruckstanz – or German Expressionist dance – flourished in 1920s Germany as a rejection of industrialization and urbanization, and as a call to reclaim what Jeschke and Vettermann (2000) describe as 'body and nature'. *Ausdruckstanz* focused on a search for origins and for essential, universal, true human expression. Mary Wigman is considered a principal proponent of the form; her work 'emanated from individual creative genius; in other words, from innermost feelings and from the mind' (Jeschke and Vettermann 2000: 58). In contrast, *Tanztheater* focuses on everyday human behaviour, exploring relationships, social perspectives and personal issues as political reality, along with struggles of human co-existence. *Café Müller* marks a pivotal point in the transition between these two forms and teeters on the cusp of contrasting styles.

The opening moments of *Café Müller* are familiar to most dance artists and scholars. Dressed in a silk slip, her arms and legs bare, Pina dances alone upstage. Walking with eyes closed, she bumps into chairs, pauses, reflects and unfolds her long, thin arms into empty space. Internally focused, expressively intense and angst-ridden, her demeanour and presence evoke the characteristic qualities of *Ausdruckstanz*. In contrast, the five dancers of her ensemble, performing downstage, represent her growing interest in *Tanztheater*'s concerns, in actual relationships and social interactions. Rather than reaching towards universal essentialism and 'nature' as expressed through the individual dancer, Pina's dance theatre takes as its point of departure ' the performers' genuine, subjective experience, which is also invoked in the audience . . . It doesn't play-act, doesn't pretend "as if"; it *is*' (Servos 2008: 21).

With Pina in the background and her dancers in the foreground, *Café Müller* balances precariously between two eras. The piece is about 'loneliness and compulsive behaviour but also the search for another dance, another theatre, no longer obliged to serve a beautiful illusion, instead exploring the depths of emotion' (Servos 2008: 61). And the movements that most represent *Café Müller*'s teeter and totter between eras and styles are performers' acts of falling.

Dancers Malou Airaudo, Dominique Mercy and Jan Minarik perform a significant series of falls. They are standing close together when Jan wraps Malou's arm around his shoulder and places his own arm under her legs. As her knees buckle and she surrenders her weight, he scoops her up and drops her into the extended arms of Dominique. She is now dead weight, collapsed backwards on the shelf created by Dominique's arms. Time passes. Dominique drops her and she falls to the ground. He makes no attempt to catch her. The entire sequence then begins again. By the ninth repetition, the action accelerates and is no longer broken by pauses. Jan leaves, while Dominique and Malou continue on their own. She barely manages to climb into his arms before she's dumped and crashes again. She springs up only to fall again, over and over. A vivid thunk underscores her every impact. Although they are engaged in intimate, tactile exchanges, the faces of the dancers are vacant, as though moving through an endlessly repeating dream.

This is a key moment of falling in *Café Müller* and one that is viscerally described by Adrian Heathfield (2006). He writes a passionate account of the performers' actions of falling and failing, the repetitive choreography, aware of the significance of this original moment of European dance theatre. Re-playing the clip, Heathfield finds himself seduced by the scene as it 'slips through his fingers just as he tries to hold it' (Heathfield 2006 :194). He eventually names the three figures that he is absorbed in witnessing and in so doing sums up the underlying motifs of *Café Müller*. Jan is the figure of Time, Malou, Desire, and Dominique, Memory (Heathfield 2006).

The shift in dance aesthetics, from pleasing to blunt, that marks this moment is driven home further when the performers slam each other's bodies repeatedly against a wall. These seemingly forceful acts and incidents of falling were interpreted at the time as sexist aggression by critics like Horst Koegler, Arlene Croce and Joan Acocella.

> When Bausch first brought her company to the United States in 1984, cruelty was the thing in her work that amazed everybody: the sheer, stark brutality, usually inflicted by men on women. Perhaps the most indelible image of that first season was the episode in *Café Müller* where a man and a woman took turns picking each other up and hurling one another directly into a wall. Again and again they did it.
>
> ACOCELLA 2013: 213–14

Yet for many spectators and contemporary dancers, myself included, the slamming flesh in *Café Müller*, the alarming drops, were exhilaratingly honest representations of abandonment and loss providing a vivid contrast to Pina's wistful, barefooted wanderings upstage. Heathfield's words encapsulate dance theatre's risk-taking, yet necessary, physical expressions of falling.

[D]ance theatre and physical theatre articulated a certain wounding in the nature of sexual (and social) relation. Positioning the performing body as the vital means through which to access and articulate this wound, they also offered it up as a promising means of cure, or at least resistance, through the exertion of movement itself. Perhaps this is why the repetition of falling became such a dominant figuration in the choreography of dance theatre: trusting in relation, in the will and flesh of others, dance-theatre's emblematic sacrificial body fell again and again, subject to the violent disregard of the other. The other couldn't catch that fall. But the fall contained an imperative . . . to recognise, remember and repair.

HEATHFIELD 2006: 189

There are less documented, less violent, though equally significant evocations of falling in *Café Müller*. They are performed by Meryl Tankard, staggering about tipsy and dipsy in her high heels among chaotically scattered, upended chairs. High heels have enigmatic and ambiguous meanings throughout Pina's work. They sometimes symbolize the oppressive and fetishistic containment of women and act as instruments of bondage. At other times, they signify female grace, power and aplomb, or serve as vicious, dagger-like spikes giving women aggressive agency. High heels – like *pointe* shoes – show off the superb flexibility of the dancers' feet, their high arches, supple toes, sculpted calf muscles and confident strides. At the same time, these elaborate, artificial, architectural accessories diminish a dancer's control, complicate her balance and render her more vulnerable to gravity. They are a constant reminder of the proximity of fragility and power. Pina's women either fulfil the fantasy of fetishistic beauty or parody it blatantly, as they stagger, totter and vividly enact the comic, grotesque and ridiculous risks of their stiletto contraptions. High heels emphasize the restrictive boundaries within which Pina's dancers are constrained, boundaries against which they exude power and test gender stereotypes. The higher their heels, the more dangerous their risk of falling and the fiercer is their fight for agency. Each high-heeled step provokes an ever-present real, and represented, potential for falling that hovers just beneath the surface of human life.

Meryl's high-heeled tottering in *Café Müller* dramatizes in particular a wobbly historical crossing. She teeters between Pina's upstage performance of *Ausdruckstanz* and the ensemble's downstage embodiment of *Tanztheater*, consistently attempting to bridge the two. She flounders erratically on the outskirts of the action, always just behind or off to the side, dithering, directionless and on her own, often obstructing choreographed events. She notices everybody, but nobody sees her. She totters unsteadily backwards and forwards from Pina to the other dancers as if attempting to maintain a thread of communication, between individualistic expression and a sense of self in relation.

A STILL POINT

Stand, sensing your feet on the ground. Relax your eyes. Let your arms drop down by your sides. Lean gradually forwards from your ankles until you tip and need to catch yourself with a step forward. Then bring yourself back to standing. Repeat as many times as you like, catching yourself from falling with a forward step each time, and coming back to standing between each topple. Lean backwards in the same way and then sideways, in both directions. You are falling and catching yourself falling, always returning to a place where you feel grounded, your weight equal on both feet. Take as much or as little physical risk as you like, while noticing where you place your boundary between anxiety and exhilaration.

Continue to play, and as you do, gradually decrease the extent of your off-balance leaning; topple less and less each time – in all directions – minimizing the angle of your leaning to be barely noticeable to an external eye. Continue until you are doing no more than internally sensing a potential for leaning. Here is a still point of grounded support. Your body, in stillness, remains animated with sensations of falling while knowing you can catch yourself from falling. You are standing, alive with the force of gravity in your body, ready to move in all directions.

This exercise provides me with a safe opportunity to explore my tolerance for gravity's pull, for expanding the space and time in which I live and function before the fear of falling is activated. Being *with* the potency of gravity – sensing the extent of risks we are prepared to take without being overwhelmed by fear – can transform physical and psychological experiences of falling, while enhancing our relational, responsive readiness to interact in the world.

PACKAGING

By the 1990s, the somatic practice of Release was absorbed into mainstream Western contemporary dance. At which point I observed how the nuances of its philosophy seemed to get lost within the structures of technical training. Admitting here to a subjective view informed by a critique of my own teaching, I suggest Release principles and innovative processes of discovery tended to be applied to dance training – and consequently to dance vocabulary – to ignite a fluidity and range of movement previously missing in modern dance choreography. This reflection invites a paradox. Release has inspired an engaging choreographic style, exemplified by the loose-limbed, fragmented movements characteristic of American choreographer Trisha Brown's repertoire. Yet in doing so Release has become a fashionable dance technique with coded movement phrases, to which teachers, students and choreographers can affix criteria of success and failure. My subjective view is validated by Nancy Topf, who taught according to original Release principles, but became reluctant to use Release Technique to describe her work, because of its associations with dance fashion. At the time of her death she was developing a programme called Topf Technique and Dynamic Anatomy to avoid being associated with Release (Buckwalter 2012).

The point of Release philosophy is not to identify a fixed pattern, choreographic style or way of moving, but to embody an ongoing process of inquiry. Even though – perhaps particularly because – Release is a practice founded in an acceptance of uncertainty, institutional teaching tends to package it as a falling style and an assessable product. Rather than encouraging its disorientating, unpredictable and curious process. By coding falling in Release Technique, sources of vitality that are consequences of engagement with gravitational uncertainties can be smoothed out and lost to habitual repetition.

DYING FOR LOVE

The year is 1993. I am chucking myself about with Nigel Charnock, the queer prodigy of physical theatre, in his performance-making workshop. Nigel sets the score which goes like this: Emilyn loves Nigel. Emilyn will do anything for Nigel. Nigel, however, does not return the passion. He tolerates Emilyn's advances, while remaining indifferent. For an hour, we improvise without speaking. It takes a full hour – not only to test endurance for withstanding this relational dynamic, but also to experience it fully on both physical and psychological levels.

Then, we exchange roles and the score is repeated. Starting cautiously, Nigel performs for Emilyn with teasing gestures. Emilyn remains unresponsive, turns away or draws back. Nigel persists and, in time, attempts a range of tactics to entice her. He catches her in a hug, grabs her hands, pulls her, holds her, flirts, caresses and smothers her with kisses. Emilyn remains cool and aloof. As the hour goes on, Nigel drops to his knees to embrace Emilyn's ankles; Emilyn drags him along the ground. Nigel runs ahead in front of Emilyn, throwing himself to the ground, demanding attention. Emilyn walks over Nigel's prone body. Nigel gets up and tries again, repeatedly falling for a love unmet.

Go back twenty-five years to the short film *Darling, Do You Love Me?* (dir. Martin Sharp and Bob Whitaker, 1968), performed by a feisty, young, creative Germaine Greer and shot during her time at the counter-culture magazine, *Oz*. Germaine's male co-actor (Alisdair Burke) plods forward in a straight line along a country path. He wears a suit, coat, hat and glasses. Germaine is outrageously clad in a long white dress and long black wig. With her heavily made-up face – featuring exaggerated outlines around her lips and eyes – she warbles 'Darling, do you love me?' in fulsome parody of operatic style. As she sings, she throws herself all over her partner, clutching his face, waving her arms and flitting about, flapping, jumping, blocking his progress. Increasingly exasperated by his lack of attention, she dives across his path. He steps right over her.

Up to this point, the material performed by Germaine and her partner parallels my experience of Nigel's score. Germaine's film continues to completion along feminist lines. She seizes her reluctant partner and wrestles him to the floor. With fingers laced around his throat, she strangles the man until he squeezes out the words 'I love you' – at which point, she abruptly stops, turns to camera and, slowly smiling, reveals the words THE END inked on her teeth. Nigel's score, though, has no completion. The process of playing the roles is both the narrative and the point. Performed twenty-five years apart, the two approaches underscore shifting engagements in the politics of desire.

The narrative of *Darling, Do You Love Me?* reflects a parodic take on a 1960s heterosexual feminist crusade to give visibility and voice to women's desires, exposing the exasperating position experienced by women when their wants are ignored by men. In this film, the role of the submissive female – vehemently contested by feminists – is overturned by Germaine's parodic take as she projects, then subverts, the role of the submissive object. Casting herself as a hysterical woman, throwing herself all over her man, she flips expectations by taking possession of both him and his emotions. Choreographically, she mocks the linear, phallic, straightforward fixities of heteronormative desire. Solid and composed, Alisdair walks upright in a straight line forward – while she runs, sings and chaotically falls, flitting maniacally from side to side of the screen. By openly flaunting *her* sexual desires, *her* wants and *her* determination to play a dominant role, she puts to scorn Freud's famous questioning of what women desire, along with his declaration that 'women oppose change, receive passively and add nothing of their own' (Freud 1925: 245).[12]

With her final smile, Germaine spoofs the fears that submission to a woman's sexual desires heralds a man's downfall – and subjects that old apple-and-Eve story to ridicule. When the words THE END appear in her satisfied smile, she effectively derides Freud's notion of Oedipal desire as a perpetual (male) quest for an unattainable Other through 'an endless network of replacements, substitutes, and representations of the perpetually absent object' (Grosz 1995: 176). Quest over, goal accomplished. Germaine gets her man, The End.

---

[12]The term *desire* seems to belong to another era of mid twentieth century, when the Western world was seduced by theories of Freud and Lacan, Oedipal narratives, psychoanalysis, phallocentrism. For feminist critique of the psychoanalytical narrative of desire based on Oedipal logic, see Mulvey 1975; Kaplan 1983; de Lauretis 1984; Phelan 1993; Grosz 1995; Schneider 1997.

Germaine's positioning of herself as submissive object (which she then subverts in order to take control) is overturned in Nigel's score twenty-five years later, signalling a shift in perspectives on desire, from feminist to queer. In this context, desire becomes a play of love and submission, a process without a goal of completion. Nigel appears to be surrendering, dying for love, to no effect, while Emilyn stays aloof. My description of the score suggests that Nigel's part is submissive and humiliating, while Emilyn plays the dominant role. Yet, improvising Nigel's role induces different sensations, tells a different story. Most participants (myself included) discover that Nigel, falling on the floor, seemingly suffering the effects of abandonment, feels empowered by the experience. Emilyn – remaining distant, upright and reserved – actually plays a supportive role for Nigel's liberation. The practice generates a physical understanding of how *falling* for love, dying for another, can become a source of agency for the one who submits. Here, pleasure is not in getting or achieving, winning or dominating, but in becoming a body of desiring, self-aware, reflecting queer perspectives. Power and agency are realized through submission.

Heteronormative psychoanalysis promotes an idea of desire being primarily concerned with reaching a goal: an original object exists for which the desiring subject is always searching, always longing, and to which she feels she belongs, while always finding it unattainable. Queer desire is about a *process* of desiring – about meandering between objects – and not necessarily about a sense of belonging. Because there is no original. As feminist theorist and philosopher Elizabeth Grosz writes, queer desiring is a rethinking of 'social relations in terms of bodies, energies, movements' (1995: 77); it does not focus on fixed, identifiable goals of desire. In her film, Germaine gets her desires met. Nigel's desires are never met; the play of desiring is both process and goal. Yet, in both Germaine's film and Nigel's score, acts of fall and surrender serve as physical, psychological and metaphorical signifiers of contrasting embodiments of desire, and of falling in love.

SUBLIME BANALITY

In her piece *Rire/Laugh/Lachen* (2008), Antonia Baehr laughs out loud; throughout the presentation she explores laughter for its variable rhythms, registers and qualities of sound.[13] She is not a comedian, does not make jokes, nor is her laughter triggered by jokes. She uses laughter as concept and content, as a sound score and choreographic tool.

---

[13]The performance was developed at Les Laboratoires d'Aubervilliers during a two-year residency to research laughter.

Antonia is dressed with queer flair in trousers, shirt, jacket, tie and sturdy lace-up shoes. In her left hand she holds a ball, which she casually drops, and as it lands, she utters a corresponding laughing sound. The ball bounces a number of times and then skitters across the floor to a stop. During its trajectory, Antonia times her laughter precisely to its rhythm and tone. The ball's bounces become the score for her laughter. Later, she drops a ball with no bounce, and when it thuds to the stage, she emits a single bark-like laugh.

Antonia is sitting before a music lectern, studying the pages it holds. She reads as if following a musical score, and laughs according to its rhythm and pitch. Her laughter swells to cacophonous proportions, oscillating between tight-teethed giggling to open-mouthed bellowing. Occasionally she turns a page with her left hand, keeping precise time as she conducts herself with her right.

Detached and aloof, she seems to be scrutinizing laughter for its unpredictable, nonsensical potential, for its tonal qualities when severed from narratives or jokes. She appears to be engaging with laughter as an art form. Her erect posture and formal, drag-king attire convey gravity and seriousness of purpose. On occasion, though, she corpses and – suddenly helpless – starts laughing, as if moved by a force not her own. 'No one can corpse without at the same time knowing the power of the injunction to "pull yourself together"' (Ridout 2006: 145). In these moments – I am also helplessly giggling.

I laugh in response to her juxtaposition of the serious and the mundane. A laughing score for an everyday ball drop is a ridiculous proposition. As is turning the pages of a laughing score – the idea that laughter can be written

FIGURE 1.2 *Antonia Baehr in* Rire/Laugh/Lachen *(2008). Photo: Marc Domage.*

in notes on a stave. Or the notion that pages of laughter might have beginnings and endings, that laughing on the next page follows laughter on the previous.

Antonia's laughter is a serious performance. Yet her workaday gestures counteract the gravity, tripping and tumbling her clear out of dignity. Turning a page, dropping a ball, her movements have the look of off-stage blunders, like the actions of stagehands working the wrong show. Her laughter and her gestures appear absurdly queer and earnestly straight. An ambiguous, comic mix of solemn silliness and sublime banality.

ENDURANCE

Marina Abramovich presents... was a live-art exhibition at Whitworth Gallery during the Manchester International Festival (2009). Two women delivered telling performances of falling: Kira O'Reilly in *Stair Falling* (2009) and Amanda Coogan in *The Fall* (2009). Kira, whose work is informed by her training in Mixed Martial Arts, rolled slowly – naked – down the gallery's grand staircase. Her compelling descent gave the impression of a series of complex, improvised negotiations with successive stair ledges. She presented the piece for four hours a day over seventeen days.

> As I performed *Stair Falling* ... achingly slow fallings, naked, down a Victorian stone staircase, the caress of stone and skin, the effect of gravity and gaze burdened and unburdened my body. It was as much a dancing of becomings and molecular shifts as anything. It was upside-down hangings and slidings, flashings of pink bits and eye holdings, feelings and touching of iron and stone through soft leather skin gloves, hairs catching and muscles softening. Tits and arse askew.
>
> O'REILLY 2017: 47[14]

In *The Fall* (2009), Amanda wore a yellow evening gown and repeatedly fell, jumped, flew from a ladder onto a yellow mattress. She did this for four hours, becoming increasingly exhausted, curious about the way duration and endurance would affect her presence in live performance (Knezevic 2009). Her work alluded to Yves Klein's iconic photograph of apparent free falling, *Leap into the Void* (1960). But Coogan included the mattress, which is not visible in Klein's photograph.

In Kira and Amanda's live-art performances, each artist's body is the subject and the object of the art work, events where physical and metaphorical falls collide. Amy Sharrocks, another live artist who has worked with falling,

---

[14]See also Duggan (2009).

states: 'We suppose and we take liberties. We are presumptuous. Falling unsettles all of our worlds. It disturbs the universe. We need to have the strength to force the moment to its crisis' (Sharrocks 2013: 55). Kira, Amanda and Amy experience the tactile sensual impact of falling, the gravitational pressure of body weight against surfaces, grazing and bruising different parts of their bodies. These are real bodies exuding a vital aliveness at moments of crisis, falling through gravity – and they keep on doing it. These women reclaim the negative symbolism of 'fallen women' by physicalizing acts of falling with artistic agency. The artists' bodies also represent a zone free from sensible propositions and reasonable judgements – one that encourages spectators to step beyond comfort and dare to take risks. These women construct falling events in which – by embodying risk and testing endurance and failure on their own bodies – they expose a vulnerable underbelly of living in the world now.

DEATH DIVES

Belgian choreographer Wim Vandekeybus hit the headlines in 1987 with *What the Body Does Not Remember*, performed by his company Ultima Vez. Critic Judith Mackrell remembers it 'as the work that pushed dance to new physical extremes, introducing a whole new vocabulary of barrelling combat rolls, high flung kicks, and bodies used as missiles' (2015).

Before forming his own company, Wim performed with Jan Fabre, a sculptor, theatre maker, video artist and director whose work *The Power of Theatrical Madness* (1984) had ripped through the Belgian dance scene, then held in the grip of ballet traditions. Jan's rebellion was extreme, defiant and urgent. 'We may speak here of a prime example of identity construction through negative self-determination: one affirms one's personal artistic identity via an overt dis-identification with an already existing genre' (Laermans and Gielen 2000: 17).[15] *The Power of Theatrical Madness* was a four-hour endurance test for performers and spectators, welding together acts of horror, beauty and terror in a series of filmic theatrical images (De Vos 2015). Scenes include: a man in a suit sitting upright in a chair sings opera and repeatedly slaps the bare arse of the naked woman lying over his lap; a blindfolded man swipes a sharp knife at another; naked men wash socks in buckets; a line of performers run on the spot for twenty minutes while reciting famous names from British theatre. Interspersed are live glistening frogs and smashing plates.

---

[15]Laermans and Gielen (2000) map out the development of an authentic contemporary dance in Belgium, which began with the work of Anne Teresa De Keersmaeker.

So Wim Vandekeybus was familiar with ways to set fire to the citadel of ballectic aesthetics, and he initiated a genre of dance and physical theatre that took Europe by storm in the late 1980s, a genre characterized by dancers falling full force. *What the Body Does Not Remember* begins when a bare-legged woman in short tunic and Doc Martens throws a brick into the air above her head . . . and waits. As it falls, a man races from stage left to grab her, they crash to the ground, narrowly avoiding the brick as it bangs to the stage. Another man, dressed in white shirt and trousers, throws a brick up and waits. He is kicked out of the way and the brick is caught by another performer. The risks are replayed in various ways. A man at full run throws a brick across the stage to be caught mid-chest by a woman who is thrown to the ground by the impact. 'The brick is real and its flight through time cannot be stopped' (Hrab 2016: 5). A running woman flings herself at a man, collapsing onto him with the full force of her weight and slamming him backwards to the ground. Feathers fall, bricks fall (and sometimes break), clothes, boots and bodies all fall. This is not the theatre of make-believe. Gravity cannot lie, nor can falling bricks. The danger is genuine: 'We threw stones so that people would understand why that feeling exists. If you fall, you don't think about the best way to fall: you just fall' (Vandekeybus in Pawlouski, VerHelst and Byrne 2016: 170).

The movement vocabulary Wim pursued throughout his work was based on instinctive actions in the face of injury or death. Gravity was the principal antagonist, the urgent signifier was falling.[16] 'You can't be polite . . . If a car is about to hit a child, you – bang – push the child out of the way' (Winship 2015b). Wim confronts his performers with extreme situations – with actions requiring instinctive reactions – where they are unable to make preconceived decisions. Each movement happens as a necessary consequence of another. Bricks are thrown; bodies are thrust harshly aside. The choreography is tight, precise and repeatable; yet the demands of the material cannot be relied upon to happen unless performers are alert and responsive to the risks posed by each action.

In Wim's later work *Blush* (2002), falling is metaphorically depicted through a kind of Dionysian debauchery having more in common with Jan Fabre's un-boundaried visual orgies than the clean abstract physicality of *What The Body Does Not Remember*. *Blush* slides down muddy theatrical slopes with ecstatic, orgiastic, irrational delight. It revels in its lurid stew of frenzied, undisciplined, recklessly uninhibited and instinctive body mess. The lights go up on a group of women and men at a bottle-strewn table. Their drunken dialogue rapidly dissolves into decadent action. A woman is cheered as she drinks the liquidized remains of a lizard; a man stands on the hair of a woman whose head is pinned flat to the table.

---

[16]Although later works were text- and narrative-based, risking death through physical falling continued in *Les Porteuses de Mauvaises Nouvelles* (1989) and *In Spite of Wishing and Waiting* (1999).

Rage of Staging (Pawlouski, VerHelst and Byrne 2016) is a book about Wim's work that encapsulates Belgian artists' radical resistance to European ballet's haughty veneer. Screaming mouths, naked flesh, tied-up bodies, wrenched-open clothing, tangled ropes, torn underwear, leering masks and billowing smoke are common elements along with Doc Martens and stained satin dresses. Bloodied skin, straggling hair, sprawling gestures, running bodies, old, young, skinny and fat bodies, up against the wall bodies, bum in your face bodies, thrown to the floor bodies, lying in the grit bodies littering the stage, streaking surfaces, smearing lenses, teetering, grasping, clawing and gasping, trampling bodies, hanging upside down bodies, bodies embracing, passionately reaching, aggressively thrusting, yanking, pulling, slapping, pushing, and collisions of rampaging horses. Every second page of *Rage of Staging* overflows with descriptions of bodies falling, wide-flung arms, adventures with gravity, surges of adrenalin, fearsome encounters with death in life.

Wim's father was a veterinarian, and as a child Wim became familiar with existential catastrophes as he followed his father on his rounds. Death – without pathos – was sometimes all that could be offered (Felsenburg 1999). 'If you make something about death, everything pulsates with life . . . From the moment you are born, death is inside you' (Vandekeybus in Pawlouski, VerHelst and Byrne 2016: 327).

In the 1980s, falling as surrender – without hope of redemption, as a violent fissure in dance's glossy veneer – became a signature element of European dance and physical theatre. Wim and his followers inspired radical rethinking and a regenerative new relationship between body, gravity and ground. Falling was an expression of aliveness in desolation, lyrical waves of harmonious movement disintegrated rapidly as body after body slammed to the floor. The stage was not a springboard. Getting up was not a rhythmic inevitability. Falling was an admission of the uncertainties of sex, love and death. Gone was the hope of a better life, as constituted by Christian mythology; gone was the external longing, the reaching for upwards and beyond, as dancers dropped to the ground or flopped lifeless in each other's arms. For me, I fell as a result of embracing abandonment, surrendering to loss and rejecting dreams of redemptive desire. Kaput went happy endings, as did ideal resolutions and transcendent heights. Yet falling was far from ultimately destructive. Yes, our bodies were often bruised, but falling generated a living force, for performers and spectators alike.

THE BUCK STOPS HERE

Partnered falls in dance/physical theatre – which I call 'splats' – have a particular dynamic that distinguishes this dance form from other genres. In a prime example from DV8's *Dead Dreams of Monochrome Men* (Newson

1988), Lloyd Newson runs and flings himself directly at Russell Maliphant, his partner who stands waiting. On contact, Russell falls backwards and together they drop to the floor. On the way down, Lloyd clasps his hands behind Russell's neck and holds him tightly, even as they hit the stage. Russell lands on his back, with Lloyd in a crouch, his feet on either side of Russell's neck. The connection is intense, as Lloyd continues to cup Russell's head in his hands. The momentum, though, ends there; they do not rebound, nor use the floor to recover.

This and similar splats are familiar to practitioners of physical theatre. What identifies it as specific to the genre is the dancers' mutual, downward trajectory, as distinct from the duet work in ballet and modern dance, where partners catch each other on the upward swing, resisting gravity through muscular efforts or with a range of arched positions. Physical theatre's splats require the same discipline and precise timings as ballet's lifts, but the partners here go as far as gravity hurls them. The dive in *Dead Dreams* ends with both partners pressed to the ground, with no suspension or upward arching. Physical theatre practitioners revel in down. Catching their partners descending from leaps, they make no effort to disguise their weight and willingly succumb to gravity's designs; both partners typically fall to the ground.

A partnered splat has some similarity with Contact Improvisation partner-work. Nancy Stark Smith describes her early experiments with CI in the 1970s.

> The catcher would stand toward the back of the blue mat with one foot slightly stepped back, to make the eventual spiralling motion easier to initiate. One after the other, the individuals in the group would run and jump into the air in front of the catcher ... The catcher would snatch the falling mass against his or her body, sometimes turning to follow the momentum into movement, often going down to the mat with the mass and following through with a roll.
>
> SMITH 2008: 22

Physical theatre and CI both emphasize the downward trajectories of partnered falls, with little interest in skyward gestures. But there is a significant difference. Contact practitioners practise falling into rolling as a seamless flow of movement or, as Steve Paxton (1979) described it, flipping vertical momentum into horizontal travel. In CI, falling is usually made graceful and continuous. In physical theatre, graceful rolls to recover from falls are rare. Splats make no pretence of achieving kinetic or aesthetic harmony. The buck stops here, where body meets ground, where flow ends abruptly, sometimes painfully, but where the exhilaration of being just might materialise. This emphasis on a downward dynamic has bearing on choreographic structures and helps explain dance theatre's use of collage, juxtaposition, nonsense, abrupt changes, incompletion and disharmony, rather than linear narratives with happy endings.

This difference is intensified by intention. CI favours falls where relationships between dancers are a function of sensory awareness and weight; the mess of humanity's emotional entanglements is left outside the door. Dancers motivated to dance by somatic impulses tend to ignore expressions of sexuality, loss, abandonment and anger, or the hysteria of behavioural, psychological or autobiographical narratives. But physical theatre embraces narratives of human existence as its basis for creativity. The splat – falling without rebound – works with risk and values expressions of human mess.

2

Falling Out

A LUMBERING TILT

On a visit to New York City in 2017, I take a walk along the High Line, a constructed, West Side walkway on a disused railway track that stretches north from 14th to 34th Street. Around 20th, I see an arresting work of graffiti on a white-washed wall. To the left, the words 'DONALD, MAKE AMERICA PSYCHO AGAIN' are written in black. Fixed on the wall to the right are three black, oblong frames, like windows, through which an image of the continent of North America appears to be dropping. It is as if the continent – once fixed – is now ripped and sliding below the frames.

The call 'Donald, Make America Psycho Again' has layers of meaning. An obvious reworking of President Trump's campaign phrase 'Make America Great Again', it also recalls Bret Easton Ellis's horror novel *American Psycho* (1991), about a successful businessman who is at the same time a deranged serial killer. It alludes as well to the billboard 'Make America White Again,' as erected by Tennessee Congressman Rick Tyler in 2016 to advertise his deeply racist re-election campaign. All of which suggests that the High Line graffiti is targeting a slew of racist and arguably unhinged impulses which surfaced in Trump's 2016 election campaign.

The window frames position America as being observed from outside, as a continent on the brink of disaster, collapsing out of its safe zone. This falling is not depicted as a clean break. The nation appears torn from its framework, its jagged edges ripped and misshapen. Like a ship hitting a rock, the continent appears to be lurching and toppling. Black against the white wall, the image can be seen as the aftermath of a fire – or a nuclear disaster – with the country sliding charred and disordered from its moral framework. The words suggest an America murdered by a psycho fanatic. And not a clean murder, not a shot to the head, but a tearing away, limb by limb. There is no ground below on which to rest, just a continuous falling, a lumbering tilt – to the right.

ABOUT SHAME

Shame is a sensitive topic. Feeling shame, witnessing another's shame, even a discussion about shame, are all uncomfortable. Shame is wrapped tightly in metaphorical, psychological and emotional associations with sinking down. But the feeling of falling associated with shame is not one that registers physically with the ground. Shame has taken me out of my body. Its falling sensations mark my disappearance into an overwhelmingly emotional space where my body hurts, but I can't find the ground.

Shame is always close to hand when I work as a psychotherapist, and always a relational, co-created event. If my client feels shame in the therapy room, I will most certainly have played a part in creating her shame, as will she have for me. For every shamed person, there is one who shames, as a consequence of her own being shamed. For myself, I feel shame as a dancer, a choreographer, a woman, an older person and as a writer. I am also ashamed for my ability to shame others – as a mother, a teacher and perhaps most of all, as a white person with middle-class privilege. Any of these kinds of shame can appear in the therapy room to entwine with those of my client's.

Understanding shame as a relational phenomenon was certainly not the case when I was growing up in the UK. I would go as far as to say that, like the word 'cancer', the word 'shame' remained unspoken, a subject of taboo. Shame was felt silently, miserably and alone. British philosopher Bernard Williams sums up the raw, corrosive slink of shame:

> In the experience of shame, one's whole being seems diminished or lessened ... The expression of shame, in general, as well as in the particular form of it that is embarrassment, is not just the desire to hide, or to hide my face, but the desire to disappear, not to be there. It is not even the wish, as people say, to sink through the floor, but rather the wish that the space occupied by me should be instantaneously empty.
>
> WILLIAMS 1993: 89

I know that feeling well: my shoulders collapse, my head burrows down, I cannot look up, I am unable to speak. That sense of unworthiness in the presence of others manifests as painful internal sensations and deflated external gestures. Pride, in contrast, manifests itself in a straight back, puffed-out chest, lifted chin and pulled-back shoulders; it walks tall, peers outwards and presents a body demanding respect. Pride lifts and expands, shame falls and deflates, and yet they are interdependent. As William Blake famously wrote 'shame is pride's cloak' (1790), although I tend to remember the maxim in reverse.

The experience of shame is like swallowing undigested feelings of never being good enough; it renders the sense of isolation from others intense.

Shame is the sound of someone's voice saying 'Who do you think you are?' And this failed sense of self is quite different to the experience of guilt. In Brené Brown's TED Talk, where she focuses on the necessity for white people to face the vulnerability of shame in any conversation about race, she says, 'Shame is a focus on self; guilt is a focus on behaviour. Shame is 'I am bad'; guilt is 'I did something bad'. Sorry I made a mistake – guilt. Sorry I *am* a mistake – shame' (Brown 2012, emphasis mine).

Psychotherapist Gordon Wheeler, who writes about shame from a Gestalt perspective, points out that in Freud's early model of psychoanalysis, shame, as an experience of isolation, was posited as a patient's problem – not the therapist's – and that it was the patient who had to resolve through therapy her feelings of shame. You achieve and fail on your own. This is a notion of Western individuality notoriously imprinted by Christianity, Victorian morality and white-centredness, where the self alone is a 'given thing, pre-existent and predefined, a font of life force' (Wheeler 1997: 32). For psychoanalyst Donna Orange, shame in this context becomes 'a hardwired response ... independent of relational experience' (2008: 86). Given how sinking gestures of shame are emotionally painful to experience in this isolating model, the idea of falling as a creative source for change might appear to exacerbate the pain.

Orange provides a more recent and radical rethinking of shame within humanistic psychotherapies, recognizing that shame 'like all emotion, is an emergent property of a relational system' (2008: 87). Shame is produced intersubjectively: there is always a humiliator and a person ashamed. To know shame is to learn to shame, a perpetually interwoven relational paradigm where avoidance of humiliation and of the vulnerability of shame is always paramount.

> There are, of course, many forms of humiliation, ranging from early shaming parent child interactions, through bullying, to rape and torture. Each of these establishes a shaming system, in which the dominator tries to overcome shame ... by humiliating the other, that is, by shaming him.
>
> ORANGE 2008: 89

The vulnerability experienced tends to produce a denial of shame through the act of bullying another. Rather than experiencing together the vulnerability of shame, people turn toward anger, hate and bitterness as safer options. Just as a bullied person can become a bully, so entire institutions can adopt bullying tactics as a resistance to vulnerability. American psychoanalyst Neil Altman (2004) identifies this as narcissistic rage when he writes of his country's ideological machismo and wrath in the wake of 9/11. Similarly, dominant systems of sexism, racism and colonialism in the UK and across the entire world can be stripped bare to reveal an underlying avoidance of shame's vulnerability and sinking sense of humiliation.

For myself, shifts in understanding come through my awareness of – and responsiveness to – shame. 'Without my own lifeworld of shame, even if the particulars are very different, I could not grasp yours deeply enough' (Orange 2008: 96). Considering shame as relational and as shared vulnerability experienced by both sides is a central tenet of empathy. 'Some have speculated that empathy is possible because we are prewired to (I would say we have the capacity to) experience both sides of interactions' (Orange 2008: 89). So, I sit with clients and we name shame as it floods into the room. In doing so, our relationship shifts away from falling into isolation and toward falling together, to understanding our mutual shame as shared vulnerability – and to resolving the issues intersubjectively. Falling is shameful. Shame is falling. And a practice of consciously falling together, provides support for all of us who experience shame.

DUST

Stand with your eyes relaxed, letting go of outward focus. Tap the top of your head at the place where it was soft when you were new born. Imagine a plumb line from this point, dropping down through the centre of your body until it reaches the ground between your feet. Envision the line falling continuously downwards to the centre of the Earth. Now picture the top of your plumb line extending upwards into space. Imagine this plumb line is all that holds you standing. The upward line does the work of resisting gravity. It is not your muscles, nor your joints that hold you upright; they are falling down along the plumb line. All that is keeping you upright is your imagined, inner connection to an upwardly stretching imaginary line.

Use this vision to release tension in your muscles – as though you were a puppet dangling on a string. Your body drops, down along the plumb line while your upward line holds your skeleton from falling. Trust your bones to align along this axis, submit to the elasticity of being drawn upward and downward toward earth's polarities. In your mind's eye, consider this elongation, your extension upward and release down, and imagine your flesh dropping away from your skeleton – like ripe fruit dropping. These sensations are internally conjured, no action actually occurs. On the contrary, action is undone.

To initiating walking, let your upward line lead you from the top of your head. Shift the line forward and upwards, and let your body follow, while continuing to fall away, down, downwards through the earth. Your body is elongating in two directions, moved by fluid, internally visualized images rather than muscular tension. Nothing fixes. Let your focus on the imaginary up and down lines actuate your walking and running. Picture your infinite alignment. Let your head and your tailbone, stretching away from each other, propel you into motion.

When I was introduced to this imagery in the mid 1970s, I was exhilarated by its impact on my way of moving. The name for the practice was Plumb Line, conceived by somatic pioneer Barbara Clark and developed by contemporary somatic practitioners such as Pamela Matt and Andrea Olsen.[1] The practice gently facilitates skeletal realignment and readjustment. More than that, my joints feel spacious and my muscles released, yet I am internally balanced. It was a revelation for me in the 1970s, as every sinew, muscle, joint and nerve in my body became free to move in a full range of directions, each distinct yet fluid. I was suspended upright simply by an image. If I let go of the upwardly moving line, I could fall to the ground without tension.

As a sensory experience, the practice of plumb line imagery overrides judgements about right or wrong ways of standing that are often embodied in habitually externalized expressions of pride and shame. Plumb line imagery encourages expansion of movement without the influences of defence or aggression. No longer held together by muscular tension, nor organized, arranged, dictated to, or constructed by, social or moral correctness, I experience my physical self as elongated between forces, stabilized magnetically like a pattern of buzzing dust particles, suspended in this moment of time and space.

PULLING UP

Throughout my childhood, I schooled my body to be taut, muscular and straight. I struggled to present myself with an upward-arched spine, with eyes up, chin up, tits up, stomach sucked in, bum clenched tight, kneecaps hoisted and hair scraped up in a bun. Inside and outside the ballet studio, I was taught that to achieve such *hauteur* – of both attitude and physique – would lead to a successful, productive and privileged life as both a ballet dancer and a woman. If I broke the upward line, thrust or circled my pelvis, crouched, squatted or danced close to the ground, my actions would be seen as vulgar or titillating or, at best, as trafficking in light entertainment. In other words, as debasing proper form. While I quickened to the rhythms of jazz dance and enjoyed learning movements that ran counter to ballet's upwardly aspiring ideals, I was conditioned to believe that jazz was an inferior form, while ballet sat imperial and dignified on its hierarchical peak.

The association of classical ballet with aristocracy and empire is, of course, not accidental. From its inception in the court of Louis XIV, to its

---

[1] My version here is adapted from Olsen's Body Mind Centering version described in Cohen (2012: 16). The *Plumb Line* process has close parallels with practices in Alexander Technique, Body Mind Centering, Yoga and Release Technique.

enduring influence on most major dance companies, ballet celebrates nobility and romanticizes the elite. Much of its canon reveres a notion of empire as a benign and desirable condition. Along with its technical requirements, ballet comprises a range of movements coded with specific meanings. Soon after internalizing ballet's haughty posture and refined aesthetics, I was taught a set of 'mime' conventions to complete its story-telling ends, many of which deal with social and political superiority. In other words, I was trained to swan about with exquisite gentility, to assume my position in the highest classes, to pretend to be royal.

So ballet would seem to have little to add to a book about falling, other than to register its transcendent and spectacular resistance. There are, of course, narrative fallings in ballet, though they are usually involuntary and always catastrophic, often representing madness or death. In *Giselle* (Coralli/Perrot 1841), the title character's iconic downfall dramatizes both of these. Giselle, an amorous young peasant girl, goes mad when she discovers she has been deceived by a disguised prince out looking for fun. In traditional versions, her madness peaks when she collapses to the stage after a frantic, full diagonal run. Early in my career I saw many a Giselle crumble into a heap before raising a face eerily transformed, pulling free her hair and staring with crazed eyes at an unrecognizable world. Her death follows shortly. While this is the nadir of her story on the worldly plane, the entire second act is devoted to her adventures in the afterlife, where she restores her verticality and reclaims a kind of spiritual nobility. At this point, ballerinas interpreting the role require the full force of their early training to embody convincingly the ethereal values of the classical ideal, its seemingly effortless upwards elongation.

Achieving these skills is an arduous process. Ballet dancers train their bodies – on which gravity so relentlessly acts – from the earliest years to express loftiness and nobility, whether political or spiritual. They strive for a sense of airiness, even when their knees are obliged to bend to cushion landings. What is one of the spurs that motivates all this upward striving and grandeur? Shame. To achieve a trained ballet body, constructed around classical ideals and the aesthetics of European aristocracy, the shaming process begins early. Many young ballet dancers experience, as I did, an ongoing war between shame and drive. On a daily basis, I could either win Madame's approving glance for successfully conforming to her sucked-in, pulled-up and upwardly straining postural standards or, when insufficiently erect, internalize the shame of her withering stare. Subjected to her targeted shame, I would feel myself slumping in both morale and posture. And so the struggle began anew.

Shame was a spur that drove me to shape my body to ballet's ideals, to adopt its manners and aspire to its social values of white European imperialism. This dream – perhaps delusion – is only achieved with extreme effort, along with considerable deprivation and suffering. In my case, the aristocratic ideals toward which I was striving, toward which I disciplined my flesh, were nonetheless part of my cultural traditions. My genes and my upbringing – and every fairy tale I consumed as a child – placed me in a relatively privileged position in relation to this quest.

GRAND SLAM

By the mid 1990s, Eurocrash – the label given to dance theatre and physical theatre's spectacular acts of falling – was being disparaged. Critic Mary Brennan (1997) claimed that Eurocrash had become a clichéd trend, with dancers crashing about for no reason and without clear intent. Falling itself became a spectacle that assumed central importance; audiences thrilled to the impact of dancers abandoning control and subjecting their safety to the forces of gravity. Many wondered if the spectacle of falling had little more depth than the traditional displays it was designed to unseat. 'While there is a variety of motives for going to extremes, the most obvious one is the visceral impact it has on the audience: you sense the shock, the risk, the pain in your own body. It's good for expressing anger, frenzy, despair – or for finding out what happens when the body is pushed to its limits' (Parry 1997: 7).[2]

While a critical backlash was inevitable, many writers overlooked key, positive aspects of Eurocrash. For us dancers, falling was a far more complex experience than simply a release of anger. What has been labelled as a Eurocrash fall was an embodied way to begin undoing the conventional codes of beauty on our bodies. Falling *had* to be bodily experienced for physical, metaphorical and psychological change to happen. Furthermore, the collective surrender to gravity of dance theatre performers played a role in shocking audiences from their complacency.

Brennan brazenly identified Wim Vandekeybus's *What the Body Does Not Remember* (1987) as the forerunner of Eurocrash. Wim's choice to work with physical extremes, to explore 'repulsion within attraction, hate within love' (Brennan 1997: 4) was picked up in the late 1980s and early 1990s by many young choreographers across the Western world. 'Suddenly, whenever tension reared its head in any on-stage scenario, there was a significant slamming of bodies; against other bodies, against a wall, against the floor ... a choreographic grand slam' (1997: 4). Brennan accepts the possibility that the phenomenon represented a resistance among dancers to formal techniques; yet she goes on to describe it as a fashion, a style 'simply

---

[2]See for instance the work of Grupo Cena 11, founded by Alejandro Ahmed, who was born with osteoenesis imperfecta (bones that break easily), who studied ballet and jazz and developed a violently spectacular dance technique 'based on the attempt to control the most out-of-control situations' (Greiner 2007: 142). Examples of the group's work are available on YouTube.

imitated without any underpinning thought' (1997: 5). Her adverse criticisms were taken up by Ben Felsenburg, who accused Vandekeybus's followers of being 'inspired only at the most superficial level' (1999: 358). He quotes critic Keith Watson's observation that 'just as Kurt Cobain's Nirvana had to suffer the indignities of identikit grunge, so Vandekeybus inspired a lamebrain bunch who thought Eurocrash was all about trashing your bones on the floor' (Watson 1996 cited in Felsenburg 1999: 358–9).

These comments are perhaps valid from the perspective of critics. Yet *doing* falling – actually partnering up with the forces of gravity – is a telling experience. For each crashing dancer, every moment of free fall is a moment of presence, of total absorption in a singular event, which kicks the senses into high alert. The moment of surrender before hitting the ground is – each time – timeless and unique. Physical acts of falling are empowering. But to execute falls without extreme alertness is both difficult and dangerous. Gravity does not seduce, nor pretend to be other than it is. It grounds, is grave and unavoidably dangerous. There can be no fooling with falling or with the high-risk stakes of physical theatre.

Eurocrash dancers hung, dropped, crashed, collapsed – furiously, brutally, completely. Whap – bam – splat. These practices proclaimed: life is not harmony, love between people is not transcendent, it pains as much as it pleasures. Through falling, Eurocrash dancers experienced an awakening to embodied misconceptions about Western progress and success. Dancers sought out the experience of falling because falling defenceless, without rebounding – feeling the impact in viscera and fibre – dislodged the falsehoods they had long been fed about lifted postures, upward lines and flowing beauty as essential to excellence – as necessary paths to perfection.

A DEAD BLACK

A white man dressed in white shirt and jeans walks down stage, and with eyes scanning the audience he says, loudly: 'We need to discuss the nigger problem.' He walks off stage. My skin prickles and I stifle a gasp at hearing the offensive term spoken aloud. Whatever is going to happen? Having paid for my seat, I am already complicit and undeniably part of this weighty contingent of white academics from theatre and dance now packing the Lilian Baylis Studio at London's Sadler's Wells Theatre.

This is the start of *A Separation* (2014), created and performed by Colin Poole and Simon Ellis, the third dance theatre duet they made together as Colin, Simon & I. Colin is black British; Simon is a white New Zealander. The work is comprised of short scenes appearing to feature Simon as the star performer, but the show is stolen by the inert physicality of Colin, who plays the role of a dead, silenced, black man.

Simon returns with a chair, sits downstage and engages us in a monologue of nonsensical words that sound like a kind of Italian-South African mix. Each phrase ends with an identifiable derogatory adjective followed by the term 'nigger' ('untrustworthy nigger', 'suspicious nigger'). Then, to the music of Lead Belly, Simon limps around the stage, in ever decreasing circles, until he turns in on himself with his arms flapping like chicken wings, in time to the music. Colin tells me that this scene was a consequence of Simon having strained his ankle one day in rehearsal; the limping became usable material. Colin says Simon is 'shamelessly going through this piece mimicking black expression, a bit like *Blazing Saddles*; that beginning on the train track when the whites sing Negro spirituals and they all start doing their dancing' (Poole interview with author 2018).[3] Simon appears to be mimicking the walk of black slaves with shackled ankles. 'Yes, he's ridiculing that,' Colin explains. The scene is double-edged. With his racist mocking, Simon is also making a fool of himself as a white man, just as the men do in *Blazing Saddles* (1974).

On stage, Simon makes vast sweeping gestures with his arms towards the audience, lunging deeply from leg to leg, while hissing short, intensely ingratiating sentences: 'After you, sir', 'You are very welcome', 'The pleasure is all mine'. Each phrase is followed by 'you big, strong, white daddy', deliberately spoken with a hateful, cynical tone and steely smile. Colin says of this scene:

> He is serving the master and being the master. I was looking at the kinds of words that would be the language of violence on a plantation. Intense anger, held and controlled, an envious politeness towards the white daddy, this supremacist white patriarchal image. In my mind I was creating a primal scene of a white fantasy of mastery, parasitic on the things it hates. As I recall, that speech is inspired by Dothraki language from *Game of Thrones*. I imagine it's the savage, repulsive and perverse enjoyment of big white brutal daddy.
>
> POOLE interview 2018

Colin's term 'parasitic' is relevant here, for shaming another becomes a necessary and well-worn method by which a shamer holds his own felt shame at bay. The parasite that is white racism needs black bodies to cling to. The definition of blackness as not whiteness becomes relevant only within a world of white racism (de Frantz 2017). Black bodies become shameful only under a white gaze.

Back on stage, Simon dances to 'Baby Love', sung by the Supremes. Then takes off his shirt and vest, wipes the sweat off his face with his vest and leaves the stage. He returns carrying Colin over his shoulder, like a sack of

---

[3] *Blazing Saddles*: Warner Brothers film directed by Mel Brooks, starring Cleavon Little in the role of Bart, a black sheriff.

potatoes, a dead weight. He drops to the ground with Colin on top of him, removes himself from under Colin's body and sits on him, as if sitting on a log. He begins to growl to the audience. Colin tells me:

> Two things here. One is the role of being inert, playing dead, and then there is the actual performance, which is quite liberating. I am trying to do nothing. I am free to be elsewhere in my mind as long as my body stays put. I kind of go in and out of paying attention. The reality is, I feel like an extra.
>
> POOLE interview 2018

He might feel like an extra, but from where I am sitting, his prostrate body is a core provocation.

> Bizarre is the idea of blackground – a term in urban slang where you have a scene with two white actors and the director says, 'Oh wait, there's something wrong'. He gets the casting book, has a look though and sticks a black person in the back doing nothing. The scene suddenly looks normal. That's called the blackground. I am interested how that blackground comes to the foreground and what happens when it starts to become very noticeable. What's interesting for me in this piece is that I am going to be seen predominantly by white audiences and I show up like this, not moving. What kind of participation is this? I am an object who objects, that's what's going on.
>
> POOLE interview 2018

Colin's previous performance work addressing racism brought his black body actively centre stage, but *A Separation* switches attention to Simon's white body. 'I guess the only way to bring out the true colours of whiteness is to play dead' (Poole interview 2018). The deader Colin becomes, the more vivid Simon's whiteness becomes. 'And the more vibrant and alive Simon becomes when I play dead, then the more figural the issue of racism becomes' (Poole interview 2018). The final scene finds Simon dragging Colin's body across the stage and into the wings, leaving his legs protruding. Simon returns to the front of the stage and says, 'I don't see any niggers here. Do you see any niggers here? We don't see any niggers here. Are there any niggers here?' He leaves the stage and then returns to take a bow. Colin stays where he is.

> People ask me, 'Why don't you get up? Why are you still performing?' People feel troubled that Simon is taking a bow on his own. We are supposed to have a clean-cut ending, get back to normal; I should get up and bow. That doesn't happen. We are not getting back to normal. 'What's going on here? Why do we have to ignore the black guy?' I want people to be left with the idea that there's a problem that they have to ignore this black person. It's about the silence, denial, gaps in conversations that

FIGURE 2.1 *Colin Poole and Simon Ellis in* A Separation *(2014). Photo: Camilla Greenwell.*

black people have when trying to talk about racism with white people. It's the dead end-ness of trying to say there is a problem going on and having it continually ignored. The audience [is] being asked to leave, to deal with the ignoring, and the problem is staying right there on the stage.

POOLE interview 2018

I get up to leave, feeling my own sense of shame. I am standing up, Colin is on the ground. I slope away, recognizing how well established I am within an institutional academic environment that flourishes on hierarchical structures composed of great, well-meaning white men and women, philosophical meanderings and liberal intellectualism. Within academic institutions, racism, for the most part, is not an obvious person-to-person shaming, but racism by default, by abstract thought, invisibility, silence. Black British writer Reni Eddo-Lodge names this structural racism; it is not about good or bad people but about the unspoken strategies of whiteness within institutional power systems. 'It is not just about personal prejudice, but the collective effects of bias' (Eddo-Lodge 2017: 65). To cease shaming and to recognize each other as equal require shame to be acknowledged within institutional systems. But as white supremacy dictates, denial of white shame perpetuates the systems.

Colin lies on the ground and does not take a bow because he is exhausted from talking with white people about what it means to be black. What's left but to play dead and let Simon get on with it, hoping that the absent, black presence on stage will provoke me to keep looking and keep talking with other whites about how to acknowledge our shame in propping up racism. Performed by two men, one white, one black, *A Separation* is a piece that grabs parasitical relations of black and white shame to its heart and presents this to audiences so that the dialogue for overcoming racism might be kept alive, at its raw cutting edge.

STIFF UPPER LIP

The pronounced upward orientation of classical ballet is deeply encoded within its stories, technique and aesthetics, and cannot be dissociated from issues of race. Ballet is shaped at its core by the history of Eurocentric imperialist power, which, in terms of race and class, is informed by white supremacy and aristocratic values. In the UK the *Royal* Ballet, performing at the *Royal* Opera House, maintains its ties with the *Royal* Family through its name. The institution of the British Royal Family continues to uphold its traditions of white, Eurocentric aristocracy and to value transcendence in mind and body.

When I was learning ballet as a child, the courtly gestures that express the values and sensibilities associated with lifted chins and arched, upper backs – along with the traditional roles of sylphs and white swans – were presented to me as quintessential aspects of the form itself. I was aware of the upwardly aspiring impulses of these roles, but their inherently racist properties were not so obvious. To write this now seems a shocking admission. Ballet training, in which I was completely, passionately absorbed, was teaching me whiteness. Young boys and girls were indoctrinated into a system of institutional racism often without their awareness. We were learning the rules of white supremacy with all of its socioeconomic advantages, through our ballet training. From an early age, white privilege was cunningly writing itself on my body, repeating its message like a Kafka tattoo – upward reach exemplifies white beauty. Furthermore, I was learning to despise those parts of myself that did not conform to the upward codes and therefore look down on others who were less capable of upward-ness than I was. Only when I began working with black dancers in New York in the 1970s did I realize how deeply engrained on my *body* this whiteness had become, zinging along sinews, winding through muscles, infusing joints, echoing through my bone structure and wiring my upright spine. Thus began a raising of awareness and personal transformation that has stayed with me ever since in the form of questions about racism in ballet.

Representation of the white Eurocentrism in ballet is now widely recognized and critiqued. Black American dance academic Brenda Dixon Gottschild eloquently compares Europeanist and Africanist aesthetics, isolating specific elements of black dance to compare with European ballet culture such as body image, movement language and choreographic structures. For Dixon Gottschild, 'the Africanist aesthetic can be understood as a precept of contrariety, or an encounter of opposites. The conflict inherent in and implied by difference, discord, and irregularity is encompassed, rather than erased or necessarily resolved . . . . This democracy of body parts stands in sharp contrast to the erect body dictated by the straight, centered spine' (1996: 13–14).

In the five decades that have passed since I was a baby ballerina, much has changed. Black dancers are more visible and move more freely between different styles and forms of Western dance and some contemporary ballet choreography is released from imperialist narratives. However, as a result of my ongoing transformative experience, I continue to question ballet's racist tendencies so subtly reinforced through its institutional training and vocabulary. So, it was with curiosity that I went to the Royal Opera House to see the Royal Ballet's performance of Crystal Pite's *Flight Patterns* (2017). This is a powerfully emotive choreography for thirty-six dancers, inspired by the refugee crisis, which in the UK is a crisis associated with immigration and therefore with people of colour. *Flight Patterns* presents a luscious spectacle of human movement; groups of bodies eddy and swirl around the stage, flowing and mingling in expansive counterpoint with other groups. These sweeps of movement are interspersed with intimate duets and delicate exchanges between individual dancers. There are no *pointe* shoes or high leg extensions. Towards the end of the piece, Marcelino Sambé, a black Portuguese man, performs a solo of powerful gestures directed down a range of descending angles. His supple limbs and fluid falls appear in stark contrast with balletic conventions.

I leave the theatre with familiar questions about ballet's racism rattling my brain. Has the institution of ballet, which I admit gave me agency and privilege, become any more racially aware of its vertical expressions of white supremacy? Certainly, the movement language of *Flight Patterns* undoes upward leanings. But I ask myself, 'Where was Marcelino earlier in the programme?' There was no obvious sight of him in the two previous pieces that evening: *Within the Golden Hour* (Wheeldon 2019) and *Medusa* (Cherkaoui 2019). Nor did the vocabularies of these ballets involve movements other than conventional, excessively upward, acrobatic extensions. But Marcelino stars in *Flight Patterns* and he does so by physically falling out of ballet's upward aesthetics. I am wondering if this role is given to white dancers on other nights. Or is it only a black dancer who gets to fall? In which case, is this racist casting? What does that say about black and white balletic bodies in the twenty-first century?

Interestingly, just as I was finishing this piece of writing, the Duke and Duchess of Sussex – Meghan and Harry – announced their decision to step back from royal duties and pursue their own lives, dividing their time between North America and the UK. Meghan is mixed race and American, while Harry is white and sixth in line to the British throne. The morning after their announcement – which came as a shock to the Royal Family – the *New York Times* quoted from a documentary about the couple in which the Duchess says: 'I really tried to adopt this British sensibility of a stiff upper lip. I tried, I really tried. But I think that what that does internally is probably really damaging' (Lyall 2020).

Two issues here draw attention. The term 'stiff upper lip' is particularly associated with white, British, upper-class aristocracy and imperialism, therefore an unfamiliar cultural characteristic for most Americans. Second, her reference to internal damage suggests that she experienced a loss of sensual awareness in her body as a result of trying to maintain it. Meghan may be referencing stiff upper lips as a metaphor for the Royal Family's institutional restraint and suppression of emotional displays, but her association with the impact on her body, of a physical resistance to gravity, cannot be ignored.

NOT A BLACK PROBLEM

A willingness to bear the inevitable shame accompanying whiteness is 'key to the project of dethroning white-centeredness' says psychoanalyst and Gestalt therapist Lynne Jacobs (2014: 301). This is not black people's problem, a 'willingness to bear' is what I am attempting to address – asking myself, how am *I* doing that bearing, as a white person in a relational world. How can twenty-first-century dance practitioners address the inherited injustice and imbalance of white supremacy? A number of social and political options exists, a range of ways to help dismantle systemic inequalities. But even before confronting those challenges, dancers begin with their own bodies.

From the 1960s, somatic practices have caused a rift in Western dance aesthetics with the shift from upward reach to downward fluidity. The health-giving benefits of somatic movement practices and their emphasis on body, gravity and ground are well recognized by a range of somatic practitioners working in the fields of psychotherapy, movement therapy and neuroscience, such as Beatrice Allegranti (2017), Andrea Olsen (2017) and Marcia Plevin (2017). Yet perhaps more vital, and perhaps less recognized, is the way somatic practices have enabled *white* dancers to undo the uprightness of body and mind nurtured by imperialism and racism.

Mabel Elsworth Todd was working in the 1930s when 'the Victorian notion of maintaining rigid verticality as a sign of uprightness of spirit was still prevalent' (Matt 1993: 15). That Mabel was aware of how a somatic understanding of movement might facilitate a loosening of embodied racism is certainly suggested in many of her writings, such as when she indicates how psychological factors of military morality caused negative impacts on fluid physicality and responses.

> We have only to try the effect of certain admonitions 'Have a stiff back bone', 'Brace up' etc., to realize that our postural patterns easily become conditioned by moral and social notions. Too often have the positions of our bodies been the result of response to some pre-conceived idea of the 'proper' (morally perfect) instead of the balanced (mechanically perfect) position.
>
> TODD 1977a: 12

Mabel's references to muscularly-held, vertical spines could apply equally well to the effects of white moral supremacy. The admonitions she refers to conjure images of red uniformed British soldiers enforcing stiff colonial uprightness on bodies of diverse habitus and skin tone. When a culture promotes verticality, linearity and steadfast uprightness – with their moral and racist underpinnings – bodies and minds alike are affected. When white bodies learn culturally promoted habits of holding and stiffening, the fluidity of physical and psychological response becomes limited. Mabel devoted her work to rethinking anatomical structure by working with gravity, integrating mental and physical abilities and highlighting ways bodies adjust to environments. 'Constant stimuli are producing constant reactions . . . Every thought, every sensation causes a change somewhere in the structure' (Todd 1977a: 9). Environmental elements and cultural norms are sensed kinaesthetically, and physical behaviour adjusts accordingly. Importantly, in relation to racism, somatic falling practices work in two ways: as a process for undoing the sense of supremacy trained into, and onto, bodies and as a grounding support for an acceptance of white shame without needing to aggress, dominate or disappear. Undoing fixed uprightness increases my vulnerability – like stepping out of a costume that has protected me with a false performance of pride – yet also supports that vulnerability in a relationship with, and an acceptance of, gravity and ground.

But there is no room for complacency. There is an overconfidence in believing that somatic practices should be recognized by all as promoting some kind of constitutional uniformity or actual equality throughout diverse dance communities. The performance styles and choreographic approaches that grew out of somatic practices do not offer anything necessarily accessible to a broad range of dancers, nor are they of interest to diverse audiences. Attention to somatic stillness has been white-centred *but also* an undoing of whiteness – *for white dancers*. Black and white dancers have different agendas regarding identity and visibility (Claid 2006). What is essential for white artists to address is not black artists' problem to solve.

This friction surfaced during the amalgamation of somatic practices with post-modern dance. As somatic dance practices became associated with stillness and minimalism over spectacle, process over product and with a multiplicity of movement directions over fixed front choreography, these practices also echoed certain attributes of post-modern dance. From the perspectives of many queer and black dancers, this association has not been particularly beneficial. Black director and dance academic Thomas de Frantz regards white artists' attraction to post-modern minimalism as white-centred. 'I will not be "postminimal cool" because some sort of paronomastic stillness is the theatrical trend for bourgeois white theater. I will not waste an opportunity to confirm my presence with my dance' (de Frantz 2017: 12). De Frantz continues in a similar vein when discussing choreographer Ishmael Houston-Jones' use of Contact Improvisation (CI) in *Them* (Jones 1985). De Frantz comments how CI, at the time, was mainly practised by 'heteronormative middle-class white men and women' (de Frantz 2018: 271). Although CI has always included 'queer people of colour', de Frantz argues that the form, with its emphasis on 'apolitical vectors of embodiment . . . seldom spoke of the world at large in a way that acknowledged gay and racialized presence' (de Frantz 2018: 271).

In a different vein – but still linked to the diverse agendas of black and white dancers – is the way the emphasis in Release dance – somatic improvisational practices of fluidity, fragmentation, sensuality and looseness of limbs – might appear to propose similarities with Africanist aesthetics. These qualities of movement led Dixon Gottschild (2003) to accuse white dancers of appropriation, and post-modern dance of indebtedness to Africanist aesthetics: 'White dance practitioners have used the black dancing body as the territory for accessing the inherent and potential sensuality of their own dancing bodies' (Dixon Gottschild 2003: 48). There is no doubt that white dancers and choreographers have greedily appropriated black dance movements across many decades, from minstrelsy to swing, from tap to hip hop. But perhaps the phenomenon of Release signalled something deeper than stylistic appropriation: there was indeed a yearning in white dancers, like myself, to unravel the laced-up postures and rigid beliefs of racially supremacist roots, to drop inherited prejudices. Furthermore, I would suggest that a reclaiming of sensuality for many white dancers has been a consequence of deposing our whiteness through somatic awareness of our bodies in gravity.

A somatic-based relationship of body, gravity and ground is as political as it is physical, providing a key to unravelling institutional racism. I am not free of shame, but the practice of conscious falling, being in touch with body, gravity and ground, generates physical and psychological support for my human vulnerability. It helps me peel away the kinetic and physical layers and patterns in which my racism has long resided. Sensing the weight of my head and pelvis, dropping shoulders, bending knees, letting arms fall is not to regain some kind of natural, essential rejuvenation, but embodies instead a conscious undoing of codes of supremacy. A somatic practice such as this will never solve the problem of racism in society, of course, but for me it's a start. Falling opens my body to vulnerability, connection and collaboration, and a clear sense with which to help me meet difference. Somatic-based falling cuts across polarities of culturally defined pride and shame. To see and be seen in the world as a body that falls is to give presence to vulnerability, 'the birthplace of innovation, creativity and change' (Brown 2012). Falling 'reminds us we are all more alike, vulnerable, and fallible, than different' (Jacobs 2014: 304). Gravity grounds us all.

KEEPING FACE

Stretch your face into a smile. Exaggerate this expression by lifting the muscles in your forehead, cheeks, eyebrows, ears and mouth. Stay with this for a few moments, letting the smile widen through you. See how the smile affects your thoughts and emotions. Notice if and how your body wants to respond to your smiling face. After a while, gradually, slowly, release all your facial muscles and let your face go slack; drop your forehead, cheeks, eyes and the area around your lips, until your mouth and chin are hanging loose. Ease the hinges of your jaw and let it relax open. As with the smile, spend time here sensing how your body wants to respond when you release facial muscles. Repeat the exercise as many times as you like, focusing on the physicality of the practice while noting any emotional effects.

Movement practitioner and psychotherapist Peri Mackintosh first introduced me to this exercise. I was intrigued by the way a physical, task-based action could register internally, could trigger emotional and psychological responses. Inviting a smile to spread – while concentrating on the activities of facial muscles – I noticed I felt lighter and more playful, yet also as if I was wearing a mask or performing a role. When I released the muscles, I felt empty and sullen, reminding me of how my mother would say, 'What a glum face', when I was not smiling, when actually I was just being thoughtful. These socially and culturally defined emotional narratives have become inseparable from the physical task of exercising or releasing facial muscles.

After experimenting on your own, try the same with a partner. Take turns to smile and then release your smile while being witnessed by your partner. Notice how you are affected by watching your partner's facial expressions. Feeling the impact of another's expressions is the basis of relational empathy, a flowing circuit which thrives on intersubjective connections and depends, for emotional resonance, on instantaneous feedback of facial messaging.

> The evoking of feelings by activating the associated facial expression by means of *facial feedback*, demonstrates the way in which a person's spontaneous and often unconscious imitation of the facial expression of the person he is observing . . . can also produce a similar feeling in him as observer.
>
> STAEMMLER 2012: 91–2[4]

A smile is a potent example of an upward lift, a facial expression that has instantaneous impact on both smiler and witness. Developmentally and relationally, an infant learns early to interact through smiling in response to the face and presence of a caregiver. When a parent drops facial interaction

---

[4] Frank Staemmler is a psychologist and Gestalt psychotherapist. See also the work of Paul Ekman, a psychologist and pioneer in the study of emotions in relation to facial expression (2003).

whilst facing an infant, that baby can grow upset within seconds (Stern 2010). In Western culture, a smile has social currency. Smiling is a socially acceptable, relational message signifying that all is well; upward moving facial muscles convey the meaning that life is good. A smile can be a genuine expression of pleasure and joy but for many – especially women – smiling is both habitual and expected, conveying loving, caring, feminine qualities and a default position of 'yes'. Pronouncing the word 'please' requires mouths to stretch into smiles. From an early age, children learn to say 'cheese' when photographs are taken which takes our mouths into wide grins.

The impact of *not* smiling in Western culture, of presenting our faces with muscles relaxing downwards is – particularly for women – often interpreted as aggressive, dominant, sullen or sad, perhaps even a sign of rejection. Humans are relational beings, so what you express, I will empathically mirror, as you will for me. If your face falls, I am affected, as are you when mine falls. In his sociological study of human behaviour and interaction, Ervin Goffman describes keeping face as a line of behaviour by which an individual is known in the world by others and himself. Face-to-face interaction is that 'class of events which occurs during co-presence and by virtue of co-presence' (Goffman [1967] 2005: 1). Keeping face is to maintain a consistent image of self in relation to others. Goffman references poise as a way of controlling embarrassment and fear, and poise in Western contexts evokes a sense of 'holding-up,' along with qualities like deportment, grace and aplomb. For dancers, poise is often interpreted as vertical balance and linear harmony. Similarly, keeping face requires us to maintain upward-ness in relation to each other. Because I don't want you to feel bad, I keep on smiling – exhausting as it is – by lifting my face muscles all day even though I know that releasing restores aliveness.

A GOOD WHITE

Simon Ellis tells me about his role in *A Separation* (2014), a duet created and performed by him and Colin Poole as Colin, Simon & I. As explained earlier, Simon is a white New Zealander, Colin is black British, and *A Separation* was a performance that explored racism, directed by Colin. In it, Simon played a white racist.

> Who is it that I imagine myself to be and who is it that I really am? I have spent a long time in my life imagining myself not being racist – I am a good white. My father was a strong leader in the fight against apartheid. I hold on to my dad's story and the work he did – this is who I am. So there was a critical moment in rehearsal, a realisation that I was out of my depth in the creating of the role. Also that I had to recognise my complicit-ness in systemic racism, that I have benefited from it, I am

complicit in it, that I am part of a systemic racist society and I have to recognise my place in that society as a racist. That was confronting, not a nice thing to admit. I started to see that as a 45-year-old white man, I am soaked in privileges and the beauty of them. I recognise the irony, the paradox, the discomfort with this – what is the point of having privileges if you cannot enjoy them? Yet how do I stop sublimating the pleasure of privilege? So my shame was about how long it has taken me to realise this, to recognise how profoundly racist I am.

It was hilarious just trying to say the 'N' word out loud. I just kept swallowing it. Colin said, 'You can't even say it!' 'Nigger' is such a vivid word, the taste of saying it, wrapping my lips and tongue around this word. Firstly I felt shame, as it is in direct opposition to the version of myself I like to imagine myself to be. Then I recognise its power to shock, and my power to shock, and what it's like to wield that power. If you go to the 'N' word – and that is the heart and soul of *A Separation* – it opens up terrible wounds for people. We had many conversations about this. Why not drop an audience straight into it? Let's not namby-pamby around. This is something disgusting. *A Separation* was a crash course in celebrating or meeting shame.

What's it like for a predominantly white middle-class audience to encounter a version of themselves, one of their own, in the world as a choreographer, teacher, dancer, presenting this version of themselves? That's a horrible encounter, and of course the audience is going to totally reject it. 'How dare you use that word, this is not me.' Yet any time we reject something outright, all sorts of alarm bells go on. What the hell am I rejecting so quickly that I cannot even entertain the possibility? I have encountered that through the work with Colin. It still makes me shake a little; I feel myself on the verge of crying, of action and responsibility. The 'N' word is not a word I can sidestep; it morphs into shame. That opening line, 'We need to discuss the nigger problem', then walking off. It is a thing of beauty, it really is. There is no escaping what is going to happen. Love it or hate it. But if all my shame is wrapped up in that word and that line, there [is] no space for [the] audience. It is just a performance of an apology. That line is super interesting because unless I recognise that it is me, then it is just a circus and façade. But if it is just or only me, then it pushes people away; people are repulsed by it. It is wrapped up in something so hot. Hotter or more troubling now than in 2014.

ELLIS interview with author 2018

WRONG BODIES

Many queer performers harness the sinking feeling of shame, embracing it, physically and psychologically, as a creative source for making work. Queer shame thrives on what gay pride keeps under wraps. Gay pride grew as a powerful, positive, liberating – and necessary – resistance to the prejudices permeating Western societies. Following the Stonewall riots of 1969, gay pride brought forward a long, morbid, traumatic history and gave human faces to the experience of queer shame, to the deep, dark, sinking feelings long lived by people engaging in the forbidden practices of being gay. Ever since the riots, gay activists have fought hard to gain respect in a Western heteronormative world. Yet now, for many in the West, gay pride has become a neoliberalized corporate package, a respectfully identified, socially acceptable celebration of gayness. Increasing numbers of queer people find themselves alienated by the 'sanitized, staid politically vacuous and generally boring official gay culture of self-affirmation' (Halperin and Traub 2009: 8). Living and performing queer shame has become a site of radical resistance to the normalising principles of gay pride, a site that

> willingly embraces those queers whose identities or social markings make them feel out of place in gay pride's official ceremonies: people with the 'wrong bodies', sadomasochists, sex workers, drag queens, butch dykes, people of color, boy-lovers, bisexuals, immigrants, the poor, the disabled. These are the queer the mainstream gay pride is not always proud of.
>
> HALPERIN and TRAUB 2009: 9

Queer performance artist Penny Arcade takes up the call in her performance *Bitch! Dyke! Faghag! Whore!* (2012): 'The queer backlash wasn't against the hetero-world – it was against those control-freak, gay community people who wanted to be accepted by the white middle class. They wanted to be officially gay. We said *queer* because it made them crazy' (Arcade quoted in Mercier 2014: 39). Professor of gender studies Ann Cvetkovich resists any 'political agenda' that 'assume[s] a gay citizen whose affective fulfilment resides in assimilation, inclusion and normalcy' (2003: 11).

For queer theorists Cvetkovich and Eve Sedgwick, shame is not a state to be eradicated through therapeutic or political strategies but a contribution to making identity. Sedgwick writes of queer shame and theatricality as a form of communication, pointing out how shame responses signal a sense of isolation but also a need to restore contact. 'Indeed, like a stigma, shame is itself a form of communication. Blazons of shame, the "fallen face" with eyes down and head averted – and, to a lesser extent, the blush – are semaphores of trouble and at the same time of a desire to reconstitute the interpersonal bridge' (Sedgwick 2009: 50). Sedgwick urges a rejection of well-meaning aims to get rid of shame, as if the toxicity of shame can be somehow dissolved through coming out as proud. From her perspective, what is missing in this well-intentioned encouragement of pride is how shame is 'integral to and residual in the processes by which identity itself is formed ... available for the work of metamorphosis, reframing, refiguration, transfiguration, of affective and symbolic loading and deformation' (Sedgwick 2009: 59–60).

Theatre writer and director Neil Bartlett remembers a time when gay men worked hard to rid themselves of shame: 'Getting rid of your gay shame, in London in 1982, was about getting rid of the negative effeminate stereotype, butching up, dressing like a real man, pretending to be American, becoming a confident, sexually active gay man – *that* was getting rid of your shame' (Bartlett 2009: 344). In the London performance world at the time, artists such as Bette Bourne and the theatre group Bloolips reacted to this masculinizing characteristic of gay liberation, advocating that queers 'plunge *into* your shame, hook, line, and sinker ... Don't give up on your shame' (Bartlett 2009: 344, original italics). Crucially, like Sedgwick, Bartlett is not suggesting that shame dissolves through performance. Performing queer shame is not cathartic or purgative in that way. The performance of shame needs to be continually repeated 'not because I'm a profoundly sick person and I need help ... no, that isn't it at all, thank you very much. But because the world I live in means that I need constant reaffirmation' (Bartlett 2009: 346). *Being with* queer shame, performing as wrong bodies with wrong desires, expands a non-belonging space where the creativity of queer performers thrives. Where we plunge into the wellsprings of queer imagination.

A COOL WALK

Many black artists – in the face of racism – have embraced the sinking feelings and gestures of shame as agency and power. Black American musician and academic Jason King addresses this inspirational strategy, setting his argument against a 1960s background of downward mobility, when in a world of white supremacy, black people carried the burden and shame of having fallen. A burden that resulted in 'ambivalent direction, perpetual meandering, purposeless loitering, sloping destiny' (King 2004: 28). In this 1960s racist frame, shame and falling were interwoven, and progress for racialized people was associated with identity and visibility. Every step upward on the ladder offered 'a higher level of socioeconomic prosperity' (2004: 27). Standing up 'out of the terror of slavery and the darkness of colonialism is necessarily vertical in direction; one moves up and out of these things into the light' (2004: 32). Bob Marley, James Brown, Aretha Franklin and Marvin Gaye urge their listeners to stand up for their rights: standing up brings euphoria and virility. 'If ascension is required for insurgency, horizontalism becomes inertia, apathy, couch potato-ism, stasis, sittin' on the dock of the bay' (2004: 34). In the 1960s, black pride was infused with potency and sexuality; it was up and hard as opposed to 'limp, flaccid, weak' and associated with shame (2004: 35).

With queer sensibility, King flips this narrative on its back by urging blacks to *exult* in shame as a powerful performative tool, to explore black rootlessness and disorientation as a kind of freedom and to transform 'the debilitating fall into stylized, kinetic movement' (2004: 29). For King, the shuffling walk of street hustlers and break dancers becomes an expression of masculine cool. This walk, made famous by actors such as Richard Pryor and Eddie Murphy and a range of rap stars, becomes a 'winning way to move in the world not so much because it announces black male power, but because it incorporates the fall, and its concomitant shame, as an intentional act' (2004: 37). Walking with a slight rhythmic lilt on every other step, dropping down and bobbing up, with one arm swinging and hand cupped, provides black men with a cool presence that 'transforms the shame associated with downward mobility into an ethics of pride' (2004: 37). Similarly, for dance academic Brenda Dixon Gottschild, the term *cool* 'is an attitude . . . It is seen in the asymmetrical walk of African American males, which shows an attitude of carelessness cultivated with a calculated aesthetic clarity' (1996: 16). A European stride expressing control was juxtaposed by the cool, loose-jointed gait of blacks, full of playful drops and rhythmic syncopations. 'The hipster walk is the only sexy, hip way of walking that holds currency in the American imagination, and so it is black shame, the freedom that is disorientation, that is continually referenced' (King 2004: 37). This characteristic amble gained popularity across the West as a mark of street credibility for black men, particularly in urban environments; as a result, downward mobility – by embracing black disorientation and shame – was reconfigured as a source of agency.

I am reminded of black American performance artist Pope L., who performed military-style crawls as durational performances. His first venture, *Times Square Crawl* (1978), was along pavements and across busy streets in New York City. He followed up with performances in urban centres across Europe, then came back to Manhattan to crawl in *Tompkins Square* (1991) and finally *The Great White Way*, a 22-mile crawl that took nine years to complete (2001–09). Although his performances did not involve falling, his crawls demonstrate falling off the vertical to embrace the horizontal – the reality of the gritty, muddy, gravelly, slippery, lumpy, hot, hard, smelly ground. Pope L.'s crawls are not about self-defeat; he is not giving up on his humanity. His crawling body screams out a critique of racism, a statement against the dominant verticality of white privilege, by reclaiming a space of black shame. Dance academic André Lepecki (2006) draws on Frantz Fanon's (1967) revolutionary and crucially pertinent anti-colonial writing to discuss Pope L.'s rejection of verticality. For Lepecki, Pope L.'s crawls make transparent the shocking 'colonialist narratives and barely hidden racial legacies which still inform . . . modes of moving' (Lepecki 2006: 102) – and modes of restraining black bodies.

Racial politics are embodied by dancers. Falling, as a source of agency, is a central tenet in break dance, hip hop and voguing. Emerging in the 1970s, these forms were seized on by alienated black dancers and queer performers who embraced the sinking feeling of shame, grabbed it by the horns and rode its downwards swirl in a celebration of creativity. Familiar to many black queer artists, for instance, is the voguing drop, when a dancer falls fast, hitting the ground with one leg straight out, the other bent at the knee and the torso arched backwards onto the floor.

> The daredevil drop in voguing, which instantly suggests the spectacular danger and terror of being black and gay, also suggests that improvisation is nothing if not bungee jumping, free-falling, the exhilaration of parachuting, leaping suicidally into the abyss . . . To witness the 'danger' of spectacular black performance is breathtaking, unsettling – disorientation becomes reorientation. . . . The thrill of fireworks exploding is not in the ascent of the shell, but in the fall, the descending shower of light.
>
> KING 2004: 41

HUMILIATE THE BOY

Queer performance artist Joseph Mercier tried his best to master ballet. He longed to follow in Rudolf Nureyev's footsteps. But he failed and was flung out into the ditch of ballet's unwanted misfits. His theatre piece *Giselle, or I'm too Horny to be a Prince* (2014) takes the feelings of shame provoked by this failure and tosses them into creative tension with queer performative excesses.[5] Underlying this creative tension, shadowing the performance, are the parallels Joseph draws between learning ballet and BDSM practices. The show is a collage of scenes composed of spoken text, movement sequences and excerpts of music from the ballet *Giselle* (Corelli/Perrot, 1841). I attended a performance in 2014.

I enter the theatre of London's Central School of Speech and Drama from the back of the stage, through a door that opens directly onto the bright, sunlit street. I sit waiting, watching the audience filing in, aware that the stage is awash with sounds of sirens, cars and hectic London clatter. Joseph is sitting naked and cross-legged on the floor, with his head bowed forward. Vulnerability oozes from him. The door closes and he stands up, slinging a dance bag on his shoulder. Standing fully naked, he tells us that his feet are no good, that he has no turnout. 'So, if you are expecting to see 180 degrees, I can do 45.'

A passage of text details Joseph's young adult life and his training in Canada at the Alberta Ballet School. He describes how he was put in a class

---

[5]Mercier's *Giselle, or I'm too Horny to be Prince* (2014) was a performance submitted as part of *Fucking with Ballet: Performing Queer Negativity* (Mercier 2014, unpublished PhD).

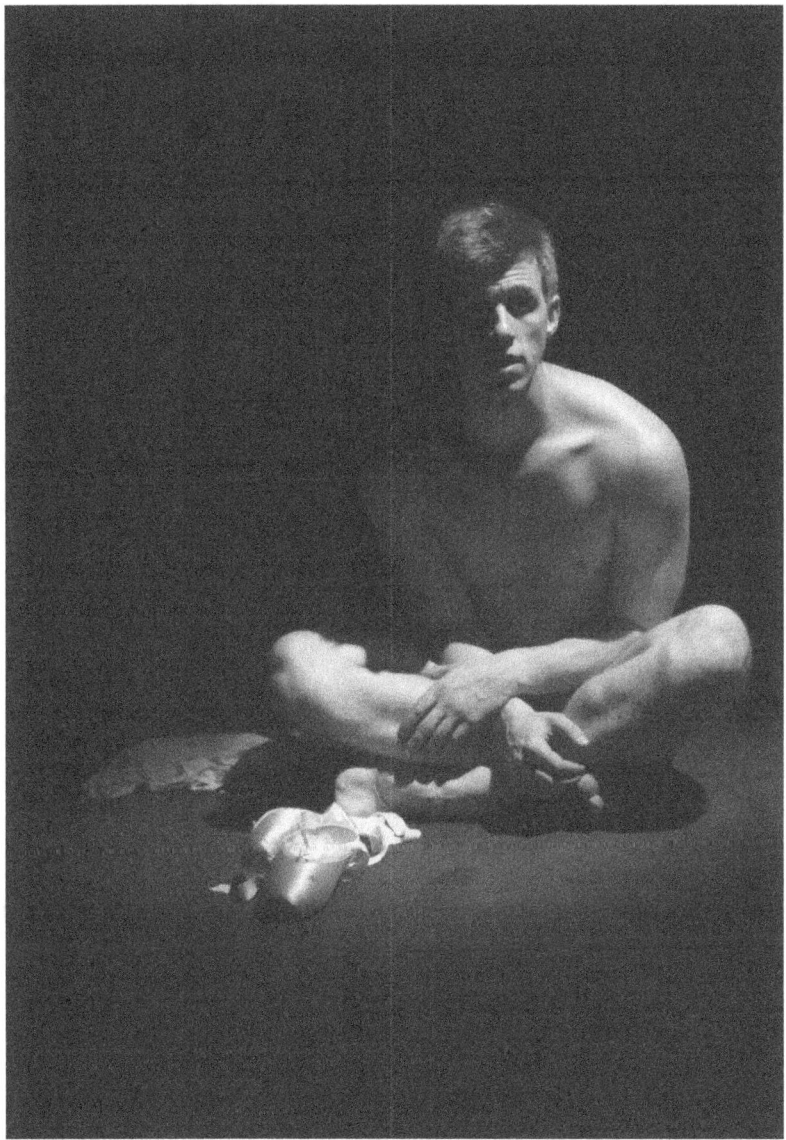

FIGURE 2.2 *Joseph Mercier in* Giselle, or I'm too Horny to be a Prince *(2014)*. *Photo: Luc Boulianne.*

with fourteen-year-old girls and told story after story about the famous dancers his teachers had taught before him. One day he was taken into a studio and taught how to run like Nureyev, while his male teacher shouted from the side. To illustrate, Joseph – wearing nothing but a jockstrap – runs wildly around the stage as if trapped in headlights, to music from *Giselle*.

With head bowed, he clamps his arms stiffly at his sides and tries unsuccessfully to point his feet as he demonstrates loud, clumsy, effortful running. I watch him doing the best he can, while sensing his – and my own – shame. For Joseph, an aim of the show is to *expose* shame. 'I am working in the context of queer negativity, accounting for myself in a queer way, which means engaging with crappy stuff, not turning that into something of success' (Mercier interview with author 2018).

Joseph again sits naked, his feet drawn up, speaking of his dream of dancing Nureyev's role as the swashbuckling pirate in *Le Corsaire*. (This was not to be.) He invites us to watch him perform a typical solo for a *danseur noble*, a male ballet star, full of jumps, pirouettes and double *tours en l'air*, all characteristic features requiring stamina, strength, clean lines and articulation. 'If you are not happy with my performance, shout out and I will do it again – as many times as you would like.' We, the audience, are cast in the role of his ballet master; he becomes the submissive student. Members of the audience insist he repeat the solo, which he does – eight times. He becomes progressively more exhausted, less technically able. He slips from positions and falls out of jumps and turns, decreasingly able to leap off the ground and increasingly lacking aplomb. He literally collapses out of ballet. Yet with every attempt, he does the best he can.

> When I was making the piece, I was going to ballet classes and trying to hire a ballet coach. I was really investing – even now it's hard to let go of the fear of failing at ballet. Then I realized that wasn't the point, so I stopped going to class. I was wherever my body was at, and my body got further and further away from ballet. That was interesting for me.
>
> MERCIER interview 2018

Joseph likens ballet training to a master–slave relationship between teacher and student, characterized by excesses of praise and abuse:

> BDSM practices were really relevant because striving to be better at ballet and then humiliated for doing it badly, or doing it naked, is similar to BDSM ... where humiliation is the point. Practitioners are not trying to transform humiliation into pleasure, it's about finding pleasure in the humiliation. The desire and the pleasure are located in the humiliation and the pain, just as in ballet. The shame of not being good enough is where pleasure lies.
>
> MERCIER interview 2018

In ballet, being shamed for not being good enough is how students learn the form. Shame and excellence intertwine.

The show continues. Joseph tells us how a primary teacher, whom he loved and feared in equal measure, had three favourite phrases of correction. When he used his arms incorrectly, she would say, 'Don't be stingy'. After correcting him on a particular exercise, she would say, 'You lazy devil'. Her third favourite phrase – spoken in front of the entire class – was 'Do you mind if I call you stupid?'

Not long after, Joseph finds himself going to bondage clubs instead of ballet class and soon gives up ballet completely. 'I was understanding a different relationship to my body through BDSM. Being there was a kind of reparative act, repairing the damage that came with failing at ballet' (Mercier interview 2018). The performance ends painfully. Donning *pointe* shoes and a flowing chiffon skirt, Joseph staggers about the stage up on his toes, lurching, tottering and collapsing against the back wall, where he balances precariously with shivering legs while crumpling with pain – yet refusing to come off *pointe*. Only by leaving the theatre do we release him from this torture.

> As performer I find pleasure in being the object of the gaze as well as in the performance of virtuosic pain/effort. The moment holds both pain and pleasure. They are located differently so the pain does not transform into pleasure. The audience . . . have permission to take pleasure in my discomfort. One audience member in a post-show discussion described the sadistic pleasure she experienced during this moment as 'watching a fly die'.
>
> MERCIER 2014: 110

Joseph's strategy in *Giselle, or I'm too Horny to be a Prince* is to render queer shame transparent. In demonstrating his longing for the artistry that emerges from ballet's gay closet – and performing his own shame at failing – he restores agency for himself as a queer man. Restoring agency to queers is not about being successful, or gaining control, in normal terms, but rather a falling out of and escape from the fixed codes of straight, gay or normal identity. Joseph thrives through performance of negativity as that which constitutes queerness, a strategy for queer living – one that does not require a return to some kind of status quo. And he performs his queer shame with a bucket-load of humour.

CINDERELLA IN DRAG

The queer closet of ballet is a slippery subject to address. The archive of queerness comprises a rich trove of trauma (Cvetkovich 2003; Mercier 2014), the result of a long history of persecution. Since the nineteenth century, when the term *queer* was levelled as a derogatory slur, the ballet world has provided a safe haven from that persecution. Within the context of ballet, gay shame is transformed into spectacular artistry, as a protective cover. The ballet closet provides safety from gay oppression, yet depends on that oppression to perpetuate its artistic expression. Ballet's gay heritage is kept behind closet doors and must remain there because the queer shame of ballet is also partly responsible for its artistic codes and narrative fantasies (Dyer 1992). Closeted queer shame helps generate much of ballet's artistry. A subject for another time, perhaps. Here I want to land lightly on the theme through personal experience.

One night in 1964, I am at the Royal Opera House, Covent Garden, watching the ballet *Cinderella* (Ashton 1948). Frederick Ashton and Kenneth MacMillan are cavorting about in drag, lavishly bewigged, clad in elaborate headdresses, jewelled brocades and fancy petticoats. They are – with absurd pomposity – performing their roles as 'ugly' sisters.[6] They revel in their travesty of femininity by playing gloriously camp, openly corpsing, barely able to contain their laughter, and fully absorbed in their homo-erotic romp. Frederick and Kenneth, two institutional pillars of the Royal Ballet, are relishing their failure to fulfil balletic ideals for either women or men – and are doing it in fine slapstick style. I am laughing, a lot.

Much performance time and space are given to the ugly sisters in Ashton's version of the story. Their choreographed duets evoke laughter through bump-and-grind flops following strained attempts at beauty and grace. Their episodes disrupt the flow of the narrative. They ridicule the institution of ballet by falling about – messy, clumsy and comically flat-footed – disrupting the dominant codes of its aesthetics and practice with skilful and precisely timed gestures. Crucially, their bumbling pratfalls and foolish efforts secrete whiffs of queerness, usually kept sealed behind ballet's closet doors.

Four years later, in 1968, I am standing in the costume department of Toronto's National Ballet of Canada, enduring a fitting for Celia Franca's version of *Cinderella* (1968). I am standing in my underwear while costume designers, fitters and makers – mostly male – are chatting over my head about my height and the size of my tits, comparing my body to the bodies of others, debating whether to design a sizeable headdress to compensate for my non-sylphlike physique. I say these men were tittering, but as I conjure the scene from the echoes of time, I remember their conversation as camp, witty, sarcastic and charming, punctuated with ornate flicks of the wrist. The headdress was created – a veritable bird's nest complete with outsized birds and a full bowl of fruit. It was so heavy that if I tipped my head forward I lost my balance. I was then fitted for an extravagant gown in velvet brocade for my role as a courtier in Prince Charming's palace. The scale of my costume meant I was not expected to dance but to be part of the scenery, a backdrop. Now, perhaps, I might wear this outlandish get-up with queer delight. But back then, I sank into shame. Now I am laughing, back then I was not. What I know now is that none of this extreme frou-frou was about *me*. I was an object of exchange in the repartee of gay men. My body

---

[6]Frederick Ashton and Kenneth MacMillan as ugly sisters, filmed in 1957: https://vimeo.com/230854201

was a medium for communal yet closeted, arch expressions of drag sensibilities.

Frederick and Kenneth understood the rules of how to parody femininity. They could openly parade a queerness that ballet habitually wraps up in a closet. A queerness that is well hidden behind Cinderella's exaggerated performance of hetero-normativity. A performance that cinema specialist and queer theorist Richard Dyer describes as 'so extreme, so refined, so ethereally idealized that it becomes rather unreal, a chimera. In a camp appreciation, this means enjoying the spectacle of heterosexuality paraded as glittering illusion' (Dyer 1992: 43). Back then I did not know how to wear the trappings of outrageous drag. The rules for this parody were kept secret and I was not ready to play. But these memories from the 1960s tease my imagination and prod me towards the possibility of future discussions, towards researching ballet's gay history. My hunch is that for it to preserve its artistic identity at a profoundly creative level, ballet must maintain, and exploit, its closet of queer shame.

TRANSACTION

Louise Lecavalier is wearing a white tutu skirt. Her naked torso is painted white. She has bleached blonde hair, a natty moustache and lipstick. Marc Béland wears a black vest and trousers. They face each other, poised and still. He lightly touches her nose with his hand, triggering a blur of stabbing gestures, an explosive barrage of 'barrel' roll leaps, fiercely flung bodies, precarious lifts and precipitous drops. This is the start of the duet *Human Sex* (Lock 1985), a work created in Montreal at the same time Wim Vandekeybus and DV8 were transforming European dance and physical theatre.[7]

To execute a flying 'barrel' roll, a dancer hurtles herself into space and spins on her axis parallel to the ground at least one and a half times before landing. In contemporary dance, performers execute this horizontal twirl but then land on their feet. Not in *Human Sex*. Louise leaps, twisting her body sideways and parallel to the floor, spins like a drill and thuds into Marc's torso. He drops to the ground without catching her; she crashes straight into his body. Again and again, she charges right at him and flings herself into his airspace. Sometimes he catches her, sometimes he doesn't. Sometimes she launches into a barrel leap with Marc lying flat on the stage.

---

[7]Originally a piece by Éduard Lock for five performers, *Human Sex* established itself as a duet. The stage version was adapted for a film directed by Bernard Hébert entitled *LaLaLa Human Sex (Duo No 1)* in 1987.

Or she flies into the air and slams to the stage alone. Or, they may face each other, pause with eyes locked, then twirl into the air simultaneously. Sometimes, he spins horizontally over her head, and thunk, they are down. When – in a reversal of traditional roles – she levers his hips up over her head and strides about with him slanted push-up style with his hands on her shoulders – her fists are clenched, her biceps ripple and her torso shivers in finely sculpted definition. Then, he plummets to the floor behind her head. She pivots, flips over and flops her full weight onto his. Between these risky, rapid-paced falls, lifts and full-body tosses, she intersperses smiles, kisses and aggressively sexual gestures. And she initiates all contact.

The duet oozes with the embodiment of 'the *trans* of transgender' (Low 2016: 64, original emphasis). Trans refers to a non-binary crossing between genders, which these performers bring alive with androgynous play. The pace and recklessness of the duet supercharge the ambiguity of its transactions. This queering of power dynamics between Marc and Louise – the signifier of which is their falling – is a continuous process of fluid changing, but never of fixing. As Louise transforms her body from states of feminine aggression to masculine grace – in endlessly compelling exchanges with Marc – their gender-markers shift so quickly as to fuse into a transitional stream – a phenomenon which defines the work. 'The fantasy I've been calling performative queerness is . . . about the unexplored spaces between expressions, the possibilities of movement, the non-names not yet imagined' (Fuchs 1996: 150). Thrilling and shocking, this raw, sensual aggressive performance of hyper-paced passions exposes 'the fluidity, instability, and impermanence of gender, and meanings of the body itself' (Low 2016: 65). Nothing straight here. Louise and Marc are two equally powerful metamorphosing creatures, leaping and falling at such dazzling speeds as to dismantle male/female gender normativity. Two erotic beings in lightning-fast circuits of desiring without goal – fall me to want you to drop me and need me to catch you to take me to throw you and fling me to drop you and fall me again yes again yes you want me to want to again.

YES TO TRASH

Queer dancers burst from ballet's closet doors and well-sewn seams. Fred Herko trained at the American Ballet Theatre School before performing with choreographers such as Merce Cunningham and James Waring. He was a founding member of New York's Judson Church in the 1960s, along with artists like Lucinda Childs, Steve Paxton and Yvonne Rainer. He made various choreographies at Judson Church but was never accepted fully as part of the group (Aramphongphan 2015; Burt 2006; Mercier 2019). Even though he 'rejected the polish of high art for the novelty of the pedestrian and raw' (Mackrell 2016), Fred continued to favour balletic gestures and extravagant style in his performance aesthetics. He was more at home with Andy Warhol, who celebrated Fred as his dancing muse and deemed him brilliant (Aramphongphan 2015). Fred starred in many of Andy's films, such as *Freddy Herko* (Warhol, 1964), *Jill and Freddie Dancing* (Warhol, 1963) and *Rollerskate* (Warhol, 1963), in which he careened across New York on a single skate, an adventure that ended with him hobbling and bleeding.[8]

In general, writings about Fred focus less on his work and more on his notorious death. By the age of twenty-eight, he was addicted to speed. Increasingly strung out on various drugs, he was rejected by Andy Warhol, who dismissed him as undisciplined (Aramphongphan 2015). On the day he died, in 1964, Fred performed naked to Mozart's *Coronation Mass* in the living room of a friend's Manhattan apartment. At the climax of his dance, he leapt from the fifth-floor window – the ultimate flamboyance for a queer artist of the 1960s, when there was little support for the shame of queer excess.

Twenty years later, in 1984, Michael Clark emerged from the Royal Ballet to form his own company, Michael Clark and Dancers. This beautiful bald-headed boy crashed into the dance scene with queer, camp, vigorously punk, sexually explicit choreographies flaunting his ballet technique with hyper-stretched, phallic limbs. He collaborated and performed with designer Leigh Bowery, whose extravagant, grotesque, drag-infused outfits with body-extending add-ons brought in-your-face edge to the dancers' bodies. Michael offset his technical refinement with naked bums, flapping kilts, bare-arsed guitarists, outrageous fur sporrans and archly effeminate, submissive gestures texturing his movements and spoofing his articulate, muscular, classical training.

Outside the safety of the ballet closet, these two queer pioneers – Fred Herko in the 1960s and Michael Clark in the 1980s – received very different receptions.[9] By the 1980s, gay pride was in full swing and support for queer performance was emerging in structures like the Dance Umbrella festival in London. Michael was swept up and swallowed by mainstream contemporary dance; his extravagance was managed, produced and given neoliberal polish. Packaged over time, his work lost its vital, outrageous, shameful queerness, and its radical punk edges were dulled. As the neoliberal arts scene increasingly embraced gay performance, Michael's style and content gradually became benign.

Fred Herko found little support in the 1960s, even in the New York arts scene. He did not belong. He was working as an artist before the Stonewall

---

[8] A re-working of this piece took place at *What Remains . . . Anatomy of an Artist: 10 New Works* at Siobhan Davies Studios in 2016.
[9] See also Javier de Frutos's duet work with Jamie Watton in the late 1990s. In *The Hypochondriac Bird* (1998), Javier, naked except for a wrap-around sarong, relishes in melodramatic, decadent, erotic movement, working to Tchaikovsky's score of *Swan Lake*, flaunting a passionate, violent, muscular sensuality around a stalwart, steady, more reserved Jamie.

Riots of 1969. He was criticized by members of the dance community for being excessively camp, self-conscious, performative and balletic. He was making performance in a predominantly white, perhaps slightly homophobic, post-modern dance scene – where dancers were purging their vocabularies of institutionalized techniques in favour of everyday pedestrian minimalism. Yvonne Rainer was working with 'no' scores at the time, such as 'no' to spectacle, glamour, trash imagery and camp, all of which define performance of queer shame.[10] Fred's queer sensibilities were out of place, misplaced. His falling was physical and psychological, yet also metaphorical; he fell out of the commonly accepted codes of post-modern dance. Although Fred found more support at the New York Poets Theatre, of which he was co-founder, the fact is – and Mercier frames this succinctly – 'he never really proved that he belonged, and I read his presence, not about belonging, but about world building, precisely in the space, the void, opened up by not belonging' (Mercier 2019).

For Fred and Michael, queerness was expressed in performance through seductive excess, as a strategy that resisted the performed heteronormative identities of men displayed in ballet. For both artists, not belonging meant continuing to flaunt balletic technique *and* flirting with trashy entertainment, emotive music, glitter, velvet, candlelight and fur, thongs and gross gestures, gothic black cloaks with star-studded heels, lilies and rose petals scattered and strewn, red lipstick smeared and eye liner bruised, leather, pink silk and long painted nails, campy flailing, low art and willies, frocks and bare arses, gestural slippage and spilling excess. This is the trashy stuff that illuminates queering in performance – nothing is upright.

BASIPHOBIA

Even though the fear of falling is inherent, humans only *know* this fear after feeling it in their bodies, as a quick dive into neuroscience demonstrates. Sitting on top of the brainstem (the most primitive part of the brain) is the limbic system, the part of the human brain that deals with sensory, emotional and pre-verbal experience, along with 'reflexive defensive processes' (Taylor 2014: 29). Primary emotions and survival instincts are all triggered through the limbic system, which also activates defences. Miriam Taylor, who draws on neuroscience for an understanding of the mind–body impact of trauma, writes how reactions driven by the limbic system can flood the body 'in as

---

[10]Later, Rainer's 'no's' became labelled by dance historians as her aesthetics of denial, her *No Manifesto*, yet originally her 'no's' were simply some of her own working principles, presented as a postscript to her article: *Some retrospective notes on a dance for 10 people and 12 mattresses called Parts of Some Sextets . . .* (Rainer 1965).

little as one twentieth of a microsecond – literally less than the blink of an eye. After all, in situations of danger speed is of the essence' (Taylor 2014: 29).

Basiphobia, fear of falling, is generated in the limbic brain. And since gravity is constant, the limbic system is relentlessly stimulated. 'Because our senses are so acutely attuned to every subtle shift in gravity, the stream of messages they deliver to the limbic system keep it in a steady state of arousal' (Soden 2003: 267). Human bodies experience fear *before* conscious thought, as reaction has already been initiated by the amygdala, which controls emotions deep within the limbic system. The amygdala increases heart rate, tenses muscles and releases neurotransmitters to prime the brain for action. Meanwhile, the hypothalamus dumps chemicals like adrenaline into the bloodstream. Only then does a person *know* fear. This also works in reverse. *Thinking* about falling as frightening – or witnessing frightening falls – triggers onlookers' limbic systems and kicks them into action to respond to fear, just as if falling were physically happening. It can be a rush. Many enjoy experiencing these sensations on fairground rides offering precipitous drops.

GRIEVING TOGETHER

Along with millions of others, I was affected by the tragic events of 11 September 2001. I watched the falling of the Twin Towers live on my TV. Never had I witnessed such a catastrophic display of destructive power as the collapse of New York's World Trade Center. I am not American, and the event occurred across a vast ocean, yet this was happening in a Western city I know and love. It could just as well have happened right here in London, where I would have been choking on the dust. As a Westerner, I felt deeply impacted by the devastating event unfolding before my eyes. That the cruel plummeting of lives and symbols was caused by aircraft – machinery designed to overcome gravity – added bitter irony and immediacy to the horror.

Over ensuing years, I have questioned my responses to the tragedy – and they are not straightforward. I was profoundly shocked to witness the fallings, and I grieved deeply for the thousands who died and for the agony of those who lost family and friends. I was angry at Bin Laden, angry at al-Qaeda and was as quick to lay blame as anyone else. Yet seeking revenge was not my immediate instinct, aggression did not seem a constructive response. American psychoanalyst Donna Orange explains her country's response to 9/11: 'many Americans, feeling terrified, shocked, and humiliated, sought to affix blame and thus welcomed the division of the world into good and evil. We were too ashamed to seek for understanding, but sought instead to restore pride by means of revenge' (Orange 2008: 95). This pattern of retaliation following demoralizing events – in which so many nations reflexively engage – seems self-defeating, never ending and hopeless.

This is a theme that philosopher and gender theorist Judith Butler explores in her reflection on America's response to the fall of its iconic towers. With her insight into the grief and shame that stoked America's need for revenge, Butler offers alternatives to her countrymen's violent reactions. In her essays on mourning and violence following 9/11, she honours the fear and shock unleashed by the breaching of US borders and the grief over those who died (Butler 2004). Yet even more compelling, she suggests that America might have missed a chance to radically reconfigure its place in the world. 'It was my sense in the fall of 2001 that the United States was missing an opportunity to redefine itself as part of a global community when, instead, it heightened nationalist discourse' (Butler 2004: xi). Butler questions whether the country's immediate response to grief and shame – a heightened nationalism and a lust for vengeance through military might – was necessarily the only course of action to follow. 'If we are interested in arresting cycles of violence to produce less violent outcomes, it is no doubt important to ask what, politically, might be made of grief besides a cry for war' (Butler 2004: xii).

Exploring ideas for what else could be done, Butler initiates a discussion into how *being with* loss and grief, along with the sharing of grief, offer alternative and constructive pathways forward. This approach to grieving means residing with loss as an instrument of change, as a transformative agent, rather than using it for forgetting or 'getting over'. It means instead, seeing loss and losing as productive forces. 'Perhaps mourning has to do with agreeing to undergo a transformation' (Butler 2004: 21). And, perhaps equally important is making that agreement together with others. Yet this is far from easy, as I discover when I experience shock and grief, as tears fall and my body collapses. Blame feels like something to hold onto, as a way to distract myself from my own falling. To share that vulnerability with others can feel shameful, but also, surely, life changing.

Following 9/11, this perspective on grief and grieving was not shared by many. The US and its allies pursued a course of retaliation that diverted attention from the nation's experience of feeling defenceless and channelled the unsettling energy of grief into revenge. Extreme vulnerability of this kind, falling out of pride and into shame, is hardly a change that any nation wants exposed to the world. The inability of countries to seek alternatives to the perpetual drive for dominance over others seems to hang on the fear of revealing their ability to be hurt, their vulnerable exposure to suffering. At a micro level – on my body and yours – we experience vulnerability, grief and loss as a visceral drop, culturally a physicality to be resisted and replaced with an armour of upwardly orientated stiffness. On the macro level, the flight from vulnerability in the West is characterized by a need to dominate, by patriotic arrogance and by blindness to the inter-relational, human connections that grief and shame reveal across race, cultures and nations.

MELTDOWN

Square Dances (Lee 2011), directed by independent dance artist Rosemary Lee, is a large-scale site-specific, cross-generational event, consisting of four different performances and involving 200 performers. *Meltdown*, one performance in this event, takes place in Brunswick Square, one of London's many leafy havens. In one corner of the square is an aged plane tree, its limbs fanning out over the grounds. At the time of this performance, its leaves are turning golden brown. At the sound of a bell, thirty casually dressed men enter the square from all directions and assemble under the tree. Passers-by are intrigued and an audience gathers in a wide, ragged circle. The bell chimes again, and the men – young, old and from diverse backgrounds – lift their arms and faces to the canopy of branches and falling leaves. On the third chime, the men themselves begin falling. Over the next fifteen minutes they gradually sink, drop or crumple to the ground in their individual ways, until each man has surrendered his weight to the earth. Tears of gratitude come to my eyes as I witness this ritual, with each man simply, slowly, awkwardly, candidly discovering his passage down, from high to low, erect to prone, vertical to flat. I gaze at bodies sprawled on the turf and a carpet of leaves. The bell rings once more, the men stand up and leave the square. The significance of their collective falling evokes in my thoughts a patriarchal crumble, a collapse of the scaffolds of institutional, monolithic, white Western supremacy.

Later that same year, Gill Clarke dies. Gill was an inspirational artist, teacher and advocate for independent dance in the UK. To commemorate her death, many members of the UK dance community gathered to perform *Meltdown* together. We met in open, outdoor spaces all across Europe, at the same time, on the same day. I was part of a group who met in north London in the woods of Highgate Hill. It was a chilly day at the end of winter. The layers of leaves blanketing the ground were crisp, brown and brittle. We fell in silence with our memories of Gill. On the way down, I heard birds singing, smelled damp earth and saw sky through a lattice of branches.[11]

MY SON AND ME

My son fell from a second-floor balcony in a Malaysian jungle. He broke his shoulder, punctured a lung, smashed his ribs, broke a leg and ripped a toe. He

---

[11]*Meltdown* was also performed by the faculty at University of Roehampton to commemorate the death of Andrée Grau (2017). Grau was a professor of anthropology who worked tirelessly to establish anthropology as a subject within dance study.

hit the first-floor balcony on his way down, cracking bones yet saving his life. He dragged himself round to the front of the hotel and cried for help. The news of his fall came to me through a mobile phone call from his father when I was walking down the ramp at the Tate Modern in London. I dropped to the ground for support. Fear overwhelmed me as I imagined him falling, his body tumbling over into nothingness. I visualized him dragging himself along the ground, sensed his will to survive, knew his pain. Anguished, I wanted to know who found him lying, broken and bleeding on the jungle floor. In my mind, I held him suspended between balcony and ground, gravity silently, invisibly on hold. I imagined him hovering, weightless and safe. The sound of his impact was too much to bear. And I wanted as well to blame someone. Devastation quickly turned to survival tactics. What could I do to help? How could I make his life more bearable? How might I get him back to London? In time, he recovered, texting with one hand from his hospital bed to organize his return. He survived; we got on with our lives. Yet for years I dreaded answering my phone when I saw his name on the screen. Any text message saying, 'Mum, can you call me?' brought a sharp ache to my stomach.

Reflecting on the event now, what strikes me is how much him falling felt like me falling, his pain my pain. As a result, trying to make him feel better was also about assuaging myself. As Gestalt psychoanalyst Lynne Jacobs confirms: 'Self and other are an indissoluble unit . . . one's sense of self is an emergent phenomenon of intersubjective relatedness' (Jacobs 2009: 135–6). Psychotherapist Emmy van Deurzen adopts an existential, phenomenological perspective: 'I only become myself as I relate to the other. There is never purely an I on its own . . . Everything takes place in relationship and encounter' (van Deurzen and Arnold-Baker 2005: 165). Identity and individuality are relational matters. My son and me understand each other to exist through how we show ourselves to each other and the world, and when my son feels the pain of falling, I sense that pain as my own. Our encounters are intersubjective exchanges where my responsibilities as a parent pre-exist my right to be (Levinas 1989). We experience each other bodily, and because this interaction holds an ethical, empathic core, falling affects us both.

My son now has a family of his own. As I watch him rough and tumble with his youngest son, my grandson, I am aware of our intergenerational, inter-relational independence. I feel his joy and find myself wondering how he might feel if his son were to fall, how might I feel to experience his grief – and how will he feel when I am gone?

APRIL 2020

I am working on structuring this book, choreographing its scenes in a possible sequence. I am also listening to the Covid-19 news – there is no other news – and I am feeling the chill on my flesh. We are in our fourth week of lockdown with no end in sight. In the UK alone, a thousand people died just yesterday and the day before, and the virus has not reached its peak. As of today, the UK has approximately 120,000 cases and 15,000 deaths, with the number of deaths climbing faster than in either Italy or Spain. I look to the statistics – to the numbers and graphs – for information, as if figures on a page could create order from the chaos. As if finding a pattern for the spread of the virus could tame its infectious fire – while trucks full of the dead roll out of Madrid, while makeshift morgues and new Covid-19 hospitals are thrown up overnight.

The psychological effects of lockdown have snowballed. First, older people and those with underlying conditions were advised to self-isolate. Sensing what was coming, we collectively panicked. Panic went viral, and we reached and grasped at anything available to avert a sense of falling. With collective desperation we hoarded, gathering and amassing vital necessities. We stacked up packets of pasta and toilet rolls into protective walls and hid from the entity the replicating virus was becoming. On 18 March, UK schools were closed, on 20 March the pubs and restaurants. Finally, on 23 March, the country went into complete lockdown. Flights were cancelled and borders closed. Large gatherings forbidden, sports events and rallies postponed. All businesses, shops and zoos – shut.

The British government's slogan 'Stay at Home, Protect the NHS, Save Lives' has replaced last year's 'Get Brexit Done'. As the number of deaths persistently climbs, the economy is collapsing. Financial aid, mostly unavailable during ten years of austerity, is offered to support businesses through the crisis. Self-employed artists are beseeching the government for the same support. 20,000 retired National Health Service (NHS) staff have returned to work to help combat the virus. 750,000 people have volunteered. Following three nights in intensive care, the prime minister, Boris Johnson, was discharged from hospital and soon after begins to speak of the virus as a *national* battle, saying we will not be beaten, that we will overcome this challenge, together, as a *nation*, collectively, as we have in the past. Nationalism rises, stoked by Brexit, enflamed by COVID-19.

The widespread use of the idioms of war casts the virus as enemy and fuels nationalist fervour. Officials speak of supplying the 'front line', while NHS workers go into the 'trenches' – like lambs to slaughter – without adequate protection, with inadequate weapons. It's the First World War and the last world war, with the additional hardship of enforced separation. 'We will meet again,' the Queen assures us, recalling Vera Lynn's hopeful wartime ballad. The seventy-fifth anniversary of VE Day will take place during the seventh week of lockdown, provoking further echoing parallels with wartime pride. The day's agenda will include a flypast – consisting of nine war-time planes shooting smoke in the colours of the rainbow, honouring the NHS.

The underpaid and undervalued of the British workforce – nurses, caregivers, food-supply workers, shop assistants, refuse collectors, dispatchers, delivery men and women – are now cheered and revered as we recognize the importance of their service. The LGBTQ rainbow – a signifier of inclusivity – has quickly evolved into an emblem of support for the NHS. Children draw rainbows for front-room windows, and every Thursday evening we stand on pavements to bang out our appreciation on kettles and drums. But despite the heart-warming stories and the burgeoning good will, what was failing before in Western social policy is worsening now. The virus itself does not discriminate, but our obdurate class system and institutional racism is helping determine who lives and who dies. Those with the space and funds to self-isolate efficiently are more likely to survive. Large, extended families living on low incomes in high-rise blocks of cramped apartments are far more likely to die. Domestic abuse is on the rise and psychological damage will keep pace with the death toll. Stuck at home, we stoically wait for a thinning of the herd and a world forever changed.

This is a grim and morbid reality, in April 2020.

Yet, humankind is infinitely malleable. This new, improvisational movement score – this social distancing – this choreographic challenge where bodies must maintain their two-metre margins – invites us to reconfigure the dance. Long stereotyped and renowned for loving to queue, Brits are now cooperatively snaking in well-spaced lines from supermarket entrances out along the streets and around the houses, awaiting the moment to edge through the aisles. We share conversations from window to street, door jamb to pavement, and across expanses of flagstones. From Verona comes the story of a woman and man falling in love from upper windows on opposite sides of the street, rewriting a classic with invisible parasites in place of a family feud. Virtual meetings proliferate apace. Zoom cocktails are all the rage and social media is thriving. Orchestra members record together from their individual homes, while theatres, museums and galleries create virtual tours of their exhibitions. Russian ballet dancers post videos of themselves performing as Giselle in their kitchens. Dancers from the Paris Opera Ballet practise to Prokofiev with their children darting under their legs. Choreography students are making virtual domestic performances; a proliferation of dance classes and yoga sessions are offered online. People in their local communities are reaching out to each other through WhatsApp groups, sharing resources, checking on each other with loving care. I exhale with intent and draw fresh support from gravity and ground. World change begins here, mid-fall, with the tiny details of our daily lives, in April 2020.

OPTIMISTIC DECEPTION

So far, the twenty-first century has been a time of precarity for humans and for the world. We feel the psychological effects in our bodies as sensations of falling out: vertigo, stress, anxiety, panic, loss and fear. How we support ourselves to coexist with precarity, rather than holding onto or hoping for what came before, is now an urgent concern. The collapse of all that was promised in a capitalist wonderland is a familiar theme to Lauren Berlant, a professor of English at the University of Chicago, who writes on social politics from a queer perspective. She argues that capitalist precarity is emerging as people realize that the promised 'good life', including 'upward mobility, job security, political and social equality, and lively, durable intimacy' (Berlant 2011: 3), the supposed rewards of hard work and perseverance, is an unreachable fantasy. Berlant calls this phenomenon 'cruel optimism', the covert strategy of Western capitalism. The attachments we form to fantasies of the good life – framed as a liberal democratic achievement – amount to deceptive optimism because 'the object/scene that ignites a sense of possibility actually makes it impossible to attain the expansive transformation for which a person or a people risks striving' (Berlant 2011: 2).

The psychological effect of decline appears like the hollowing I feel in my stomach when I stand looking down a flight of steep stairs. In the same way I clutch at the hand rail, so people inevitably reach out for something to hold, a steadying rail for managing decline, a means of ordering descent in the world. On a political level, strategies for avoiding the physical and psychological consequences of capitalist decline take shape in isolationist and protectionist policies. Or, in extreme situations where no hand rail is available, in aggression.

Western decline is not a new phenomenon. On BBC Radio 4, media editor Amol Rajan (2018) responded to Trump's demand to make America great again by recalling a previous Western decline in Europe after the First World War. A decline, that in no small way, activated people's attachment to the devastatingly cruel optimism offered by Nazism (Spengler 1922). Rajan noted that out of the ashes of the Second World War came an end to decline, a return to prosperity and the creation of a welfare state – a cause and effect of liberalism and democracy. Led by America, a golden age of democratic capitalism emerged as a new world order, proclaimed as a superior model the rest of the world should follow. Institutions were built to bolster its greatness, such as the United Nations and the International Monetary Fund, meaning that international conflict could now be resolved – under Western terms. Yet the imperialist construction of a prosperous, capitalist, democratic, white 'I' neglected to consider how cultural, political, religious and racial differences across the world might coexist under its umbrella.

As a consequence, the tools that were so successful after the Second World War in lifting the West back up into prosperity are no longer so effective. Democracy has failed to bring economic growth to the poorest and has paid little attention to the consequences of hypermobility (Rajan 2018). Perhaps the term 'prosper' is worth re-considering, given its associations with generating wealth, flying high, flourishing, being at a high career point. Attempting prosperity, forward and up, might be just another cruel tease of optimistic attachment. Perhaps alternative strategies exist for rethinking global relations using other criteria than those associated with prosperous production.

Thinking differently is crucial to Berlant's thesis. She introduces the term 'impasse' as a way to *be with* the current shakiness of 'race, citizenship, labor, class (dis)location, sexuality and health' (2011: 3–4). Impasse for Berlant means to live without optimistic narratives and to wander where directions are enigmatic. Impasse is 'an aspiration ... holding pattern ... a temporary housing' (2011: 5).[12] In a parallel yet different vein, cultural theorist Jack Halberstam speaks of failure as a positive conduit for change and as a way to displace or step aside from capitalist systems of production. Halberstam intentionally explores low art, minor films and silly performances in her book *The Queer Art of Failure* (2011). Failure, in terms of capitalist production, becomes a strategy for political, cultural and artistic change. To work 'outside of success' (Halberstam 2011: 93) is 'to fall short, to get distracted, to take a detour, to find a limit, to lose our way, to avoid mastery, to forget' (2011: 120). This subversive strategy owes much to 'queer, postcolonial and black feminism' (2011: 126). Mirroring Berlant's impasse, Halberstam values failure as 'a shadow archive of resistance [that] articulates itself in terms of evacuation, refusal, passivity, unbecoming, unbeing' (2011: 129).

Berlant and Halberstam propose alternative, queer strategies for dealing with Western decline by encouraging – rather than resisting – uncertainty, unknowing, unfixed identity and non-conformity as viable sources of action. While relishing their queer thinking, I look as well to ground these theories in practice. How do I physically/bodily abide with uncertainty? Letting go of optimistic attachments, *being* with failure, sounds intriguing in theory, but what does it mean in daily life?

Just as psychological condition affects physicality, so the body influences the mind. Physically falling safely to the ground – as an intentional practice – can build resilience for psychological falls. Focusing awareness on body, gravity and ground prepares us to survive not only the precariousness of life but 'also rescues us from the relentless ascension and striving for success that marked the late twentieth century' (Albright 2017: 72). Kinaesthetic connection with gravity develops resilience. Physical, intentional falling comprises a process of becoming confident with disorientation and off-balance states. Falling sees precarity as potential support, much as Derrida considers pharmakon (1981) and Hahnemann describes homeopathic potency (1996), poison in small doses can act as a cure. Somatically informed falling induces psychological release from the endless search for the good life of fantasy. Familiarity with gravity provides emotional resources for

---

[12]As a psychotherapist, I acknowledge the term impasse as it defines a state of being between growth and resistance. Seemingly nothing is happening in an impasse; yet this suspended state of uncertainty holds potential for change.

accepting uncertainty, for getting lost and not-knowing as a viable way of being. Falling, I am supported by the ground to *be* with failure without seeking revenge on the world. Falling, I am vulnerable and collaborate with gravity as the constant force that has provoked precarity from the beginning of things and will do for as long as things last.

STRIPPED

Six men run onto the stage from upstage left, or rather, they spill on, tumbling into the space facing different directions. They pause. They stand, gaze about and blink as if freed from a box for the first time into the light. Then they walk off stage. They had entered as if an energized performance was going to happen, but nothing did. What catches my attention, as physical impact, is a sensation of doing not doing. This is the start of Joe Moran's performance piece *Arrangement* (2014). Trained in Release Technique by Joan Skinner, Joe draws his choreographic influences from the postmodern frameworks of artists such as Deborah Hay, Siobhan Davies and Rosemary Butcher. Unsurprisingly, given this history, Joe prefers absence to excess, and a stripped-down approach to queering performance, rather than a strategy of hyper-indulgent drag performances of gender stereotypes. Both strategies represent queer efforts to escape static, heteronormative expectations in performance and encourage transmuting, transgressing and traversing boundaries – especially around identity. Similarly, Cuban-American theorist José Muñoz (2009) describes a model of queer utopia as living practices that – though evincing constant potential to be something – never materialize. 'Unlike a possibility, a thing that simply might happen, a potentiality is a certain mode of nonbeing that is eminent, a thing that is present but not actually existing in the present tense' (Muñoz 2009: 9).

> I made *Arrangement* as reaction to the heteronormative male work that was proliferating UK dance at the time. Through working with Deborah, Siobhan and Rosemary, I became interested in performing and choreography as a perceptual practice. I introduced this to my dancers through questions: what if we witness what we do to hold ourselves together – for instance, am I performing heroic, or dramatic? – and what if we undo, let go of these ways of holding? What if we engage in an active dynamic of not doing, while doing? What if I see where I am in order to surrender where I am? As with Deborah's work, these questions are not resolvable – the practice proves an impossible task. Trying to find the answer will always fail. As Deborah says: what if I just focus on the question, what if this is what I need?
>
> MORAN interview with author 2019

FIGURE 2.3 Arrangement *by Joe Moran (2014, 2019), performed by Andrew Hardwidge, Alexander Miles, Sean Murray, Erik Nevin, Christopher Owen and Yiannis Tsigkris. Photo: Camilla Greenwell, taken at Sadlers Wells.*

The performers meet on stage and merge into a single mass, their torsos entwining, their legs and arms knitting together. Moving slowly, simultaneously pushing and pulling each other, the clumped bodies travel towards the audience as a single entity of many parts. Joe explains: 'When the men become an amoeba mass, rolling together, they are engaged in something that exceeds representation, becoming an otherness. Yet we see it becoming actual, it is already representing itself to us as something. So, the question becomes: how can we show something that we can't show?' (Moran interview 2019).

Underlying Joe's practice is a tension between presence, representation and the challenge of undoing representation, which itself poses an additional dilemma for performers. Joe encourages his performers to question how they are representing themselves and then to avoid acting out the obvious consequence of that representation. This presents a challenge, as performing is always an act, always a representation of something. At every moment of being present, each man is already representing himself. 'Un-performing is the work's central concern, disrupting notions of the representation of men and masculinity. Male privilege is constantly reasserting itself so, for me, practicing un-performing is how we get to the edge of personhood, the edge of self' (Moran interview 2019). This practice of un-performing heroic male imagery becomes a continuous process of falling away from heteronormativity.

Arrangement comprises a collage of scenes, where beginnings, endings and transitions between movements happen without narrative progression or climax. When a man lifts his arm to the side, he does just that and then drops it again. After dancing a physically strenuous choreographic pattern, he stops and stands, looking vulnerable. There is no 'look at me, I'm special'. When they run, grab and shove, chucking each other about in a burgeoning mayhem, they resemble a group of kids who have forgotten why they're fighting but are thoroughly enjoying the rough-and-tumble.

Joe's practice of not-quite-here-ness (Muñoz 2009) suggests parallels with the work of Ishmael Houston-Jones and his choreography, *Them* (1985). Both choreographers, working with male performers, seek a queerness in performance that unravels 'normal' representation of men. In achieving this, both choreographers face failure – to conform – a theme Thomas de Frantz explores in his writing about *Them*.

> Queer includes gestures that don't quite add up. These nonnormative, mismatched attempts to succeed that ultimately fail are to remind us of how fragile anything like "normal" might be ... Throughout the work, physical encounters fail, and conventional theatrical dancing also fails.
>
> De FRANTZ 2018: 273

Towards the end of *Arrangement*, a man walks on stage to stand facing the audience. He says hello. Two more men join him. They also say hello. They wait, doing not doing. Spectators laugh and ask questions. What's your name? The men spontaneously answer. After a while, each man walks off. 'As a queer gesture, there is no heraldic, heroic moment, there is no getting anywhere, nothing that is achieved. Rather than doing anything, the gesture goes somewhere else. Performers peel out of what they are doing, in a way that is a kind of collapse into itself. How to disrupt representation being core to queer performance' (Moran interview 2019).

As the men stand facing the audience, spectators laugh because the men do nothing other than look exposed; they fail to be 'men', they appear uncertain – foolish. So strong are heteronormative male stereotypes in contemporary dance that even in 2019 – when I again see the work in London – a man standing on stage doing nothing conjures such uncertainty of identity it evokes laughter. Much like what happens in contrasting cases of drag excess.

EXCESSIVE SLIPS

After leaving DV8, Nigel Charnock conceived a series of solos that he performed until close to his death in 2012: *Resurrection* (1991), *Original*

Sin (1993), *Hell Bent* (1994), *Human Being* (1999), *Frank* (2002) and *One Dixon Road* (2010). To label him or his performances as queer is not to categorize Nigel, but to recognize and honour his continuous project of image transformation through movement, text, character and song. Deeply critical of religion, homophobia, institutional power, heterosexuality, conventions of beauty, any named dance forms (modern, postmodern, physical theatre), and 'isms' of all kinds, Nigel's shows oozed with conviction and camp humour, with drag excess, sardonic wit and sheer, naked vulnerability. In memory of one of the UK's *most* queer and outrageously shameful performers, I gather images from his solo shows that continue to shiver my skin.

Wrenching himself between Gollum grotesque and Greek-god gorgeous, Nigel thrived and prevailed, nourished by his own and the world's contradictions. As lizard, clown, hostess, queen, conductor, lover, wizard, boy or sacrificial victim, he grappled with anger, pathos, laughter and the sublime, along with serious intent. Nigel took his chances with gravity. Pain was no barrier. With boundless imagination he chased his desires beyond his own flesh into stormy exposures. He chatted with a skeleton, carried crosses on his back, threw toy babies, dialogued with dolls – the blow-up kind – and grandly held court from bed. White boxers, suit trousers, silk slips, dress shirts, sunglasses, blond wigs, sequined dresses and high heel shoes were among the accoutrements he wrapped himself in . . . if he wasn't appearing stark naked. He skipped, he minced, he flicked his spine, clamped his knees, hunched his shoulders and distorted his whole person. He screamed, he wanked and toyed with audiences, floundering through the rows, perhaps to dance with hesitant spectators. He roared popular songs in rich alto sound, sang opera with gusto or played jazz and blues on harmonica, saxophone and piano.

And words words words – Nigel loved words. Delicious, lavish, extravagant words – fanciful sounds – spiky, loving, dirty words, splitting off his tongue, gurgling in his throat, dangerously resonant like hot sonic gold. Nigel's audiences loved and laughed at his agile, cruel, humorous debates, the argumentative monologues he had with himself about sex and desire, where he scorned all sexual currencies. He barked outrageous remarks, swore like gunfire at night – yet however much he shouted, however coarse his language or harsh his tone, he always loved – his audience, his fellow performers, his theatre.

Until his final fall, Nigel was strung between limitless imagination and the limits of his frame – his human dimensions – contorting his way around comedy and tragedy, a consummate artist and entertainer. Nigel Charnock openly, pleasurably, ridiculed and flaunted the shame of being queer. He was a tragic queen and romantic poet, his gestures sliding from powerfully virile to flippantly feminine excess. He was achingly thin, a bruised, bony figure with colt-like legs, knobbly knees, a sharp-boned rib cage. All thrashing, flapping, flicking and thrusting, he tested and fought with mortality.

3

Falling Away

SHOLIBA

Sankai Juku is a Japanese Butoh dance company. In their signature work, *Sholiba* (1979), the performers descend slowly from the roofs of iconic buildings around the globe. In 1985, a large crowd gathers to watch *Sholiba* at Seattle Pioneer Square, where the performers will descend from the Seattle Mutual Life Building. Spectators gaze up to the top of the building – fearful and excited – as two men appear, naked and painted white in traditional Butoh style. They tip their bodies slowly over a support bar and begin their gradual descent, upside down, suspended by ropes tied to the bar and attached to their right ankles. Barely four minutes into the descent, one of the ropes breaks. Yoshiyuki Takada hurtles to the ground. Spectators cry out and rush forward, while a camera pushes into the crowd to capture him where he has fallen. People surround his broken body. He dies on his way to hospital.

In 2018, with voyeuristic curiosity, I am in the British Library watching a YouTube video of the event. Even though I am prepared for what is going to happen, and even though the fall is far away in time and space, my gasp of terror when I witness Yoshiyuki's fall echoes through the silent reading room. The spectacle of humans performing highly staged, slow-motion falling events suddenly becomes real – real falling, felt in real time by real people. Felt in real bodies, like mine. This is not art, not representation, this is death by falling.

FORGETTING

Working *with* gravity as a way to enliven ageing may seem contradictory or nonsensical. To advocate for falling – the actual physical direction of dying – as a resourceful pathway appears to be promoting danger and pain.

I certainly sense this contradiction in my own body. As I get older, I have learnt to adapt to various physical disabilities, particularly an arthritic left foot, with the right side of my body taking more weight and my spine compensating for this restriction. To deal with this skeletal and muscular imbalance, I am tempted to hold my body stiffly, in one piece, away from the ground to avoid pain. Yet when I do that, physical stiffness and tension worsens and so does my fear of falling. Therefore – since physical and psychological instincts are connected – my thinking also stiffens, becomes fixed.

Somatic movement pioneer Thomas Hanna was adamant that growing older should not mean decreasing physical activity. Slowing down is not only treacherous, but a 'pathway leading directly to decrepitude' (Hanna 1988: 39). Integral to Hanna's somatic research was his understanding of how to reverse the typical consequences of ageing. His key insight concerned the stiffness of old age, which he ascribed to sensory-motor amnesia (SMA) – a loss of memory about movement – rather than to the number of years a person has lived. To explain: the sensory-motor system encompasses the relationship between sensory nerves and motor nerves, 'two sides of the same coin' (Hanna 1988: 6). Sensory nerves carry information to the brain from the outside world, which the brain integrates with outgoing commands to the motor nerves, which initiate action. This is a 'feedback system ... [We] require a constant stream of sensory information from the outside in order to maintain ongoing control of our muscular movements from the inside out' (Hanna 1988: 7). When something goes wrong with this system, bodies malfunction.

Living in stressful environments, and with injury, pain or the aftermath of trauma, means that things do go wrong. Sensory nerves are immediately affected by physical and psychological environments. With stress, anxiety or fear, motor nerves are affected, muscles contract and withdraw, a reaction that Hanna calls the 'red light reflex' (1988: 49), an automatic protective response to distress. This reflex has evolved as a primal response to threats and activates itself prior to any conscious awareness of danger. If situations are repeatedly stressful, the red-light reflex remains switched on, and without conscious awareness, a body will continuously withdraw, leaving muscles contracted and putting additional strain on the motor nervous system. Whatever the threatening external conditions, restrictions on motion and mobility become habitual through repetition and register even less on the conscious mind, hence sensory-motor amnesia. This is also known as conditioned learning (as opposed to somatic learning) – learning imposed by outside forces. Conditioned learning produces automatic responses, independent of somatic awareness.

Gravity is one such external force that, throughout our lifetime, has an impact on sensory nerves, for the most part, unconsciously. Not only is gravity an environmental constant – always provoking fear of falling – its effects are exacerbated by cultural aversion to the shame and failure associated with falling. Constantly subject to gravity, the body is always prone to the red light alert with its motor system ready to trigger withdrawal and the contraction of muscles. Tension accumulates when the red light reflex does not turn off – because the body has forgotten how. Even without specific falling traumas, the red light response to fear of gravity becomes a habitual condition and brings on the stiffness, pain and physical restrictions characteristic of old age. Yet, as Hanna asserts, complaints by the elderly of stiffness in backs, necks, knees and hips have nothing to do with ageing but with the 'functional problems of disuse' (Hanna 1988: 43) caused by forgetting how to release the red light reflex.

According to Hanna, once a person understands how her physical stiffness accumulated and regains enough voluntary muscular control to release tension through somatic exercises and awareness, then the so-called problems of ageing begin to ease. Most of Hanna's somatic exercises are practised lying on the ground or on a table, where the influence of gravity is the most diffuse and where bodies can more easily be encouraged to switch off the red light reflex. Here, voluntary muscular control that has been forgotten can be relearned 'by making direct and practical use of two abilities that are the unique properties of the human sensory-motor system: to unlearn what has been learned; and to remember what has been forgotten' (Hanna 1988: xiii).

VERT LEAPS

Vert, short for vertical, is a term used by skateboarders to describe feats on high-sided, U-shaped ramps, as opposed to their exploits on horizontal surfaces. Riders plunge off the lip on one side, skate down to the curve at the bottom and then up the other side, where they free-sail into the air, perform a variety of flips and somersaults and career back down the steep-sided ramp to repeat the adventure on the opposite slope. Throughout the manoeuvre they somehow manage to maintain the connection between skateboard and feet. The speed of their downward flights provides impetus to power up the other side. The more speed a rider creates going down, the higher she sails before flipping to hurtle back down; the higher she flies, the more time there is to develop and refine her aerial stunts.

Participants of extreme (X) sports, such as skateboarders, take the driving force of gravity seriously. Playing X sports means being prepared to take risks, being ready to tumble: 'The more serious the risk, the more extreme the sport' (Soden 2003: 225). Practice begins with learning to fall properly: not catching yourself with your hands, but falling onto well-padded knees or in a full body slide. When attempting the vert leaps, there can be no holding back. The weight of the body must be slammed forward onto the board to go *with* gravity. Pulling back causes a dangerous crash and burn. Here is a paradox. Falling off a ride signals failure in X games, yet falling *with* a ride is essential to success. These daring athletes – skilled in the air, on wheels and on those treacherously curved surfaces – develop intimate understandings of physics; they know in their bones the difference between falling skill and falling failure.

NOT GOING GENTLY

I would like to believe I am honing my curiosity about dying – wide eyed and laughing – actively seeking its creative verve, hungry for adventure and eager to learn. I am certainly working on achieving that philosophy. Yet, as a dancer and a woman, I am also afraid, saddened and frustrated by my dying body with its stiffening joints. I stare at my ageing skin, a landscape of furrows and creases. My underarms are slack, elbows and knees scaled like the skin of a turtle. My stomach folds over like Bridget Riley's artwork *Fall* (1963), and my neck is as scraggy as remote Scottish cliffs. Age exerts its gravitational drag all over my body. It pleats my flesh with its inexorable patterns of decay. As my body caves to gravity's pull, my spine gets stiffer, and the ground, once so familiar to my younger self, only gets further away.

I want to spend time in this writing with the loss of youth and of youthful dancing, by paying respect to Martha Graham, who fought against that loss till the day she died. Thinking about Martha, I am reminded of Dylan Thomas's famous villanelle which begins: 'Do not go gentle into that good night / Old age should burn and rave at close of day; / Rage, rage against the dying of the light' (1947). Written after the Second World War – when Martha was in her prime – Thomas's poem urges resistance against death and celebrates those efforts so familiar to dancers whose bodies are the medium, the vehicle through which they realize themselves in the world.

Accepting ageing is a challenge for most people. For dancers, it is particularly difficult. Our livelihoods and identities are inseparable from our physicality. In the West, dance continues to be associated with youthful power, stamina and elan. Not only is the ageing process physically debilitating and irreversible, drooping flesh is a tell-tale sign that a dancer can no longer maintain the control and extreme muscular strength that characterizes many Western dance forms. No matter how much a dancer pushes to maintain herself at top performance levels, the ageing process will silently and inevitably enfold her in its gravitational embrace. And when a dancer is also culturally elevated, a celebrity in her field – as was Martha – then her resistance to ageing and desire to continue are exacerbated both without and within.

Martha's story is particularly relevant because her resistance to dying is symbolized clearly in her choreographed falls, which so pointedly fight against gravity.

> In one of Martha's great falls, she went to the earth with her usual mastery but was unable to rise again and struggled for a second or two helplessly on the ground . . . Bertram Ross, who was dancing with her, swooped her up, performed a remarkable step and laid her on the nearest Noguchi support.
>
> De MILLE 1991: 373

A performance of dying was not Martha's intention when she found herself unable to rise during one of her final performances of 1969, when she was seventy-five years of age.[1] Rather, her struggle to get up highlights how challenging her falls actually are, the demands they make on age-worn muscles and nerves. Whereas a somatic practitioner might yield further into the ground to gather the support to rise, yielding is not a feature of Martha's falls. Without yielding into the ground, pushing up again requires intense muscular effort.

Even in her seventies, Martha found it hard to give up her life as a performer. She became 'morbidly sensitive to any possible threat to her position, to her power, to her privileges, and looked upon rebuffs, even the most natural and the most reasonable, as a direct questioning of her rights' (De Mille 1991: 372). She railed against her failing body, turned away from her company and scorned young dancers who performed her roles. When I was training at her school in 1969, Martha's appearances were rare and rumours were rampant. Understood in the deathly hush of our respect was the fear that perhaps she would burn down the school, so adamant was she that her work should *not* live on without her. Inevitably, she collapsed. In her own words: 'I had lost my will to live. I stayed home alone, ate very little, and drank too much and brooded. Finally my system just gave in' (Graham 1991: 237).

After a long spell in hospital, Martha returned to her company in 1973 to focus on making choreography, heralding what dance writer Mark Franko calls her 'afterlife' (2014: 3). She created some thirty works over the next two decades until her death in 1991. These choreographies, however, were a 'distorted and disjointed replay of what had already transpired in the 1940s' (Franko 2014: 3). When she returned, she was hyped as an American legend. In 1976 she was awarded the Presidential Medal of Freedom by

---

[1] The exact date of Martha's final performances differ. Freedman (1998) claims it was 1969, for De Mille (1991) it was 1968, while Martha herself claims her final performance took place in 1970.

President Gerald Ford. Pop star Madonna, who studied with and idolized her, declared her desire – across the media – to portray Martha in a film. A legendary force, Martha was raised on a pedestal as a national treasure of American modern dance. The media packaged and sold her along with her work as commodities, and she 'lent herself to this commodification' (Franko 2014: 3).

I understand her commodification as a consequence of both the artistry – and the fixed disposition – of her technique and her choreographies. Because her works were codified and fixed, they could easily be repackaged and sold. Her company, along with following generations of dancers, re-taught and re-constructed them without her active engagement, except in the role of figurehead. Even now, her company continues to perform her works.[2] Propped up by the media, Martha remained in the light. Why would she not want that for herself, if it helped her maintain her relationship to dance and her image as its diva?[3] Yet without her physical engagement in the studio – dancing, choreographing, performing – her artistic instincts and innovative spirit shrivelled and died. From the hotbed of her own expressive flesh, she reached out to inspire her dancers. Having achieved and accepted star status, the new philosophies that had bubbled to the surface at Judson Church during the 1960s, ideas based in collaboration, improvisation and somatic awareness, were not available to her. Her artistry brought success and renown, yet also restricted her potential for change.

Martha was working at the height of modernism in the 1940s and 1950s, when achieving star status for individual artists was the principal measure of success. Martha did not want to die, but neither was she allowed to. She was trapped by the media, by the dance world and by the strength of her own will, a combination that could only bring tragic results. It led to 'Graham-fatigue', which did much to spoil her earlier reputation as an inventive choreographer and performer (Franko 2014: 3).

Like myself, readers will be thinking times have changed, dance has changed and that dancers are continuing to dance into old age, working *with* ageing in their dancing. Yes indeed. And while Dylan Thomas's words make beautiful poetry, they are in fact terrible advice. But right now, as I get older and attempt *to be with* ageing, I acknowledge that this is not an easy acceptance for a dancer and a woman. Sometimes I feel the decline of my dancing body as a mammoth loss, and some days dying feels just too dark to face.

---

[2]That Martha was willingly caught up in this commodification is the issue Franko addresses in seeking to 'rehumanize' her through a deep analysis of her early works (2014: 5).
[3]Richard Move is renowned for portraying the diva image of Martha in his drag performance *Martha@Mother* (1996).

WILLING TRANSITION

Begin standing somewhere, with enough floor space to stretch out fully when lying down. Let the muscles of your face grow heavy, relaxing your eye sockets, cheeks and forehead; let go of smiling and drop your jaw. Allow your head to drop forward, followed by your shoulders and torso, letting the weight of your skull lead you downwards. Your arms are soft and hanging easy; your hands loosely weighted towards the earth. As your body rounds over, allow your knees to bend and your tailbone to loosen and drop. Allow your skull to be heavy, to curl you forward and down, while you anchor yourself by your dropping tailbone. Let your hands flatten and spread, and your knees as well touch the ground. Here you are, on your hands and knees with your head dropping forward.

Continuing your downwards trajectory, support yourself on your left arm while sliding the right ahead along the ground and your right leg back along the ground behind you. Slide outwards in two directions until you settle inevitably down flat with the weight of your torso. You will find yourself lying on your stomach with one arm and leg stretched out, yet aware of a slight tension and resistance to gravity in your other leg and arm as you lie in this position. Continue releasing all your limbs and coming to rest where all parts of your body are surrendering to gravity, which might entail rolling onto your back. Here you can drop fully into gravity and let the ground support you. To get up, you might follow the actions suggested in 'Infant Wisdom' (see page 37). Repeat your passage of falling, as many times as you wish.

With time and practice, you will find your own trajectories, discover your own versions of falling in different directions. Sometimes I find myself dropping into a squat and then sliding one arm backwards along the ground to facilitate releasing my weight onto my back. Or I land on one hip and slide sideways to the ground. You might gradually increase your speed of falling, taking risks with gravity that are appropriate for you. Practise intentional falling every day, just as you stand, walk and run, and you will experience an increase in physical confidence to move about in the world. With confidence comes fluidity; as a result, if you should experience an accidental fall, there is less likelihood of injury. In relationship with my 'oldest friend, gravity' (Olsen 2017: 181), I can relate to others with curiosity and respect, without the need to dominate or possess, nor to eliminate differences. The implications – in the face of radical uncertainty – of resettling my outlook in this way are vast.

RIGGED FLESH

The original version of Trisha Brown's *Man Walking Down the Side of a Building* (1970) takes place on Wooster Street in New York City. Safely harnessed and hoisted by a set of ropes, a man steps off the building's roof and stands on the façade horizontally. Facing downwards, he walks calmly down the side of the building to the street below. Trisha's purpose in her wall-walking series of the 1970s and 1980s reveals her conceptual curiosity, her questioning of what constitutes dance by placing a natural activity within an unnatural setting. 'The paradox of one action working against another is very interesting to me . . . you have gravity working one way on the body and my intention to have a naturally walking person working in the other' (Brown 2002).

Elizabeth Streb performed a version of Brown's *Man Walking Down the Side of a Building* at the Whitney Museum in 2010. In her own world of performance, Elizabeth is not concerned with conceptual innovations in dance. Her *raison d'être* is physical risk. She wants only to see humans fly. Elizabeth creates high-flying, extreme, action-hero events, which have been documented in the film *Born to Fly: Elizabeth Streb vs. Gravity* (dir. Gund 2014) and in her book, *How to Become an Action Hero* (2010).

To realize her impossible premise, Elizabeth converted a Brooklyn garage into SLAM (Streb Lab for Action Mechanics), home to Streb Extreme Action Company. Activities there focus on circus, trapeze and extreme action performance. Her manifesto includes: 'Do not camouflage the impact of gravity; stop being careful; agree to get hurt; invite danger; defy transitions; explode' (Streb 2010: 134). The Lab is equipped with a range of equipment: trusses, scaffolding, trampolines, harnesses, ropes, steel girders, trapezes, seesaws, wheels and various apparatus for flight. To highlight her obsession with risk, Elizabeth integrates mechanical structures with live bodies in all her performances. As she says in Gund's film, 'Anything that's safe is not action'. Working more in the realm of extreme sport than in dance, Elizabeth pairs living, breathing humans with industrial-grade machinery and urges them to attempt ever more dangerous flights and falls. She describes her performers as action specialists, action engineers, movement methodologists, modern-day gladiators or action heroes. 'Their number one question has to be *how*, not *why*. They can never say no' (Streb 2010: 40, original emphasis).

The pounding heart of Elizabeth's work – and of her abrasive manifesto – is her insistence that performers and spectators alike come to the edge, that they approach high-risk falling as closely as possible. These brutal activities attract those seeking adrenalin highs, people wanting their nerves, emotions and senses fired up, their tolerance for fear severely tested, especially their fears around gravity and falling. I have an enduring impression of the eagerness with which Elizabeth's performers and spectators enter into a pact, urging her on to fly and to crash, to challenge the physics, ignore the risks, seek spectacular ways of experiencing the thrill of life in the extreme. 'The combination of Streb's dogged pursuit of the physics of the crash and her childlike desire to escape gravity and fly gives her work a sometimes contradictory character, it is at once punishing and beautiful' (Phelan 2010: xviii).

For both Trisha and Elizabeth, establishing hybrid matrices between body and tech, between equipment and flesh, is central to their experiments with (not) falling. Yet these two artists are inspired by contrasting personal manifestos, by polarized approaches to gravity play. As might be expected of early American post-modern performance, the element of adrenalin-filled excitement is played down in *Man Walking Down the Side of a Building*. By juxtaposing pedestrian actions with extreme disorientation, Trisha considers the objects of her fascination through a conceptual lens. Elizabeth's work is produced and performed by whipping up a state of excitement in viewers, by stoking the sense of immediacy; for spectators and participants, the experience is vital and dangerous. Trisha's performers walk slowly, with their equipment exposed. The rigging is functional, integrated into the performance as a necessary element, enabling performers to complete their tasks. Elizabeth's equipment certainly supports her performers, but is often used to increase the risks and exacerbate the danger: blocks and planks ricochet and fly, imperilling performers who must dive out of the way. The equipment itself performs. Trisha's performers focus on the everyday actions of walking in highly unusual places. Elizabeth's performers crash through the barrier of pedestrian effects to a place of spectacular showmanship. Trisha turns attention away from fear, asking her audience to engage abstractly with displacement of pedestrian actions. Elizabeth's performances seduce her audiences into a space of wonder, spectacle and fear.

CAUGHT ON THE BLINK

I know that what I am looking at is a trick, but my body responds viscerally. I am standing in London's Hayward Gallery, transfixed by a woman thrown into a backbend and suspended off-balance with her arms flung outwards, pelvis thrust forward, both legs bent and only one foot touching the ground. She is caught just above the floor in a frozen moment, a fraction of a second before impact. As I walk up close to her, the woman is visibly breathing and blinking, and I experience a vertiginous thrill and fear of falling, a seductive yet unsettling sense of liminal disorientation.

In Just a Blink of an Eye (Xu Zhen, 2005/2012) occurred as part of the exhibition *Art of Change: New Directions from China* (2012). It is a living sculpture where a moment of falling, too fast to witness in real time, is timelessly arrested. For Shanghai-born Xu Zhen, this live-art work represents a metaphorical falling. The work is a socio-political comment on present realities in contemporary China, the plight of Chinese workers, the status of marginalized people and the instability of a global market. For me, the immediacy of witnessing the luscious physicality of a free fall frozen in time is an experience of suspension in gravity. I am entranced.

In Just a Blink of an Eye is a live-art installation, with a performer whom I observe as an art object. Distinct from such live art is the genre of photographic imagery dealing with falling. *Leap into the Void* (1960) sees Yves Klein suspended in time, seemingly in full flight, leaping from a building on a Parisian street. This photo-montage, created by Harry Shunk and Janos Kender, offers a breathtaking moment of falling-flying. Yves's leap represents freedom from the conventions of an increasingly industrialized era. As an artist, he has painted himself into space, in defiance of gravity, heroic in his suit and tie, arms outstretched, back arched, suggesting a desire for spiritual transcendence. In dance, there is an overabundance of photographic images of falling. As just one example, on the cover of *Caught Falling* (Koteen and Smith 2008), Nancy Stark Smith is captured with her head, torso and arms thrusting forwards, horizontal to the ground. While Yves's fall resembles flight, Nancy is clearly diving in a manner that excludes fantasy and transcendence.

These images in live art and photography were *constructed* for artistic effect. Xu Zhen's performer is lying on a wire frame camouflaged by her clothing. Yves is in fact leaping into a tarpaulin held by friends, which was edited out of the image. Later in *Caught Falling*, the entire photograph is revealed, and Steve Paxton is seen providing a counter weight, holding Nancy's hips while she drives into a forward fall. Even though these are constructed images, they unleash seductive adrenalin. The role technology plays serves to expand and unfold moments of falling, drawing spectators further into vertiginous dizziness. These artistic images allow viewers to experience safely the sensuality of falling, the beauty of surrender and the thrill of abandonment to gravity.

Photographic images of captured falling can also serve to highlight social issues. *La Chute* (*The Fall*, Darzacq, 2006) is a series of photographs of young hip-hop dancers in the suburbs of Paris caught in falls only inches from the ground. Darzacq was inspired by the French riots of 2005 and a disempowered youth culture: 'an entire generation in France in free-fall, ignored by society, their energy untapped and unused' (Chrisafis 2007). Darzacq captures these young men falling for the camera against banal, urban landscapes where shutters are drawn and streets deserted. The images reveal a milieu of poverty and displacement, of falling as an abandonment to nothingness.[4] The hip-hop dancers fall without the hidden safety nets that enable the work of Xu Zhen, Klein and Smith. Physically fit and seemingly fearless, they assume the risks and perform spectacular drops straight onto concrete, captured on camera.

---

[4] See Albright (2013) for discussion about Darzacq's *La Chute* images, alongside falling in contact improvisation.

In horrendous contrast to these images of artistic falls is *The Falling Man*. The photograph by Richard Drew of a man falling from the North Tower of the World Trade Center in New York on 9/11 continues to appal viewers as a reminder of their vulnerability in the face of adversity. This is not art, this is not a constructed performance image, nor is this man in control of the risks of falling, as in the previous examples. He dies. A real person falls from a great height. The photograph makes vivid the audio and visual shock of that day.

Since its publication, images of falling that have been applied as metaphors in Western art, literature and poetry are forever freighted with trauma. This line of inquiry is pursued by Pozorski (2014), for whom the 9/11 photograph brings real and representational fallings forever into tension. Representations of falling can no longer be simply literary tropes, social or political references or linguistic abstractions. Falling imagery can no longer be figurative, or connote 'a moral or spiritual fall, which is where the literary resonances first found [their] greatest power' (Pozorski 2014: 25). For Pozorski, *The Falling Man* means that artistic and literary images of falling are now perpetually infused with personal and national trauma. Artists and writers who wish to represent gravitational falling as symbolic or metaphorical must now respect the traumatized sensibilities of a different global reality. *The Falling Man* is a photographic image triggering horror, shock, pain and loss. Pozorski refers to an excess of meaning as a consequence of *The Falling Man*, in that representations of falling in photography, art and poetry now exceed their metaphorical references as they will always call to mind the horrific images of that day. Dance academic Ann Cooper Albright draws attention to the fact that the events of 9/11 have conditioned people's subjective experience of their bodies. She suggests that since that date, the fear of falling itself has been intensified, has taken on additional peril and metaphorical overtones, 'a fear of losing stability in a world that is already so chaotic' (Albright 2013: 41).

This is not the first time a photograph has ignited traumatic memories in specific communities. *The Death of a Loyalist Soldier* (Capa 1936) captures a man falling just after being shot during the Spanish Civil War. The difference here may be that the loyalist falls in an already established context of war, where death was predicted, and the image is accompanied by silence, abstracted from the sounds of conflict. In contrast, prior to the 9/11 attack, the American people were oblivious to its imminence, and the invasion of Afghanistan followed, rather than preceded, the events of 9/11, which were so brutally epitomized in *The Falling Man* image. Furthermore, this photograph brings to mind a confusion of nightmarish imagery and sounds indelibly stamped into our memory.

I propose that witnessing images of falling in art and photography *always* carries potential to trigger traumatic memory, regardless of its close associations to actuality. This is an element of its imagistic attraction, which draws people to look. For the most part, photographic representations of bodies falling offer spectators safe, accessible, sensations of falling, a combination of anxiety and exultation. These images tap into the thrill and fear of falling, even when, and perhaps because, the fear is secondary. That is, fear provoked by thoughts or memories of falling rather than in-the-moment terror. So deeply primal and universal is basiphobia – fear of falling – that it is triggered even when the image is constructed. Like all trauma, knowing and sensing are intricately intertwined when it comes to fear of falling (Rothschild 2000; Taylor 2014). The 9/11 image stands apart. It takes viewers beyond the point of a safe thrill, the height is too high, the fall too deep, the accompanying sounds and visuals too shocking. There is no safety, no escape, no relief.

A COLD STAGE

Celeste Dandeker performed with London Contemporary Dance Theatre. In 1973, she fell while on stage. Now, as a wheelchair performer and founding artistic director of Candoco Dance Company, Celeste remembers the accident that left her disabled from her neck down.

> We were on tour with *Stages* (Cohan 1973), all about a hero coming from above to save us from the creatures of the underworld. It was the last night at the Palace Theatre in Manchester and it was very, very cold. Those were the days when we did eight shows a week with two matinees. There [were] the miners' strikes, the theatre wasn't heated properly, the lights didn't go on till fairly late into the evening and I had a terrible cold.
>
> There was an acrobatic section in *Stages* that involved me doing a handspring over two men, who were lunging forward in a wrestling position. They made a surface for me to go over; they didn't have to do anything. I could do that move; they did not have to assist me.
>
> I had to run, handspring over their backs and land on my feet. As I was running forward I was thinking, perhaps I am going a bit fast. I do remember this. Then as soon as I put my hands down and flipped my legs up, I knew I was going too fast. I just thought I am going to fall and then I don't remember. I remember I put my hands down on their backs and flicked my legs up with a *WHACK* instead of a *TA-DAAA*. [*Celeste uses her hands to describe how her legs went up too fast and then to describe the suspension mid-air that should have happened.*] What you are supposed to do is go over in an arch position and land on your feet. But I went half again. Instead of one rotation as you would do in a somersault, I made an extra half a rotation and landed upside down on my face, with my chin like this [*she lifts her chin so her head tilts backwards, she places*

her hand under her chin to represent the floor]. Apparently, I was on my elbows and knees with my head on the floor and knocked right out cold. I didn't move. There were two or three doctors in the audience who immediately stood up because they knew something had happened. Apparently, one of the dancers picked me up and took me off stage. I woke up in the wings. I felt like I was floating and when sensation kicked in, that's when it began to hurt. It was frightening, not knowing what I was doing there. I couldn't move anything, except my head. I had broken my neck at the fifth and sixth vertebrae.

And the show went on.

With 100 per cent of me, I wish it hadn't happened. Of course. I have not had a bad life this last forty-five years, and Candoco wouldn't have happened, but I would certainly give it all up to be able to be me again, me as I was. Even with all the good things that have happened, I still think I would have given all that up and that's honest.

DANDEKER interview with author 2018

DEFIANCE

Aerial performers defy gravity, develop somatic desensitization, surmount physical pain, and ride fear while testing fear, to fully engage with risks-taking feats in the air. For Lindsey Butcher, director of Gravity & Levity, this is a way of life. Lindsey, who defines herself as dancer, choreographer, aerialist and teacher, is dedicated to pioneering interdisciplinary practices in the fields of aerial dance and performance.

I met Lindsey in 1983 when she was dancing in Extemporary Dance Theatre, of which I was artistic director. She first took to the air in 1984 with her new hobby – skydiving – which she did during company holidays. She remembers it being about pushing boundaries, testing her response to fear.

> Somebody gave me a parachute jump for my twenty-first birthday. It was a big plane we jumped from, a sky liner. Students go out three at a time, and I was towards the back. All along the line, people were bailing out, 'I don't want to do it, I don't want to do it'. So, the plane would go around, and the instructors would ask them again. I was crying with nerves. I could see the instructors nudging each other, thinking 'We're going to have a problem with this one'. I could not stop crying. But when they asked me if I was ready, I said, 'Yes'. And out I jumped. One of the instructors met me as I landed and said, 'We thought you would never jump. But then you were like our best student ever, perfect position out the door, your body awareness is incredible, do you want to go again?'

FIGURE 3.1 *Lindsey Butcher in* Rites of War *(Gravity & Levity, 2013). Photo: Mark Morreau, with thanks to Scarabeus Aerial Theatre.*

He got me a parachute, and I jumped again and again that weekend. By the end of the summer I had moved on to free fall. Sixty seconds of free fall – just falling – before the parachute opens.

Apart from your face, it does not feel like falling. More like flying than falling. It takes a few seconds to reach terminal velocity, about 120 mph if you are in stable, belly-to-earth position. Diving in a head-down position you can reach speeds of up to 180–200mph. If you get out at 13,000 feet, then you are falling like that for around sixty seconds before you deploy the parachute.

Landing was the thing I was always fearful of. When you get it right, it's beautiful, like stepping down from a ledge and then running for a few steps. People who are really good can land on a 50 pence piece in the middle of a sand pit. I always thought, 'If I am going to hurt myself, this is where it is going to be'. It was always about the landing, never about the falling, that was my biggest fear.

BUTCHER interview with author 2018

In 1988, Extemporary Dance Theatre commissioned Sue Broadway from RaRaZoo circus to create an aerial ballet, *When the Moon Rises*.[5] The project required dancers to perform rope work and web spins. Lindsey, already competent with anti-gravity, calculated-risk manoeuvres, was quick to learn. A web spin uses a length of hanging rope with a loop secured in it. The performer climbs up and inserts a hand or foot into the loop. A spinner at the bottom cranks the rope, winding up speed until the performer is whizzing around horizontally with just a hand or foot through the loop.

In order to defy gravity – to orbit at speed around their ropes – aerial performers require a respectful understanding of the force that keeps us on the planet, a defiance that Lindsey exposed by inviting somatic movement practitioners Gill Clarke and Caroline Scott to work with Gravity & Levity. The performers explored ways to release their breathing because harness and other aerial work 'constrain[s] the rib cage and breath' (Butcher interview 2018). The problem was, after the somatic sessions, no one wanted to get back on the trapeze. Traditionally, aerial techniques involve a desensitizing process.

Building up callouses. It's often about overcoming pain and blocking out nerve pathways and neurons. People ask me why I don't get sore doing harness work and I say, 'I have killed off those nerve pathways'. Of course I haven't; I've desensitized them.

BUTCHER interview 2018

---

[5] Artistic director of RaRaZoo, Sue Broadway was an Australian female aerialist at a time when there was no circus training. In the UK in the 1980s, a few individuals, such as Helen Crocker and Deborah Pope, trained with Sue and formed a women's circus troupe called Cunning Stunts.

Working with Gill and Caroline, the performers became intensely aware of their breathing – both in and out – and began experiencing a somatic sense of gravity. In doing so, they became hyper-sensitized; they could locate precisely the pains that needed to be overlooked in order to achieve the spectacle of flight.

> So, here's the interesting point. If you want to push your potential, if you want to get anywhere, there are times when you have to *not* listen to the danger signals, you have to block them, or you wouldn't do anything.
>
> BUTCHER interview 2018

Lindsey acknowledges a daily requirement to repeatedly blank out sensations of pain, in order to accomplish excellence. For many dancers and aerial performers, success and the sense of personal agency that is achieved by transcending gravity come at physical cost.

ANGEL WINGS

The Golden Gate Bridge is an ideal place to commit suicide (Soden 2003). It has earned its status – thanks not only to the convenience of there being no fence, but also because death is certain. Many of the thousands who have jumped from the iconic bridge in San Francisco, chose it for aesthetic reasons: their final sight was a spectacular view of the city. 'Unlike any other form of suicide, falling to one's death is tangled up with aesthetics, both private and public' (Soden 2003: 107).

In the UK, dance performer Lea Parkinson jumped to his death from the roof of The Lowry, a Greater Manchester arts complex. He was thirty-four. Lea had worked professionally with V-TOL Dance Company and Candoco Dance Company. V-TOL – taking its name from vertical take-off and landings performed by V-TOL aircraft – was renowned for its demanding, crash-and-burn performances of falling.

When I was working with Lea, making *The Castle of Slow Death* (1992)[6], he told me that he had always wanted to fly. He then made himself a pair of angel wings, which he wore throughout the performance. The role he devised for himself was of an angel entrapped. He began the show by skirting the stage of The Place Theatre (London), shimmying up walls and dropping to the boards. Later in the piece, he fluttered and stumbled like a dying butterfly – shod in black boots, a grey silk tunic and his homemade

---

[6]Devised by Lea Parkinson, Russell Trigg, Shirley Pickles, Angela Asew, Kuldip Singh-Barmi, Steven Long and James Flynn. Directed by Emilyn, music by Sylvia Hallett.

wings – while chanting a poem. Lea was not afraid of falling. He ran and leapt all over the stage, dissolving with gravity in the way treacle folds and spreads when poured. Falling was not a challenge for Lea – but flying was. He wanted to fly. He did not fall by accident from the roof of The Lowry. He jumped. He flew. He purposefully fell, and landed on his back with his arms spread wide.

THRILLS

For extreme sports enthusiast Garrett Soden, 'The paradox is that we're born with two conflicting instincts: one designed to protect us from gravity, the other urging us to play with it' (2003: 206). He charts the history of risk-taking sports and follows the careers of pioneers who pushed play with gravity to life-threatening limits. People such as motorcycle daredevil Evel Knievel; Cannonball Richards, who flew backwards from the impact of a cannon ball hitting his gut; Shipwreck Kelly who perched on flag poles atop Manhattan's skyscrapers; escape artist Harry Houdini; Philippe Petit on his high wire, who said, 'Life should be lived on the edge of life' (Petit quoted in *Man on Wire*, dir. Marsh 2008); and Sonora Carver who, in 1920, repeatedly leapt on horseback into a tank full of water from a platform sixty feet above ground. Bungee jumpers, tight-rope walkers, parachutists, trapeze and rope artists, mountaineers, divers, wall climbers, BMX riders, skateboarders, surfers, wave-sliders – all are identified by Soden as gravity performers, gravity daredevils and gravity heroes.

The human craving to witness or experience ever more dangerous and spectacular gravity adventures has pushed advances in technology towards safely increasing risk and, as a consequence, thrills. The roller coaster, for example, which allows ordinary people to experience their own gravity challenges, developed from mountain ice sliding and tobogganing in Russia. In mid nineteenth-century St Petersburg, the slide was transferred away from the ice and transformed into machinery, allowing the public – in any season – to experience the adrenalin-filled rush of falling.

> The roller coaster ... was a machine that amplified the sensation of falling ... By stripping away control, increasing the magnitude of the falls, and distilling it all into a few minutes, the roller coaster isolated, packaged, and fetishized the sensation ... once people tasted it, they couldn't get enough.
>
> SODEN 2003: 37

As he ponders the interest so many share in gravity and heights, Soden advances intriguing theories and cites tantalizing glimpses into historical trends. He sees possible sources for the fascination with challenging gravity in eighteenth-century Romanticism and the glorification of individual heroes 'who arose from the masses to face seemingly insurmountable odds' (Soden 2003: 38) and undertake death-defying feats. Advances in technology in the nineteenth century may also be a factor, along with growing enthusiasm for the Enlightenment's concept of progress: 'Man as nature's master, not her victim' (2003: 38). Soden also cites Freudian psychoanalysis, noting that wire walkers, mountaineers and others who risk falling are often motivated by a desire to prove their 'mastery over the death instinct by actively courting death and then defying it' (2003: 118).

A theory that Soden develops more fully as the reason why humans are enticed by gravity dares, is based in the idea that we are not 'truly land animals' (Soden 2003: 206). He intimates that dealing with gravity has played a creative role in human development and he adopts an anthropological perspective. Neither Soden nor I are anthropologists, but he notes that humans became land animals only through evolution, and only 'after aeons evolving an extraordinary ability for an entirely different environment' (Soden 2003: 206) – trees. For over 65 million years, primates lived in trees, developing hands that grip, joints and spines adapted for climbing, and eyes that look forward. Soden suggests that most of these adaptations occurred to deal with the threat of falling. To move within trees required a constant negotiation with gravity. A significant shift came as some primates evolved to be too big to manoeuvre easily through trees, which separated monkeys from apes. Monkeys, being smaller, are far more agile in the trees, while a great ape must learn to test a branch to see if it will hold its weight. Testing requires choices that must be made to avoid falling because falling will hurt. Referring to the theories of primatologist Daniel Povinelli and physical anthropologist John Cant (1995), Soden hypothesizes that experiencing fear as a survival mechanism 'is what the common ancestor of the great apes and humans learned, and that by doing this, it began to understand that it was an individual who could cause things to happen, that it could make plans and reap benefits. In short, it became self-conscious' (2003: 215). Fear has been learnt as a survival mechanism to avoid falling, and consciousness has developed in relation to that fear.[7] Falling and the threat/fear of falling have been essential to propel 'the qualities we call human into being' (Soden 2003: 215). Embellishing this with a flourish, Soden suggests that 'many of

---

[7]Testing whether fear of falling is an innate fear, psychologists Eleanor Gibson and Richard Walk experimented with creating a 'visual cliff' (1960). A checkerboard platform was constructed, which led to a drop-off to the ground below, and then the platform continued on the other side of the drop. The entire construction was covered by strong clear glass, acting as a bridge across the two platforms. Thirty-six babies aged between 6 and 18 months were tested to see if they would cross the glass to get to their parents. Only 8 babies crossed the glass; most refused, backed away or cried because they could not reach their parents.

our cherished intellectual abilities are just a fantastic side effect of trying not to fall out of a tree' (2003: 219).

Soden's anthropological musings explain how human consciousness developed *in parallel* with fear of falling in an evolutionary adventure from trees to ground. Perhaps more profound is the notion that consciousness and fear of falling are inseparable. Therefore, fear of falling is a deeply innate emotion, and a measure of human-ness. Fear of falling is a universal, evolutionary trauma; fear that is constantly triggered by being alive and present in the world.

OUT OF CIRCUS

In his performance of *Head* (2018), John-Paul Zaccarini unravels his life-long allegiance to the world of circus. As I enter Jacksons Lane Theatre in north London I see John-Paul dressed in a dapper grey suit and white shirt.[8] He sits on the side of the stage, welcoming his audience, waving to those he knows. Structuring the performance are twelve poems addressing issues of abuse, mental illness, suicide and personal trauma – written and spoken by John-Paul. He presents his poetry with ironic wit and neat, precise, expressive gestures. The physicality of his words energizes his body – while his body in turn enhances the text with nuanced meanings; the interplay appears in the way he times a smile or completes a joke by turning his face, twisting his posture or clenching his fingers.

At centre stage, a rope attached to ceiling rafters dangles down into a child's paddling pool. Six life-sized, rag-doll figures with balloon heads, scattered around the stage, are attached to scaffolding by ropes that are later used to hoist them into the air, where they flop, helpless and forlorn, the picture of physical despondency. Interspersed with his poems, Jean-Paul climbs the rope, only to fall. He exaggerates the impact of his falls and invests them with more importance than he gives to the climbing. A theme he develops throughout the performance is his love affair with the audience – 'I fell for you' – weighty with its ambiguous blending of the meanings in falling and loving. His previous experience seducing audiences with high-flying skills is juxtaposed with tonight's deliberate falling – off the rope, out of circus conventions. He cracks the veneer of circus spectacle to reveal its underlying effort and danger.

John-Paul, a vertical rope artist, performer, poet and academic researcher, reflects on his compulsion for risk-taking feats. In his writing, he peels back

---

[8] Performed as part of Circus Fest 2018. See https://www.upper-circle.com/home/review-head-circusfest-2018-jacksons-lane for review (Esme Mahoney April 11th 2018)

the gloss, 'the heroic caffeine rush' of his vertical rope performances. He seeks to reveal the 'uncooked meat, bones and nerves' of circus (Zaccarini 2018: 6), articulating and developing a method of reflection that he calls circoanalysis.[9] He draws on Lacanian psychoanalytic theories – melancholia and trauma, nostalgia and desire – to understand his own practice, which keeps failure, falling and death connected to the allure and thrill of spectacle. He deconstructs the workings of his circus acts and shows failure to be essential to the success of vertical artists. Circus performers develop their skills through a relentless relationship with failure. Training methods require them to push

> something almost to failure and then take a step back to recover and reflect. But rather than withdraw from failure and go back to what is known to be achievable, it attempts to push the failure further. It treats failure as the condition of creativity – breakdown and breakthrough are contiguous.
>
> ZACCARINI 2018: 5

Training for – and performing – circus work inevitably involves courting death through risk-taking gravity play. 'We were running-towards-death ... the only truly authentic experience, rather than running from it' (Zaccarini 2018: 100). Accepting that a deconstructive analysis of his courtship with death might also kill his desire to perform, John-Paul gets at something beneath the fantasy that holds circus acts aloft: admitting to a death drive that circus performers experience daily while they tango with the desire to live.

> Trauma lurks behind that grin we associate with circus. These are the origins I have to ignore in order to climb the rope. Uncovering those drives might do something to that enjoyment, it might problematize this frictionless performance that works so very well; night after night. We want pretend near-death; we don't want suicide.
>
> ZACCARINI 2018: 5

EVOKED COMPANIONS

What if, from the day a baby is born, falling were integrated into her movement vocabulary in the same way as standing, walking and running. Falling is not on the list, of course, because of the associated fears. There are only two innate human fears: the fear of falling and the fear of loud noises. We adapted both of them as survival strategies over millions of years. Now,

---

[9] For Zaccarini, philosophical thinking and writing is a practice 'as rigorous, thrilling and potentially dangerous as somersaulting in the air over concrete' (2018: 7).

in 2020, our instinctive fear of falling functions to keep us from dropping off dangerous heights – unless we consciously by-pass or play with that fear. But I am curious about the difference between innate and conditioned fears. When is an innate fear of falling an appropriate response, and when is it unnecessary? Or, to put this within a familiar frame, I wonder – when it comes to fear of falling – what nature actually is and what might be reconsidered as nurture. With full respect for those suffering fear as a consequence of traumatic falls, I am suggesting that, during our day-to-day pedestrian activities, fear is passed on intergenerationally and often triggered unnecessarily. By way of loosening the tightly woven intersection of instinctive and conditional fears of falling, I am proposing a whimsical narrative, which wanders into the territory of developmental psychology (Stern 1998).

Around the age of six months, babies discover how to sit, their little spines flow upwards and they balance on their sitting bones, with legs folded at the knees and flopping outwards. Their heavy heads are still a bit wobbly, and as a result, they slump forwards, sideways or backwards when they lose their balance. The distance of the drop, from sitting to lying, is relatively short, and a baby is likely to remain relaxed, her joints free of tension, her body soft and malleable. The baby is unlikely to be hurt and injury is rare. What often happens next is, a carer appears, shows concern, perhaps with a gasp of worry, and uprights the baby from where she sprawls, fallen. The carer puts cushions around her body so that when the infant falls again, she'll be protected from the ground. As a mother and a grandmother, I recognize this response, this spontaneous, bodily reaction, which is triggered by my own fear of falling rather than the baby's.

At this age and stage of development, a baby learns about the world through relational, bodily sensed interactions with carers, rather than through spoken language. Infants sense their carers' concerns and pick up on the speed of their reactions. Inevitably, if such interactions happen habitually – as babies become toddlers learning to stand, walk and run – carers' fears are integrated into babies' understanding of falling as something frightening and wrong, something to be avoided. Shame sets in, and babies learn to be ashamed of falling. As children grow, they make adjustments in relation to carers' responses, such as learning to tense at the moment of falling, or holding away from gravity. So falling becomes less supple and more painful. Fluidity of movement with gravity towards the ground becomes compromised, causing tension and resistance and increasing the likelihood of injury when falling. These interactions between children and carers are conditioned responses we pass down generationally, causing an unnecessary triggering of the instinctive survival strategy. This perspective can be understood further, and embellished, by psychologist Daniel Stern's writings about the development in a child's core self.

After the first interaction around falling between infant and carer, the infant lays down a memory. After many interactive episodes similar to the first event, the infant forms a 'Representation of an Interaction that has been

Generalized' – a RIG (Stern 1998: 97). A RIG is a prototype to represent all the different experiences – episodic memories – which include the interactions with the carer, whom Stern refers to as a 'self-regulating other' (Stern 1998: 102). The carer regulates the infant's self-experience through his/her own responses, which are integral to the RIG being incorporated in the child's developing sense of a core self. From then on, the memory of the interaction is retrieved 'whenever one of the attributes of the RIG is present' (1998: 110). When the growing child faces an act of falling, the entire RIG is activated: the memories of past falling, the carer, the carer's responses, the encouragement to remain upright and the sense of something wrong are all retrieved. When the RIG is activated, the self-regulating other – who was directly interacting with the child in the past – is now encountered as 'an evoked companion' (1998: 111). The other is integrated as an element of the child's core self and, crucially, as part of the self evaluating the current experience.[10]

> [I]f a six-month-old, when alone, encounters a rattle and manages to grasp it and shake it enough so that it makes a sound the initial pleasure may quickly become extreme delight and exuberance . . . not only the result of successful mastery, which may account for the initial pleasure, but also the historical result of similar past moments in the presence of a delighted and exuberance-enhancing (regulating) other . . . The current experience now includes the presence (in or out of awareness) of an evoked companion.
>
> STERN 1998: 113–14

The infant's evoked companion is a part of herself that evaluates the present experience as exuberant and joyful, a consequence of the past interactions with a self-regulating other when the RIG was established.

What if experiences of falling could stimulate a similar joyful RIG? To do so, the inter-generational passing on of fear (and shame) needs to be interrupted. This is where somatic movement practitioners have knowledge to share, having discerned, through practice, when to trust an innate fear of falling and when fear is a conditioned response. Sharing this embodied knowledge suggests people might then interact differently with their babies, encouraging rolling, tumbling and playing together rather than anxiously righting them upwards, activities they can maintain as their children grow.[11] A different RIG is then established whereby these children grow into

---

[10] Stern describes four senses of self: an emergent self, a core self (formed between the ages of two and six months), a subjective self and a verbal self. They are 'not viewed as successive phases that replace each other. Once formed, each sense of self remains fully functioning and active throughout life' (1998: 11).

[11] An outlook much favoured by somatic pioneer Barbara Clark. 'Rolling, crawling and squatting favour the development of the deeper muscles of the body, the ones closest to the bones . . . Adults like to see the child march – run around. But the child likes to wrestle, to lie on the floor and to tumble around . . . the child is doing what he needs to do to achieve strength and balance' (Clark quoted in Matt 1993: 36).

adulthood experiencing their psychologically evoked companions as pleasurable supports for falling, without triggering unnecessarily their innate fear. These infants become adults who interact with infants, and over time, perhaps a few generations, associations of falling with fear and shame become undone, mitigating the oppositional, metaphorical binary of up-good-pride and down-bad-shame by giving equal credence to both orientational stances. Being on the ground becomes as familiar as standing up. Shame of falling dissolves and my fantasy expands. People fall in the streets, lie down on pavements, meet for falling picnics and parties, fall while dancing at clubs, in ballet class, learning maths, waiting at stations, at airports, at bus stops. Couples converse while falling. An old person experiences gravity without fear; their falling no longer means helplessness – off to the care home – but signals innovative converted living space. Furniture is redesigned; door knobs, refrigerator handles, shower taps, light switches are placed within easy reach of a fallen body. Floors are strewn with knee pads, books, pens, a TV, a mobile phone, electric sockets, a tea-making device, a laptop, a mattress, blankets, clothes, a potty, toilet paper, a radio, bread, biscuits, towels . . .

[S]he fell very slowly, for she had plenty of time as she went down to look about her and to wonder what was going to happen next. First, she tried to look down and make out what she was coming to, but it was too dark to see anything; then she looked at the sides of the well, and noticed that they were filled with cupboards and book-shelves; here and there she saw maps and pictures hung upon pegs. She took down a jar from one of the shelves as she passed; it was labelled 'ORANGE MARMALADE', but to her great disappointment it was empty: she did not like to drop the jar for fear of killing somebody, so managed to put it into one of the cupboards as she fell past it.

'Well!' thought Alice to herself, 'after such a fall as this, I shall think nothing of tumbling down stairs!'

CARROLL 1865

SEX IN CRISIS

By 1980, the art scene in the UK was throbbing with political energy. As feminist, gay and black dancers, we were proclaiming our identities, rustling our differences and preparing the ground for explosive ruptures in conventional dance performance. At the forefront of these fissures was *My Sex, Our Dance* (*MSOD* 1986), created and performed by aesthetic innovators Lloyd Newson and Nigel Charnock. In *MSOD* they embodied the risks and crises of a generation, while flipping conventions and galvanizing awareness of the complacency at the heart of mainstream contemporary dance.

Alarmed at the spread of AIDS, Nigel and Lloyd made work in defiance of the institutionalized, heterosexual morality being enforced by government policies like Clause 28 (1986), which forbade the promotion of homosexuality by local authorities. This defiance – along with his rejection of the hierarchies and codes of institutional dance – drove Lloyd to question profoundly the meaning of dance and inspired the issue-based work he produced throughout his thirty-year directorship of DV8 (1986–2016).

> In the mid 80s, HIV had just started rearing its head, AIDS was decimating the gay community, friends of mine were dying and I thought, how far can you trust another man in terms of having intimate relationships? Because ultimately if you had unprotected sex you could die – I'm not even sure if there were HIV tests available then.[12] That is what the duet was about: how much can you trust another man . . . It also encompassed ideas about intimacy and risk – which we tried to physicalize.
>
> NEWSON interview with author 2018

In *MSOD*, the light comes up on Lloyd and Nigel seated on either side of the stage. Lloyd is shaving his legs on a bare mattress. Nigel sits playing a toy trumpet. Clad in only long johns, they appear stark and vulnerable in the cold white light. A fully dressed man and woman chat and drink at a downstage left table – absorbed with each other in a warmly lit café. Dressers appear and assist Nigel and Lloyd – who appear somewhat reluctant – in donning manly attire of shirts, trousers and ties. Adjusting their ties, Lloyd and Nigel walk to the centre of the stage and stand facing each other. They pause, just looking. Lloyd extends his hand in greeting. Nigel accepts it, but instead of shaking, they grasp and pull, testing each other's strength and balance, jerking about at off-kilter angles while maintaining the standing grip. Tension grows; so does the speed and range of their movements. They teeter on the edge of losing balance, then clasp and grapple in a contentious hug, from which Nigel thrashes and frees himself.

Lloyd then runs and falls, but Nigel catches him just before he hits the floor. A sequence ensues where Lloyd falls backwards, forwards and sideways; in every case, Nigel catches him before he crash-lands. Sometimes, they hit the stage together with the full impact of gravity. Again and again, Lloyd cartwheels into the air and into Nigel, who clasps him round the waist upside down. They continue, Lloyd falling, Nigel catching, until both are exhausted.

> Nigel and I began this process of improvising in the studio, and one of the simplest things to do was – I trust you to catch me when I fall. The most

---

[12] 1981 – first case of HIV reported. 1984 – HIV was identified: Human Immunodeficiency Virus. 1985 – first test for HIV was licensed. 1987 – first Western blot blood test became available.

amazing thing about Nigel was his determination, his passion, his agility and speed. I was running around and deciding to fall in positions where he would have to get to me, and this was completely improvised.

NEWSON interview 2018

Lloyd then resumes his position at centre stage. Nigel runs and leaps into his arms, but Lloyd does not catch him. Nigel drops. The audience laughs. Nigel runs and jumps again, grabbing Lloyd around his neck, with his own legs stretched out in front. Again, Lloyd does not catch him. Changing tactics, Nigel runs around the stage, dives into the air and crashes to the mattress. Over and over. Each flying leap has a moment of suspension where – with spine arched and limbs outstretched – he hovers in the air before plummeting flat. Lloyd repositions himself to lie on the mattress, but moves away when Nigel flings himself into the air above. Finally, though, Nigel runs, dives and Lloyd does catch him. They lower themselves gently and curl into the mattress in a caring embrace.[13]

Nigel liked to catch me falling, he liked to catch me in the air. I said, 'Let's try and change these roles, let's try me catching you'. He didn't like that. He didn't want me to catch him. He liked being in a position where he saved me at the last moment; so we built this idea into the piece. He flings himself at me and I do nothing. It was also a bit of a gag, but he wasn't into being caught. So we found our roles within it.

NEWSON interview 2018

It was 1986, HIV was charging every sexual encounter with unknown terror, especially for gay men. This duet brought that fearful uncertainty to the fore. Intimacy was risky, sex a complete danger; friends, colleagues, dancers, lovers – people were falling and dying. Gay sex was an absolute venture. Love and desire were killing. Each fall in *MSOD* signalled the presence of death, each leap into the air a gamble. Can I trust him? Will I be caught? If I fall alone, am I ready to die?

I'm not sure how much information I knew about using condoms, other than intuitively knowing I needed to practise safe sex. There was so much confusion at the beginning of the AIDS crisis as to how HIV was actually transmitted, what it was, how it could be stopped.

NEWSON interview 2018

---

[13] Arditti (1993) interprets this duet as 'the emotional danger of lovers attempting to make contact. The intensity and integrity of the dance was itself a vital affirmation in the age of Clause 28 and Aids'.

In the 1980s, Contact Improvisation (CI) was blossoming in the UK. *MSOD* began as basic trust exercises, like those of CI, where dancers learn lifting skills, weight exchange, catching, tumbling and falling, and as part of a vocabulary of movement for improvisation. While CI pursues kinetic explorations, the movements in *MSOD* were driven by human narratives of desire, trust, love and abandonment. Falling in *MSOD* was

FIGURE 3.2 *Lloyd Newson and Nigel Charnock in* My Sex, Our Dance *(1986)*. Photo: Eleni Leoussi.

performed with a faster, more violent dynamic and is mixed with pedestrian movement and body language ... Hurling the body onto another at speed, climbing up a body, falling or being thrown, often repeated until a state of real exhaustion and desperation is reached to evoke the nihilistic aspect of relationships in an unsympathetic society.

LEASK 2011: 298

It is about intimacy in relationship. When it works, you can be lifted higher than you can propel yourself; so the fall is greater. Nigel was a total free spirit. That last image – him running and diving – there was a strobe light and as he jumps ... the strobe light flashes, catches him mid-air, so you never see him fall. You only see him flying.

When we did the shows, we were regularly bruised and sometimes there was even a bit of blood, due to the risky nature of the choreography. It was taxing on our bodies, incredibly exhausting. The aerobic level in the work made us incredibly lean. But it was wonderful dancing with Nigel.

NEWSON interview 2018

The unreserved leaping and desperate catching in *MSOD* represent the specific risks of love and trust between Nigel and Lloyd, while highlighting the work's broader concerns with gay sexual politics and the fearful uncertainties of HIV in the 1980s. The couple downstage continue to chat, seemingly oblivious, suggesting a heteronormative complacency in the face of the uncertainty and risk experienced, and expressed by Nigel and Lloyd. Catching someone in free fall requires total commitment and presence, without hesitation or doubt. Such living – fully in the face of death – can forge an enduring relationship.

The two of us had a huge commonality, in our working-class backgrounds, our sexuality, our lack of respect for mainstream authority – which we often saw as arcane and ridiculous. But it was actually doing *MSOD* which left a life-long bond between Nigel and myself, even after he went off to pursue his own work. When someone catches you and you trust someone so deeply that they will stop you falling and injuring yourself; that imprint on your body is profound. It was deeply intimate. When Nigel was at the point of dying, we hadn't seen each other, other than a couple times, for maybe twenty years. The fact he asked me to be around when he was dying I put down to our duet, to the depth of that experience.

NEWSON interview 2018

FAILING SUCCESS

'Ever tried. Ever failed. No Matter. Try again. Fail again. Fail better' (Beckett 1983). This phrase echoes through the years as a call to allow failure in order to collapse theatre's 'certainties of knowledge, competence, representation, normativity and authority' (O'Gorman and Werry 2012: 1). Taken literally, Beckett's words appear to recommend failure as a methodology for performance. Yet failing is not usually anything that anyone sets out to do, a goal in neither life nor performance. Failure in performance is usually the consequence of doing something not as well as hoped (Bailes 2011).

Trying to fail is a kind of oxymoron, of course, because trying implies aiming for success. In performance, to succeed at failing is usually a failure to succeed, which is a product of skill and hard work. Failure happens – not as a consequence of attempts to fail, but in spite of best efforts to succeed. As theatre academics Róisín O'Gorman and Margaret Werry confirm, failure is 'the hallmark of performance – with its endless interruptions, accidents, breakdowns, flops, misfires, dead-ends and surprises, moodiness and messiness' (2012: 2).[14] *Trying* to produce a flop, or taking failure as a theme for making, could well result in something entirely different being created. Something that might indeed be successful, therefore not a failure. Let failure, then, settle in where it's most useful, as a possible consequence after the trials and errors of making the very best performance. As a planned objective, failure cannot exist.

A practice of falling is not a prescription for failure, even though falling connotes failure across Western culture. With falling as artistic practice, there is no intention to either fail or succeed. Where falling and failing *do* correspond is in the opportunities provided to drop the pace, to take notice of affects associated with failure, rather than turning quickly away. Being with failure is perceived through the body as a sense of falling into shame. Despite this, failure's misery can be – perversely – what unites us. 'It allows us to imagine ourselves as members of response-able communities: individuals in a state of openness to moving and being moved by others' (O'Gorman and Werry 2012: 5).[15] The shame of failure – when experienced deliberately as a collective sense of falling – becomes a resource for productive reflection and change. 'Failure is a metaphor ... Failure is the shadow on the thing. Success is too. The major difference is that success gets a party. While failure is simply one of the strongest agents for change the universe has to offer' (Stanley 2012: 4).

---

[14]See also Ridout (2006).
[15]An attitude towards failure embraced by Berlant (2011) and Halberstam (2011). To read more on failure in performance, see the special issue of *Performance Research*, *On Failure* (O'Gorman and Werry 2012).

MORO REFLEX

The Moro Reflex is a physical response to falling deeply embedded in human movement patterns. The phenomena was first observed by paediatrician Ernst Moro in 1918 and occurs when a newborn infant experiences her own weight, such as when dropping backwards or when her head is out of balance. The Moro Reflex describes a baby's autonomic response to finding herself out-of-kilter, that of instantly extending her arms and fingers outwards for support. This instinctive reaching out happens during the act of falling – *before* experiencing the pain of landing – as an innate survival mechanism. Developmental movement psychotherapist Ruella Frank confirms that until infants 'feel the weight of their bodies falling through space, the act of extending into the orld is not readily available to them' (2001: 85). Just like baby birds, infants learn through falling to reach out into the world, which explains perhaps their delight at being tossed in the air and dangled upside down, or their enthusiasm for climbing, rolling and tumbling about.

Somatic practitioners such as Barbara Clark agree that babies love the sensation of gravity play while being safely supported. By playing with gravity, they develop physical confidence because boundaries between safe and unsafe experiences are established and repeatedly tested. When a child rough-and-tumbles with gravity, she senses acutely her presence in the world. When falling in contact with other bodies or with the ground, she experiences the full range of developmental movements: yielding, pushing, reaching, grasping, pulling and releasing. Experiencing gravity through the full range of these movements fosters physical and psychological confidence and a sense of security in the world. Gravity play often provides infants with greater feelings of comfort than the experience of gentle rocking because the sensation of falling spurs a reaching into the world. 'Falling is part of a deep grammar. From there ... the language of movement develops' (Frank interview with author 2017).

ARÊTE

Kate Lawrence directed the feminist dance company Nomads during the 1990s. Then she discovered rock climbing.

> When I started climbing, it was just like dancing really, moving off rather than on the ground, defying gravity and using all fours as opposed to being on two legs. Climbing outside is all about balancing your weight,

reading rock faces and rock texture and finding places for your feet and hands – it's improvisation. Climbing practice is generally with ropes. If you lead climb, you are taking the rope up with you, and the aim is not to weight the rope at all. It is just there for your safety. In traditional climbing you squeeze camming devices into cracks in the rock, where they expand and you attach the rope to them.

You don't know what you are going to find on the rock, so you have to make immediate judgements, assessing risk all the time. I am constantly thinking about falling whilst I am climbing, always questioning. What's going to happen if I fall off here? What am I going to hit? Am I prepared to make this next move? Am I prepared to continue going up even if I don't know what is ahead? I talk to myself. I don't want to down climb because it is too difficult, but I have put myself in this situation and I have to find something. Philosophically, it's banging up against assessments of risks and then working out what risks I am prepared to take. I had a bad accident soon after I started. I fell ten metres and my heel smashed into the rock below. I guess it is about conquering gravity, yet it can't be aggression towards gravity.

There's the athletic joy when something works really well, setting myself challenges and conquering physical and mental challenges. I read the rock and transfer that into a set of moves, the way you might in contact improvisation. Partnering with the rock face – a rock-solid partner! The other joy is the environment, being in the mountains, fresh air and the thrill of that.

There was a climb that was just so beautiful. It's called an 'arête' – where two rock faces meet and form a vertical edge. I climbed up this edge so I was constantly exposed and I had this amazing view of mountains. I was really fit at the time and confident, nervous because it was a colossal climb and at the edge of my comfort zone in terms of difficulty. It was a day where I could say – it's just happening. I was just flowing. I live for those days.

LAWRENCE interview with author 2018

Integrating her new skills into her artistic life, Kate began specializing in vertical choreographies danced on the sides of buildings. Slow, gradual descents from the tops of buildings develop into suspended falls during which choreographic events take place. Kate explains that vertical dance is

> A performance practice in which the performer is suspended above the ground, usually against a wall (which is used as a floor), using rock-climbing equipment. You might hear it referred to as 'harness work' or 'aerial dance'. We use the term 'vertical' to indicate the orientation of the surface that is used as a floor, be that a wall, a balcony hand rail or a rope. Climbing is the opposite to vertical dance. The only

time climbing comes close is when you abseil down – that's the vertical dance bit.

In the harness there is a constant awareness that the ground is below you, but sometimes you forget because you are involved in choreography and suddenly you go upside down with the crown of your head pointing to the ground. That's when you tend to think, 'Hmm . . . I really don't want to fall now'. It's a relationship between falling and trust in equipment, which is different to climbing, where you have to trust yourself and trust how you use the equipment. In vertical dance once you are in the harness and over the edge, you've given yourself over, your questioning has gone, your ability to change anything has gone. If you jump off a wall, depending on the length of your rope of course, you might have lots of time in the air to experience being suspended. What an amazing thing to be able to experience – falling (not) falling.

LAWRENCE interview 2018[16]

Kate's work draws on a hybridity of body, rope and harness to achieve ultimate performance. Technical equipment, essential for gravity-defying performances, has become ever more sophisticated to meet the (not) falling demands of performers' aerial adventures. On rock-face climbs, the ropes are for safety – devices to avoid falling – while for vertical dancing, ropes are used to provide performers with falling experiences, albeit controlled ones. The equipment becomes a partner in the dance, a vital element of choreographic method and content.

A THUMP

Sarab is a circus troupe composed of young performers from a circus school in Palestine. I saw Sarab performing at Jacksons Lane Theatre in London on 14 April 2018. The work was troubled and sincere – awash with themes of anguish, loss and displacement. Animated young men tumbled over each other with a sense of purpose, balancing precariously, sliding down poles, throwing suitcases and juggling hats. Towards the end of the show, a woman fell from a trapeze with a sickening thump – followed by a moan of pain. The show was stopped and an ambulance called. Gasping with shock and

---

[16]Kate is a founder member of Vertical Dance Forum with six other choreographers with funding from the Creative Europe.

concern, we stumbled out of the theatre and into the night to await news. The following morning I was informed by email that she was okay. I remember the date because the same morning, 15 April, an alliance of Western nations, United Kingdom, France and the United States of America, contributed further unrest to a deeply troubled Middle East by dropping more bombs on an already bombed-out Syria.

NEUTRAL BUOYANCY

Simon Ellis dives in the deep sea. Besides being a dance artist, a research scholar and co-director of Colin, Simon & I, he sinks to the bottom of oceans. In contrast to most dance and aerial performances, where skills and equipment are in place to *avoid* falling, deep-sea diving's skills and equipment are there to *enable* falling. When diving, the instinctive fear of falling is compounded by a fear of rising up.

> On the boat, we go through checks every time before diving. The equipment is so painfully clumsy, a total faff, really heavy. Then there is this absolute pleasure, falling backwards into the water. You put a load of air in your jacket, so you are really buoyant when you first go in.
> In the water, you release all of the air out of the jacket and have this lovely experience of descending. You tip onto your front and start free falling. I am trying to be calm as it's a feeling of immense pleasure – in falling. In the UK, bad visibility makes for a dis-falling, falling into nothing or darkness. Descending quickly is not a problem, it's just falling. It's pretty special, that moment.
> Putting a little bit of air into my suit creates balance, stops the falling. The key skill is achieving a state of neutral buoyancy under water, neither ascending nor descending, a delicate balance, a feeling of weightlessness. Most of my diving experience is spent focusing on buoyancy, seeking that sensation. Water is more dense than air, so you don't fall as quickly. You know you are neutrally buoyant when you inhale, take air from the cylinder, your lungs expand and you go up ever so slightly. When you exhale, you go down. Your breath is constantly drawing your attention to your weight and weightlessness. The aliveness and sensitivity to breath and weight through weightlessness is like taking something away in order to recognise what it is. Breathe in you go up, breathe out you go down. Simple, and very, very beautiful.
> Neutral buoyancy is a special feeling of release or freedom, like being given a reprieve from gravity. Dance is a constant negotiation with gravity. Diving, I get forty minutes of dancing without it. If I choose to close my eyes, to tune myself to buoyancy, it is also like a forty-minute

meditation. A sensitizing of the body that has very little to do with what I can see, more about bodily sensations, bodily experience.

Once I was with a diver, penetrating a wreck, going into a very, very dark space. I turned my torch off and had a beautiful feeling of 'how am I here?' So, so dark. As we were finning towards the wreck's entrance, my heart started racing. I saw a mass of expansive ocean, going from really dark to really open, and I had a strong desire to bolt to the surface. Maybe I got some vertigo – it happens at a certain depth, thirty metres, like getting drunk, feeling a bit euphoric, or a bit down. I am confronting a particular feeling of fear, something I don't know about, a fear of the unknown. Powerful stuff. Very beautiful and very terrifying. The volume's turned up on everything, everything is a little bit more. A fascinating philosophical and bodily experience of being alone. Pretty cool. And again, not cool at all.

You need to ascend slowly, allowing your body to acclimatize to returning to the usual amount of air pressure, and that has to happen slowly. I like that, something about the otherness of it. The desire to be at the surface is strong, but the training says that you need to go slowly, in a constant negotiation with buoyancy. Paradoxically, as you get closer to the surface, the pressure is decreasing, so you actually have to dump air from your suit because if you don't you would be like a champagne cork. It is really lovely going slow. I try to go as slowly as possible, emerging out of the ocean. I can see why people get addicted. There is a slightly quasi-spiritual aspect. It's a reminder of very basic things: breath, sensation, weight, pre-birth – big metaphors – tubes and all.

ELLIS interview with author 2017

Simon's telling of his diving experiences provides an antidote to my writings on aerial performance. Writing about both in close succession, I find myself drawn to the elements of air and water and the different requirements these habitats demand of human bodies in relation to gravity. Aerial performers fear a fast fall downwards, whereas divers fear a fast rise upwards. Yet performing in both habitats brings a vast sense of spatial nothingness, a disappearance of earth's horizon, disorientation, suspension of time, vertigo, and, without a doubt, a dependence on technological equipment for survival.

A CLIFF EDGE

Traumatic experience and its triggers are primarily stored in the body (Taylor 2014), and sensorimotor psychotherapists draw on somatic movement and sensation as primary sites for developing restorative procedures (Ogden and Fisher 2015). Of particular relevance to therapists' handling of traumatic fears of falling is the notion of a 'window of tolerance', which is an embodied zone of 'autonomic and emotional arousal that is optimal for well-being and effective functioning' (Siegel 1999: 253). Situations perceived as threatening – like falling – cause states of hyper arousal, which prepare us 'to flee, fight or freeze,' but also of hypo-arousal where we shut down and 'become immobile and still' (Ogden and Fisher 2015: 225), as happens in the grip of overwhelming vertigo. If my world becomes unsafe (physically and/or psychologically), my body stiffens, my breathing grows shallow and my movements freeze. I resist gravity or I collapse into dullness. If fear of falling becomes overwhelming, it can trigger a desensitizing process, which psychotherapist Miriam Taylor likens to 'splitting … a natural response to managing the feeling of overwhelm; it makes trauma containable … To different degrees we dissociate from traumatic experiences, making them less personal, less real' (Taylor 2014: 2).

A window of tolerance is a safe zone between the extremes of hyper- and hypo-arousal within which psychotherapists and clients can explore fearful triggers, and where emotional and physiological experience can be processed without further anxiety. For each person, the window of tolerance varies, depending on context and on individual traumatic experience, but it is generally a calm and stable state suspended between polarities, often experienced as boredom by those used to being sustained by a 'chronic overload of adrenalin' (Taylor 2014: 64). Finding a window of tolerance, where I feel safe yet am not cut off from sensation, is an initial and essential point of departure for working with trauma. Without the window of tolerance, I risk re-traumatizing myself each time I talk about the precipitating event and can succumb repeatedly to hyper or hypo arousal. By working within a safe window of tolerance, however, therapists and clients can experiment with minuscule, off-balance movements, gradually exploring tolerable levels of fear, making note of which actions trigger an increase in hyper-arousal beyond the window of tolerance and which thoughts facilitate a return to the safe zone.

Importantly, undoing traumatic behaviour does not happen from an entirely safe middle space in the window of tolerance. Change happens on the edge of safety (Ogden and Fisher 2015), in a state of excitement generated by a managed sensation of fear. It happens when the limbic system is aroused – not to the extent that the sensory system is overwhelmed, but not so little that sensation is dormant, a state I would describe as sofa-comfortable. Change and growth happen when a person experiences enough fear to be excited, but not so much as to move into extremes of hyper- or hypo-arousal and anxiety.

Psychologist Michael Apter offers a similar model with his notion of the tiger and the cage, an allegorical reflection of Siegel's window of tolerance: a tiger without a cage would be too fierce, a cage without its wild animal would be boring. Danger *and* safety are required to process trauma. 'One buys excitement with fear and the greater the cost, the better the product' (Apter 1992: 39).

> The psychological landscape we cover when we do anything that involves risk is like a plateau near a cliff. Apter defines three regions: a safety zone, far from the edge where there is no danger of falling; a danger zone, near the edge, and a trauma zone, over the edge to injury (or in day-to-day experience – emotional trauma). In the excitement-seeking state, we will try to come as near to the edge as possible because here is where the prospect of pleasant arousal is highest. Yet we can only go there if we feel safe.
>
> SODEN 2003: 270

When considering my own and my clients' traumatic experiences, there is frequently a compulsion to resolve the original disturbance through re-enactment. Managing this compulsion by using the model of a window of tolerance from which to test, discover and experiment with gravity allows us to venture towards the edge, but not over the cliff.

The attraction of the cliff edge helps explain the seductive appeal of witnessing – or performing – gravity-defying physical feats. The fascination performers and spectators hold for circus, vertical performance and extreme sports provides a way of playing within their windows of tolerance as a means to process evolutionary, post-traumatic fears of falling. I advance this theory as a reason so many seek gravity thrills in a constant need to meet with – and possibly overcome – fear of falling through safe but not risk-free experiences.

Circus artist John-Paul Zaccarini confirms that gravity performers harness their fears of falling as sensations of adrenalized intensity. John-Paul himself works at the extreme edges of his window of tolerance. To be at a great height 'gives me a rush of adrenalin, instigates the fight or flight mechanism, not inherently a pleasurable experience, more like a state of emergency wherein everything is at stake' (Zaccarini 2018: 16). Gravity dance artists bring themselves to the edge of danger, constructing precarious safety, to contend with the traumatic fear of falling. Extreme sports and circus practitioners seek out fear in their drive to repeatedly experience hyper-states of adrenalin – in order to feel fully present. Engrossed in extreme, spectacular gravity play, performers experience a state of optimum consciousness and innovation.

Spectators also test their fear of falling as observers. When I witness a frightening event, or anticipate that it will be frightening because of the potential for falls, my limbic system kicks into action, just as if I were actually falling. I feel the adrenalin rush even though fear in this context is a secondary emotion. The reason that – along with millions of others – I am drawn to witness such events is that when the limbic system arouses itself to the edge of tolerance, my brain processes information differently. The world appears crisp and clear, my presence feels more vital.

LEAN ON ME

Gather seven or eight people together in a room, people who feel comfortable and safe in each other's presence. Take turns with the following exercise. Stand in the centre of the group, with everybody else in a circle around you. Take time to notice your breathing and to sense both feet equally on the ground – your support. Leaving your feet where they are, tilt forward. Allow one of us in the group to catch you, rather than saving yourself with a lunge or forward step. Allow whoever catches you to bring you back to standing on your own feet. Try it again. Lean out in any direction and one of us will catch you and restore you to your still point of standing in the centre. Experiment with leaning out in all directions – forward, sideways, backwards. Begin with very small tilts, sensing when and where your fear of falling kicks in. As you develop assurance and confidence in your safety, expand your window of tolerance; allow yourself to fall a little further – not enough to trigger fear or cause you to stiffen, but sufficient to increase excitement and bring you to your own edge of safety, before letting us restore you to your ground. After each person has had a chance to experiment, discuss what develops when you perform the task. Are you afraid? Can you surrender your weight to another? Do you trust someone to be there? Can you fall backwards into another's arms? Do you prefer independence? Is acting alone a safer option?

Lean On Me is a physical experience that has psychological impact, with parallels in everyday life. Even contemplating the possibility of another person catching me brings me smack up against my core belief that I am too much – too heavy or too demanding – and am therefore better off independent. I can catch myself, thank you. How many others feel this or something similar? Yet performing the task, in that sliver of time between being steady on my feet and then collapsed over someone, I feel something else taking place. Just for a moment I am out of control – in a strange and uncertain space of not knowing what will happen. I cannot go back, I can only continue to fall and be caught. By someone. My habitual independence and other psychological patterns must instantly adapt to the requirements of trust.

With each new adventure into unknown paths comes a moment to waive familiar patterns, testing physical and psychological behaviours; a point when we are, as psychologist Elizabeth Friedman says, free falling 'into empty space ... to deal with the unknown, the as-yet-to-be experienced, the open space' (1993: 112). Lean On Me offers a physical ritual that allows us to experience free falling within a field of safety. Yet more than that, this process empowers us to develop trust in the support of others. This is a physical practice to experience in small groups that has far-reaching social, political and metaphorical implications for undoing distrust between people and communities worldwide, particularly following times of radical uncertainty and crisis.

BAREFOOT

Footwear is normally constructed to provide safety and protection from the ground. Across the world, styles and fashions of footwear are loaded with cultural significations of power. In the West, the higher the shoe, the higher the status. Ironically, walking *without* shoes – sensing the interface between foot and ground – brings physical stability and motor control that many Western styled shoes do not. Yet there are also stigmas attached to walking barefoot, linked to historical issues of gender, poverty, status and class. In Western culture, barefoot walking comes with a history of shame, particularly for women. Walking about with feet uncovered brings a woman's body closer to the ground – a symbolically lower place – the terrain of animals and sexual desire. Walking physically lower to the ground, barefoot or in shoes that are flat rather than high-heeled, enhances a woman's physical stability while reducing her status, gives her freedom to run from danger while labelling her as a fallen woman, increases her movement capacity and provides environmental support yet renders her invisible in the workplace.

The relationship between footwear and falling was highlighted by Amy Sharrocks in *Time to Fall* (2013), a live-art installation at the Royal British Society of Sculptors. During the installation, members of the public could experience gravity by climbing a ladder and falling onto a mattress. Amy also conducted group walks on London streets, during which any member of the group could fall and be caught by the others, before continuing walking. One of the gallery's exhibits featured an assortment of shoes displayed on rostra mounted at one side of the studio, items such as *pointe* shoes, high heels, stilts and Chinese clogs. The shoes were chosen to draw visitors' attention to embodied experiences of falling, or not falling, when wearing different kinds of footwear. Visitors were invited to try on these shoes to experience the necessary postural adjustments and shifting points of balance. Pairs of butter and ice shoes were also included as an artistic experiment. Their slippery, unstable qualities exacerbated risks of falling while also provoking laughter.

As I walk barefoot I can sense every movement of my uncontained feet as a small falling, yet simultaneously I feel in control of my movements. In contrast, Amy's shoes, which appear as constructed architectures and provide artificial frames for our feet to *prevent* falling, actually take me out of control into the uncertainty of gravity's force. These shoes demonstrate

FIGURE 3.3 Keeping Up (butter shoes), *Amy Sharrocks (2013 still)*. *Cinematographer: Iris Long.*

how, culturally, we restrict ourselves with fixed and binding constructions to keep us from sensing the ground, but which exacerbate fear of falling in an effort to create safety.

> You're walking.
> And you don't always realize it,
> but you're always falling.
> With each step you fall forward slightly.
> And then catch yourself from falling.
> Over and over, you're falling.
> And then catching yourself from falling.
> And this is how you can be walking and falling
> at the same time.
>
> ANDERSON 1982

SAND WALKING

I am walking along sand dunes on the Norfolk coast, the ocean to my right and to my left, gullies and slopes colonized by marsh pennywort, Marram grass and reeds. My feet plough into the sand, heels first, then my toes, with a pouring, folding, spreading sensation unpredictably strange with each sinking stride. My weight slips downwards and outwards and my balance shifts off centre. The horizon wavers, my eyes no longer lead, and my path meanders without consistent direction. If I try to hurry forward at my usual pace, I am quickly tired. But if I let go of the need to proceed in a straight line, if I accept the sand's sliding, shifting and collapsing surface – then I experience a new kind of walking. Wobbling, lunging, sinking and scrabbling. My perspectives are altered, for the sand does little to encourage me onward. My journey takes longer; the process replaces my goal of arriving. Walking on dunes is disrupted by falling. Walking on sand reshapes the *meaning* of goal-orientated travel, converting a time-based practice into a spatial activity.

My imagination drifts from these gentle Norfolk dunes to the sands of the Australian deserts. I am reminded of writing by Australian dance and theatre academic Rachel Fensham (2010), who in discussing failed attempts by Europeans to colonize Australia's deserts, refers to the disruptive qualities of travelling on sand as a metaphor. Fensham describes how, as a consequence of this failure, Australian imagination now occupies two distinct landscapes: the cities, houses and gardens of European culture; and the untameable wilderness of vast desert spaces. During European exploration the desert was seen as unconquerable and uncivilized, as the 'dead heart ... an empty or hostile centre' of Australia (Fensham 2010: 197). To conquer terrain and colonize land, flat, hard horizontal surfaces are the most amenable to travel and expansion; sand disrupts the goals and progress of colonizing forces. As a consequence, the relationship between cities, suburbs and desert became one of 'alienation, repression and separation' (Fensham 2010: 197).

To imagine how suburb and outback might merge into a single spatial poetics particular to Australia, Fensham cites two performance pieces: *Fiction* (Adams and Hilton 2004) and *Still Angela* (Kemp 2002, 2004). In *Fiction*, 'a fantasy desert turns into a psychotic domestic space' and in *Still Angela*, 'the world of a kitchen chair expands to include the trauma of a desert interior' (Fensham 2010: 198–9). Both pieces reflect suburban anxieties and fears of desert spaces and both use acts of falling to express colonial unease. Following her analysis, Fensham suggests that to integrate suburb and desert into a comprehensive Australian poetics might require 'spatial practices and bodily movement with a less certain trajectory, one that I characterize as not walking falling' (Fensham 2010: 208). Fensham draws politics and poetics together through the metaphor of desert walking, which is 'to fall into consciousness of the European social and imaginative failure to accommodate an indigenous or postcolonial intensity of space ... By not walking falling ... falling could be an act of love' (Fensham 2010: 212).

So I walk these ancient dunes acknowledging that I cannot *master* walking on sand, I am transformed by my body's surrender to unsteadiness. Slipping and sliding, I ponder Fensham's metaphor – not walking falling –

for its proposed reintegration of spatial poetics and racial sensitivities for Australians; for its suggestion that significant changes of perspective could result, similar to – perhaps epitomized by – what happens when humans give in to walking on sand.

TORTUROUS DELIGHT

Walking is an action the able-bodied take for granted, and awareness of the falls that occur between each step go unnoticed. This is not so for Celeste Dandeker, wheelchair performer, founder and co-director of Candoco Dance Company (1991–2007), a fact she poignantly highlighted during the making of *Across Your Heart* (1996). When I asked her what she most wanted to do she replied, 'Stand up and walk'.

Across Your Heart was a full-length piece for Candoco which I devised with a group of performers: Helen Baggett, Celeste Dandeker, Charlotte Darbyshire, Jon French, Kwesi Johnson, Kuldip Singh-Barmi, and Sue Smith.[17] The work was loosely based on carnival extravaganza, a collage of scenes exploring androgyny, gender play, eroticism and dark humour, while interweaving themes of power and pleasure. The piece begins when Helen – naked, except for a loincloth – endures an energetic mauling by Kuldip. Wearing a sleek Lycra dress, he ravishes her thoroughly with grotesquely distorted movements. The work ends with Helen in her loincloth hanging from a scaffold upside down, dripping blood onto the dinner table below. The others take turns catching her blood in their wine glasses and making luxurious toasts. Celeste sits in her wheelchair at the head of the table.

Earlier in the performance, Celeste is placed on stage in a blackout. When the lights come up, we see her standing, no wheelchair. In long white dress and veil, she projects an image reminiscent of Frieda Kahlo. 'It was amazing, I was upright, quite a surprise for the audience, who were probably wondering, what's going on under that dress' (Dandeker interview with author 2020). Flanked by a charming suitor, Kwesi, she is carried further on stage. The scene progresses as Helen, Sue and Charlotte, dressed in leather and Doc Martens and wielding chains, tease Celeste mercilessly, rocking her side to side, tipping her back and forth, and eventually stripping her from the wedding dress. They then deposit her – vulnerable and exposed – inside what appears to be a solid, full-length white casing, which encloses her body while leaving head, neck and arms free. Celeste called this contraption her swivel walker.

---

[17]Music composed by Stuart Jones. Designed by Roger Kitis.

Swivel walkers were used for many years for children with spina bifida, giving them an opportunity to stand up and put pressure through their bones. When I was recovering from encephalitis, after my accident, I was asked if I would like to volunteer, try one out, to see if it might be any good. I jumped at the opportunity. What I used to do was sit on a bed, lean the brace against the bed, then get in it by going over the top, so to speak. My feet touched the foot plate and a device, like two metal hoops, came over the arches of my feet to trap my feet. There was a brace over my knees, and then a large leather brace that went around my hips and up over my torso as I have no muscles in my back. Once I got the hang of how it works, I was able to walk and see the world from a different level.

DANDEKER interview 2020

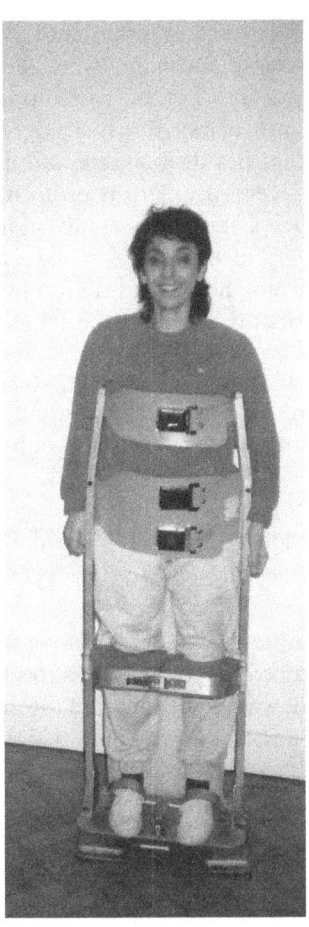

FIGURE 3.4 *Celeste Dandeker in a swivel walker (1984). With thanks to the Orthotic Research & Locomotor Assessment Unit (ORLAU) at The Robert Jones and Agnes Hunt Orthopaedic Hospital NHS Foundation Trust in Oswestry. Courtesy of Celeste Dandeker. Photographer unknown.*

Pause with this image of Celeste in your mind while I describe other scenes which contextualize Celeste' upstanding moment. Performers stomp onto stage beside a carnival float. They wear animal masks and engage in fake sodomy while Jon sits up high on the float, on a throne – his wheelchair – wearing a feather headdress and lashing a whip. A funeral ends in hysterical laughter with mourners teasing Kuldip, solemnly focused in his role as the corpse. A sedate formation where all performers dance in wheelchairs disintegrates into a chaotic, erotic jumble of falling chairs and bodies, then re-aligns for a tensely performed tango. There are choreographed group dances interspersed with individual performers portraying strange gothic figures. Such as Sue, bent forwards, wearing a full body cloak with hood, holding two long sticks stretched out in front like another pair of legs. A monstrous creature, she travels slowly across the back, sometimes catching Kuldip within her extended limbs, trapping him like an insect while casting a dark stalking shadow over an intimate love scene taking place downstage. Images flip from sweetness into horror, worship into obsession, beauty to the grotesque, laughter into tears. *Across Your Heart* is a work of queer imagination in which, identities disintegrate and desires become sinister or excessive, while routine events transform in bizarre and surreal fantasies. This is the context in which Celeste now stands alone on stage, a vulnerable, disabled figure propped up in her swivel walker. She begins to rock from side to side, gradually turning herself, a fraction further with each sideways rock, until she faces towards the back of the stage.

> You know those toys with the big flat feet, you put them on a slope and they walk down? Walking was a bit like that. I would swing my arms over to the right, leaning forward onto my right leg, release the left foot, not my actual foot, but the brace, then with a swivel movement I could move my left side forward a bit. Then I swing my arms over to the left, lean my weight to the left and swivel forward again. Like a duck.
>
> DANDEKER interview 2020

There is no music as Celeste makes her arduous way upstage, an inch at a time. When she reaches centre stage she begins to sing. 'La li la li la la la'. She is light-hearted, delighted, waving her arms in the air with carefree abandon. She continues to walk upstage alone, gaily singing, lurching laboriously from side to side in her rigid, white walker. 'The only time I felt really nervous was when we were in Hastings. We performed on a raked stage. Going down was fine, but going up at the end was quite scary. I didn't want to fall backwards' (Dandeker interview 2020).

Since her accident in 1973, Celeste has been unable to stand up. This scene in *Across Your Heart* offered her an experience of freedom and pleasure. She was face-to-face, at standing level, with non-disabled people, wearing a long white dress, where her disability was hidden. Yet like other scenes in *Across Your Heart*, this apparent able-bodied-ness disintegrated.

When the stark white walker was revealed and she was alone on stage, spectators were voyeurs to her vulnerable efforts to walk. Time was suspended. As she slowly, awkwardly travelled upstage, happily singing, the walker took on aspects of an instrument of torture, trapping her flesh, hindering her freedom of movement. In contrast to her wheelchair, in which she moves with speed and efficiency. As witness to her walking I smile with her pleasure, yet I am disturbed by her loss.

An excruciating five minutes later, after a walk of agonizing joy, Celeste eventually reaches upstage. As the lights fade, we hear her singing louder, irritated with Roger, the well-meaning production manager trusted with carrying her off stage. The show goes on.

4

Falling About

PRATFALLS

What better reason for falling than falling for laughs? The physicality of laughing is, for the most part, a benign act of falling. When performers fall for laughs and – in response – spectators fall about laughing, then falling, and falling about laughing about falling, are shared gifts of vitality between performers and audience.

Most stand-up comedians rely – to a large extent – on words to provoke laughter, whereas body-based humour depends mostly on movement. A signature movement of physical humour is the pratfall – an act of falling as a source for laughter. Pratfalls, familiar from slapstick films, circus and comedy, turn attention from intellectual wit to physical action, disrupting traditional theatrical production values. A pratfall is the *high*light of a physical joke, one that interrupts – purposefully – the flow of heroic action and linear narrative. Furthermore, artists who perform pratfalls manipulate success and failure simultaneously. A pratfall is a constructed failure that becomes successful when it achieves its desired effect of a laugh. The success of a pratfall is in the skill of falling, of falling as failure.

Circus clowns are indomitable practitioners of the pratfall, which is purposefully used to fail the task of thinking logically through any given physical challenge. At the circus, clowns offer an antithesis to aerial acts, setting out purposefully to counteract upward achievement, as American clown and comedian Bill Irwin's clowning routine demonstrates.

> Irwin cheerfully begins running around in a circle, trips at a certain point and falls down; he gets up, dusts himself off and sets off eagerly around the same imaginary circle, only to trip and fall at the same point; the third time around, he slows up his approach to the tripping point and, emphasizing for the viewer his incipient cleverness, steps over it successfully, then, triumphantly launching back into his run, he trips and falls once again.
>
> WEITZ 2012: 80

A historical home for pratfall humour is in the slapstick routines of silent films. The term 'slapstick' originated from 'a circus prop consisting of two thin slats joined together, so that a loud clack is made when one clown hits another on his backside' (Crafton 1995: 108). Slapstick formed the underlying principle of Keystone Films' silent comedies (Sufrin 1987) and, as visual performance, has a history in seedy, anarchic acts of indecency, exaggeration, depravity and gross incompetence by skilled, professional performers whose bodies 'were those of sly flawless acrobats' (Sufrin 1987: 21). Within this arena, skilful acts of falling on one's prat, as a way to induce laughter, were welcomed and encouraged.

Emerging from the early years of slapstick comedy in silent films (1912–16) were pratfall stars such as Charlie Chaplin, Harold Lloyd and in particular Buster Keaton with his droopy, deadpan face, whose early stage experiences were of being thrown about in his parents' vaudeville acts.

> Even in my early days our turn established a reputation for being the roughest in vaudeville. This was the result of a series of interesting experiments Pop made with me. He began these by carrying me out on the stage and dropping me on the floor. Next he started wiping up the floor with me. When I gave no sign of minding this he began throwing me through the scenery, out into the wings, and dropping me down on the bass drum in the orchestra pit . . . I did not cry because I wasn't hurt.
>
> KEATON 1960: 12–13

Buster was a performance artist with charismatic presence and choreographic precision in his use of objects in time and space. Falling was his trademark and as a consequence he became known as a 'gravity handler' (Benayoun 1982: 105). His pratfalling offered a philosophical and performative challenge to slapstick – as undertaken by circus clowns – providing inspiration for later live art, theatre and performance artists. Buster did away with the clown's excessive trappings of 'makeup, wigs … porkpie, slapshoes, outsized garments' (Keaton 1960: 176) to create 'the comedy of grateful annihilation' (Benayoun 1982: 101), playing pratfalling with serious and existential intent.

Buster often employed stage sets and gadgets rather than his own body to deliver pratfalls, to represent sabotage and chaos (Knopf 1999; Bailes 2011). Unforgettable is the moment in *One Week* (1920) when he stands looking to camera, absentmindedly, and the façade of the house behind him (which he is in the process of building) falls forward. He just happens to be standing on the spot where the window opening will land, framing his feet; he remains standing there, fortuitously unharmed after the façade hits the ground. Whether he falls, or objects collapse, Buster's films are funny. Additional layers to his pratfall humour accrue as he casually disassembles any sense of heroic masculinity, presenting himself with precise timing and adept physicality as a lost, floundering shipwreck of a man.

Samuel Beckett admired Buster, who influenced in turn the playwright's existential representations of failure (Diack 2012). After Buster had failed in Hollywood and suffered through alcoholism – falling in performance and in life – Beckett asked him to take part in a film, *An Odd Couple* (Schneider 1965).[1] In this film, which reeks of existential emptiness, the camera pursues Buster along an empty street, up a dark staircase and into an apartment. Shuffling along as an old man in a long black coat, he avoids the camera until the very last shot when his weathered face is finally revealed, his posture and whole being infused with resignation and with his signature drooping, deadpan demeanour.

Live-art practitioners such as Bruce Nauman, Bas Jan Ader, David Shrigley, Frances Alys, Gillian Wilding, Joseph Beuys and Sarah Lucas have also been influenced by Buster. Bruce's *Failing to Levitate* (1966) echoes back to 'a long lineage of pratfalls' (Diack 2012: 79). This live-art performance is documented by two superimposed photographs. One image shows Bruce lying stiff as a board, horizontally supported between two chairs, his head on one, feet on the other. The second image shows Bruce having slumped to the ground when the chair supporting his feet was pulled away. The caption states that he is attempting the impossible task of levitating, a term easily confused with levity: the treatment of a serious matter with humour and lack of respect. His attempt at transcendence is thwarted. 'The reality of human limits is brought tumbling back down to earth in a conceptual pratfall' (Diack 2012: 76).

Sarah Bailes (2011) also draws on slapstick's pratfall gag, mapping its history and impact in her comprehensive study of the poetics of failure in contemporary theatre. Bailes emphasizes that 'the blundering practicalities of failure have long been exploited for their humorous potential' (2011: 39). She focuses on the work of theatre companies Goat Island and Forced Entertainment, which rough-and-tumble with failure in their artistic productions. For Goat Island, a method of creating failure focused around achieving 'the impossible task', and with Forced Entertainment, a 'radical amateurism' (Bailes 2011: 56). Both companies use slapstick's signature gag as a theatrical strategy of failure, to become 'undone, whilst at the same time managing the absurdity of trying to get it "right" on stage' (Bailes 2011: 8).

This stumbling meander through a history of pratfalling as a creative source concludes with a reference to British slapstick comedians Jennifer Saunders and Joanna Lumley in the BBC television show *Absolutely Fabulous* (created and written by Saunders in 1992). These two women unashamedly flag pratfalling as a failure to conform to cultural expectations of women. They execute their downfalls in exquisite slapstick style. Their extensive repertoire of pratfalls serves as vital prompts for viewers' laughter: down

---

[1]Directed by Alan Schneider and written and conceived by Samuel Beckett, *An Odd Couple* is called *Film* in Ross Lipman's documentary on Beckett, *Notfilm* (2016).

stairs, out of cabs, off the porch – they fall about drunk, collapse through indulgence. The stairs in the *Absolutely Fabulous* house are prominently positioned to frame the motif of their trips and falls. And they are splendidly colourful, extravagant falls, fully orchestrated cadences of gesture, clothing, scenery, props and unravelling composure. So I give space here to Jennifer, in her interview with Caitlin Moran, where she talks of being inspired to pratfall through her friendship with the female pop group, Bananarama.

> The nights with Bananarama were some of the best nights of my life, and I got a lot of gags from Bananarama because they were big vodka drinkers ... When I started doing *Ab Fab*, I remembered all of the falls that I saw Bananarama do. I once saw one of them coming out of a cab bottom first and hitting the road and I thought, that's class.
>
> SAUNDERS on *Chain Reaction* 2012

Spectators laugh, not just as a consequence of a performer's constructed misfortune, but to experience respite and relief from their own attempts to exist upright and secure. Pratfalls provide onlookers with a chance to value absurdity. Performers construct events of shaming to prompt and sanction the pleasure of laughter.

STAR STUMBLES

During his life in dance, Israeli choreographer Ohad Naharin has worked with choreographers such as Martha Graham, Maurice Béjart, Merce Cunningham, William Forsythe and Pina Bausch, before becoming the director of Batsheva Dance Company in Israel (1990–2018).[2] This background, in diverse choreographic styles, suggests Ohad has a complex understanding of the different aesthetic and metaphorical associations of dance with gravity. *Mr. Gaga* (dir. Heymann 2016) is a film about his life and work. At the beginning of the film, he is working on a fall with Maya Tamir, while the company rehearses. Maya is alone on stage in a body-hugging, all-in-one unitard. Ohad directs her from the auditorium. Maya stands with arched back, upturned face and violently shaking legs, shoulders and arms. She arches further and further until she falls back on the ground, using her thighs to control her descent and catching herself on her arm, in a manner reminiscent of a Graham fall.

'Let's stop,' Ohad calls from the auditorium. 'Maya, you need to create a rhythm of the fall – you are really slowing down.' She tries the phrase again,

---

[2] Martha Graham founded Batsheva Dance Company with Baroness Batsheva de Rothschild in 1964.

cautiously. 'Way too much control,' says Ohad. 'Can you sense it? You need to lose consciousness when you are up. Not when you're down, but before you fall.' She begins again, arching backwards, when Ohad demands, 'Lose it now'. She falls – with less control and without using her arm as support – yet continuing to tense her thighs to protect herself from the impact. 'Are you OK?' says Ohad. 'You need to find a way to let go.' He gets up to demonstrate. He stands on the stage, lets his knees give way and collapses to the ground like a sack of marbles. 'Just let it happen.' Maya watches him fall, then tries again. 'Almost, almost, but you are guarding your head too much . . . the more you let go everywhere in your body, the softness of your flesh will protect you.' There is a pause while she appears to negotiate with her fears. He says, 'Are you stressed?' 'No,' she says. 'Then do it again.' She begins again, compelling herself to extremes of shaking and arching; suddenly she drops – a spectacular collapse. She's got it.

The film continues with choreographic excerpts from a number of Ohad's works, interspersed with personal stories that highlight his positive qualities. He is presented as an exceptional man and choreographer, with a dramatic childhood and adventurous career and with a combination of virility and charm – a celebrated figure across Israel. He is also portrayed as an aggressive director who intimidates his dancers (Quinlan 2019). The film, however, increasingly undercuts his star power. Toward the end, he admits that some facts about his childhood are false, that the idealized portrait is not entirely true. He purposely tarnishes his own shiny image. In the final scene, he mocks his celebrity and casts doubt on his heroic stature in Israel as a leading choreographer. Carrying his bag and with a coat over his street clothes, he walks up a flight of steps towards a monolithic, red-brick building. He stumbles, catches himself on the hand rail, gets up again, turns and smiles to the camera. He carries on climbing but stumbles twice more, looking back and smiling to camera each time.

The film begins and ends with falling, with falls that offer contrasting visions, one of an iconic choreographer, purveyor of spectacle and director of dance theatre, and the other as a person openly vulnerable, fallible and unstable. Mocking his own image as an Israeli dance hero, Ohad Naharin pratfalls himself.

ABOUT LAUGHTER

> Laughter literally rocks the body. And if you believe . . . that there exists a reversible link between one's inner life and its outer traces, a performer who has an audience rolling in the aisles will have reached inside those laughing bodies to exert a formidable effect.
>
> WEITZ 2012: 79

Plunging contractions of diaphragms, heads thrown back, bodies doubled up, mouths open, tears streaming, knees weak, balance out of whack – this is laughter. Raucous belly laughs, unrestrained roaring and howling. High-pitched cackling and chortling, punctuated and rhythmic, cascading and descending, refreshing and haunting. Nervous, embarrassed laughter, giggling, tittering, snickering and snorting. Delirious corpsing, as something suppressed, a deliciously painful helpless state. Laughter promotes health and has therapeutic effects. It reduces stress, increases energy and enhances positive thinking. Laughter is physical, an act of precarity. Often contagious, laughing spreads, un-possessed, belonging to no one, sweeping between bodies. Someone starts laughing and the rhythms spread in a rapturous, rippling falling about. Laughter is rarely experienced alone; it slops into the liminal spaces between bodies. It may be unleashed by a joke, a gag, a wicked bit of wit, irreverence, contradiction, insult, satire, or even by a thumping good story. There may just be shared physicality – and the mystery of infectious mirth.

Laughter is a focus for theoretical wanderings. For the French feminist Julia Kristeva, laughter is one of the first expressions of semiotic impulses between mother and child. 'Oral eroticism, the smile at the mother, and the first vocalisations are contemporaneous … During this period of indistinction between "same" and "other", infant and mother, while no space has yet been delineated, the semiotic chora . . . relieves and produces laughter' (Kristeva 1980: 284). For Bergson (1913) and Bourdieu (1984), laughter requires a shared social understanding and complicity with others of a group; those outside a group's customs and ideas may not laugh along. 'Laughter must answer to certain requirements of life in common. It must have *social* signification' (Bergson 1913: 8). Bergson also attends to the sounds of laughter: 'Laughter appears to stand in need of an echo. Listen to it carefully: it is not an articulate, clear, well-defined sound; it is something which would fain be prolonged by reverberating from one to another, something beginning with a crash, to continue in successive rumblings, like thunder in a mountain' (Bergson 1913: 5–6). Walter Benjamin finds 'there is no better starting point for thought than laughter; speaking more precisely, spasms of the diaphragm generally offer better chances for thought than spasms of the soul' (Benjamin [1935] 1998: 101). Theatre academic Nicholas Ridout writes on theatrical problems that spice up performance, such as stage fright, actors' embarrassment and corpsing. He describes laughter as an act capable of unravelling ideals of individualism, since laughing is always a 'collectivising moment'. Laughing undoes 'a modern bounded self', and any passage towards one-ness 'will always be interrupted' (Ridout 2006: 146). Post-structuralist rhetorician Diane Davis carries this view further, writing about how the irrepressible and shattering impact of laughter takes over reason and breaks up the solidity of language. 'To be spoken by a language contorted in laughter is to be spoken by *language on the loose*' (Davis 2000: 9 original emphasis). For Davis, laughter becomes the subject and her body is an object that is laughed.

My body feels overwhelmed, intoxicated by an inexplicable force; I feel weak, out of control. My whole being wants desperately not to laugh, and yet it's clear to me that my will is not in control; something else has hold of me . . . I hear myself beginning to lose it, 'I' am beginning to 'crack up' both literally (the stability of the 'I' is challenged when it becomes the object of this laughter's force) and figuratively.

DAVIS 2000: 22

Self-dissolving laughter decisively topples into the framework of falling as a creative source for change. Laughter erupts between bodies as a shared gift, undoing the fixed sensibleness of an upright 'I'.

NIHILISTIC OPTIMISM

One Dixon Road (2010) was the last solo show Nigel Charnock made before his untimely death in 2012. As with all his shows, *One Dixon Road* included a fast-paced, passionate rant. Performing in Jerusalem in 2011, he paced across the stage back and forth, gesticulating wildly and raging into a hand-held mic. He began by brazenly declaring that he had not wanted to come to Israel, and by berating the Israelis for defending their territory. The tirade continued:

Ah, fucking hell and the Palestinians are just as bad and the fucking Muslims and the bloody orthodox Jews and the this and that. Oh please, I mean if there *was* a God – which of course there fucking isn't, OBVIOUSLY . . . it doesn't work. Haven't you got it yet? All this praying . . . and even the fucking Buddhists with ya fucking meditation, it doesn't work – how many times – IT DOESN'T WORK. OK? OK? Christian priests are as bad as second-hand car salesmen, just selling you something – selling you Heaven, selling you the future . . . it doesn't work, OK? There is no past, there is no future. OK? [*Changing his tone to a mincing whine, he impersonates a mindful stereotype.*] 'Oh Nigel, we live in the now, in the here and now, be in the now.' [*Ranting again loudly*] Rubbish. Shit. There is no now. Hello! All there is, is this. Just this. Nothing else. Nothing else. It's nothing. And what does this mean? Nothing? It doesn't mean anything. [*Mincing again*] 'Oh, Nigel, I'm on a journey, searching for the meaning of life. I've got to find Nirvana . . . I'm going to reach somewhere.' [*Ranting*] NO! There is no past, there's no journey. You're not going anywhere. It's absolutely, totally, beautifully, divinely, amazingly MEANINGLESS. OK? Right I'm glad we got that sorted. [*A Beatles song belts out and Nigel starts dancing.*]

Nigel embraced the monstrous chaos of nihilism lurking under establishment values and commonly recognized meanings of existence. He lived his life believing that nothing – the absurdity of nothing – underlies all that is constructed. Religious institutions are built on fabricated lies; there is no single truth. Nihilism is often associated with pessimism, destruction and extreme scepticism. Not for Nigel. Living with nothingness was never *only* nihilistic; on the contrary, his belief in pervasive nothingness was exciting, joyous, funny, exhilarating. He told me, 'Nothingness – 'tis your greatest lover. It will never leave you'.[3] He lived out his existential dread as nihilistic *optimism*, as a source of creativity which propelled him to work with a ferocious drive in spite – almost because of – nothing.

His dancing said it all. He would fling his arms, twist his torso, whip his spine and kick his legs, running, falling, always racing, attacking space and audience sensibilities with savage abandon. Nigel's dancing was excessive and brash, requiring endurance in the extreme and often leaving him bloodied and bruised. His creative impulses were too reckless and risky to conform to fixed codes. He seemed to be powered – to be *danced* – by the energy of nothingness itself. Mere movements meant little to Nigel, and he often dismissed them; yet he always performed them with a raging force that became his signature, his aesthetic identity. He revelled in a void of meaninglessness, dropping to the ground, again and again, to remind his audiences that there is no saviour, no continuity, no promise of life after death. Love and live with uncertainty, he urged, because dying is all there is. *One Dixon Road* ends with his rendition of *Cabaret*. He belts out the line, 'When I go, I'm going like Elsie' with everything he has and wrings it for all he is worth.

Nigel lived his philosophy of nothingness through a fully charged, vehement, commitment to performance – as though longing to break into hyperspace at hyper-speed – to go on long enough – to perform fast enough – to reach exhaustion – to arrive at a place of absolute nothing. A year after his performance in Jerusalem – he was dead.

IT'S NOT FUNNY

Toronto, 2018, in the middle of winter and the snow is thick and deep. I am climbing the side of one of the city's many ravines, as a shortcut to somewhere else. The crest of the bank is covered in a layer of translucent ice. I drop to my hands and knees and crawl. I find traction and safety by spreading my

---

[3]Transcribed from a mobile phone text correspondence between Nigel Charnock and author in 2011.

weight across all four limbs, rather than just relying on my feet. My friend – also struggling to climb the steep wall – reaches the top and turns to see me on all fours. He chortles and continues to laugh until I am upright again. I laugh too, yet feel just an inkling of shame that my reasonable solution to travelling on ice has triggered such mirth.

> [L]aughter cannot be absolutely just. Nor should it be kind-hearted either. Its function is to intimidate by humiliating. How it would not succeed in doing this had not nature implanted for that very purpose, even in the best of men, a spark of spitefulness or, at all events, of mischief.
>
> BERGSON 1913: 198

Laughing when someone else falls down is rarely comfortable – outside the frame of performance. An outburst of laughter can generate shame and a sense of failure on the part of the faller; it suggests indifference on the part of the laughing witness. Onlookers might see the humour in a ridiculous attempt to maintain balance, but the person falling does not. Analyzing why people laugh and the psychology of humour in film, David Innes draws on the importance of social context and discusses the superiority theory, which 'requires the observer to pass judgment, whether consciously or subconsciously ... this theory can be expanded to encompass anything worthy of derision: an idea, an institution, even an inanimate object' (Innes 2014: 5) Laughter springs from a sense of superiority the witness experiences at another's misfortune. People laugh seeing someone trip in the course of a dignified stride, or fall out of fixed, mechanical, everyday, repetitive actions and behaviour. In this way, laughing at falling can be unethical.

Ethical questions emerge when the joke goes only one way, when a disconnect occurs between a subject who witnesses and another who falls and becomes the object of the witness's gaze. This paradigm harks back to the Enlightenment view of the individual self – standing alone, falling alone – a subjective I, as separate from You. It is a view of the self that owes much to Christianity and to Victorian morality, one that prompts philosopher and writer Gilbert Keith Chesterton to claim laughing about falling is 'a gravely religious matter. It is the Fall of Man. Only man can be absurd: for only man can be dignified' (Chesterton 1908). In the same vein, philosopher Henri Bergson (1913) considers laughing about falling to be a consequence of the collision between body and soul, whereby the human struggle to morally transcend the physical body is always beleaguered by the body itself. Incidents of falling draw attention to the failure to maintain moral uprightness, which provokes laughter in others.

> A man, running along the street, stumbles and falls; the passers-by burst out laughing ... They laugh because his sitting down is involuntary ... He should have altered his pace or avoided the obstacle. Instead of that, through lack of elasticity, through absentmindedness and a kind of

physical obstinacy, *as a result, in fact, of rigidity or of momentum,* the muscles continued to perform the same movement when the circumstances of the case called for something else. That is the reason of the man's fall, and also of the people's laughter.

BERGSON 1913: 8–9, original emphasis

Here, laughing at the misfortune of another is neither just nor kind-hearted. It acts as a form of humiliation.

In visual, body-based performance this is rarely the case. Pratfalls jolt spectators into laughter as a consequence of a *shared* habitus, a shared ridiculousness, a delight in ludicrous efforts. Faller and witness together experience a release from shame. To fall on her face is the performer's gift to her audience. Her falls are skilfully constructed mistakes, calculated to disrupt cerebral transcendence. Uninvited laughter at the fall of another is something completely different.

GRAVESTONE LAUGHS

Six women are standing in a line, centre stage, facing the audience, as I enter The Place Theatre in London to see dance artist Wendy Houstoun's *Stupid Women* (2015).[4] The performers are casually dressed in trainers, tracksuits and T-shirts. They hold a banner on which 'Welcome' is boldly written. They look slightly sheepish, as if observed waiting for a bus. A variety of objects litter the stage, including a drum kit, a clothes rack, a projection screen, fairy lights, a shopping trolley, a baby buggy, white plastic office chairs and an American flag. Wendy, the director, is downstage right, seated at a table with a lighting board, sound desk, laptop, cables and writing materials. Wendy has full command of lighting and sound. Throughout the performance she trawls through a range of music: electronic rock, bells, texts, echoes, bagpipes, Charlie Chaplin, Noël Coward, religious, classical, TV shows, hip hop. The following snippets provide a glimpse of the dynamics – captured from memory, scraps of grainy video documentation and performers' tales.

Annie throws her body about in the space. TC begins a slow journey across the back of the stage, wriggling her legs and shuffling her feet, body

---

[4] *Stupid Women* had four outings (Liverpool, Leeds, Nottingham and London) involving different casts of women. Making began with a week-long workshop at Winlab, at Siobhan Davies Studios in London (2015). Performers included Jane McKernan, Rachel Krische, TC Howard, Jo Fong, Sophie Unwin, Anna Williams, Annie Mesmer, Emma Murray and Victoria Malin.

hunched over, fists clenched, like a little old man making his way along the side of a building on a winter night. Victoria marches around the space, lifting each leg high with every step. Jo speaks into a mic: 'We have the power ... to do something ... stay with it ... give us feedback.' Sophie enters, waving madly to the audience. Wendy runs into the space and demonstrates a gesture, which Sophie copies. Wendy runs out again. TC sings fragments of songs, hardly recognizable over an echoing sound score: 'I could give you the moon, I could sing you a tune ... I've got what it takes to hold you, but I'd just as soon let you go ... I beg your pardon, I never promised you a rose garden.' Someone offers her a plastic rose for a mic.

Jo tumbles down to loud rock music; she gets up and falls again and again. Wendy runs in, wheels the empty clothes rack in front of her, and Jo falls once again through the frame. Jo rattles off a list of words, speaking into a mic while Wendy sets up a scene behind her. Three women sit in white chairs, framed by the clothes rail, each holding a piece of a cloth. Wendy runs back and forth, demonstrating how she wants them to cry, hysterically, while they tap their chests. She changes the music and wraps Jo in a cloth. Jo stands on a chair, in humdrum parody of a Greek statue. Victoria plays a red toy electric guitar. Wendy runs in, takes away the clothes rail, gets the three women down on their knees, palms pressed together praying earnest prayers. Wendy runs back to her sound desk, then runs in again to show Victoria where to sit behind the praying women. With her feet on another chair, Victoria casually plays the guitar, a blond wig perched haphazardly on her head. The praying continues. Wendy cries, 'Show us,' from the side, which the performers shout back. Wendy runs in, throws her arms up into the air and again shouts, 'Show us'. The women mimic her actions and cry 'Show us' in response. Wendy throws a flag at them and runs in a circle, runs out, runs back in, changes directions, creates havoc, shouting 'Show us the way'. Like her, the women run about the stage, shouting, 'Show us the way'. Pause ... I'm laughing.

The challenge for women in dance to make fools of themselves is linked, in some ways, to second-wave feminism. In the 1970s and 1980s, feminist discourse waged a long battle to counteract patriarchy's judgement of women in dance as sexual objects. Female dancers, myself included, committed ourselves, through feminism, to contest our roles as objects by establishing our subjectivity and identity as 'women'. Enlivening and enhancing that commitment to change, however, was our use of humour (Claid 2006). UK artists such as Jacky Lansley, Rose English, Sally Potter, Blood Group (directed by Anna Furse), Liz Aggiss and myself often used a humorous feminist strategy of install and subvert. That is, by installing stereotypes of sexual objectification, we could then subvert those images through excessive parody. Those parodies were often designed to make the sexual object stereotypes appear purposely silly, foolish, even stupid – certainly funny – in order to honour the earnest subversion into serious, powerful, intelligent feminist subjects.

Wendy works with humour differently, I could even say, in opposition. In *Stupid Women*, rather than install female stereotypes, Wendy calls on the foolishness of earnest worthiness in women dance performers and herself as director, as a strategy for humour. Her tools have developed, in part, from her experience with the theatre company Forced Entertainment, whose humour is often based in human blunders and in *Stupid Women* Wendy skilfully directs her performers to underachieve, to metaphorically fall about, to fail at performance tasks through maintaining serious intention. Talking with Wendy, she begins by telling me about the challenge for women to be stupid in dance, describing her strategies for making *Stupid Women*.[5]

> Stupidity is, apparently, not something I should be selling in relation to women. I had to clarify that for people, so that when I say stupid women, it is about a *desire* to be stupid. It wasn't about calling women stupid. In a weird way, I think making an idiot of yourself is really key to ever being taken seriously. In my mind, if you want to be taken seriously, you also have to be considered a fool. Theatre seems to allow much more collision; dance tends to enjoy consensus. My main learning from Forced Entertainment is that it's fun when people don't know what the other person is doing but they carry on trying to do what they are doing. In a way, *Stupid Women* was my attempt to bring that collision into a physical world and the almost arbitrary, sometimes valiant, but often misled attempts by the director to steer the action.
>
> HOUSTOUN interview with author 2018

TC and Jo are jogging on the spot; TC holds the handles of the baby buggy, Jo the shopping trolley. They pant along, side by side, at centre stage, facing front, barking into a mic placed between them. They play a word-association game with Wendy directing from her table. 'Just drinks,' she says and they list alcoholic concoctions, randomly straying into other themes. Wendy directs them to go faster, louder, to elevate their buggies off the stage, to adapt their pace to a kind of side shuffle timed to the repetitive soundtrack. Their bodies are silhouetted on the screen behind and lit from the front by floor lights. The mic drops down, so they follow it with buggy and trolley held stiffly in front of themselves. Wendy changes the soundtrack and a front wheel of TC's buggy falls off. Wendy sits a yellow toy donkey in the buggy. When it tips off the side, she runs back in and places it upright. Jo speaks quietly to the donkey. Donkey is centre of attention. TC grabs donkey and buggy and launches herself wildly into a jig, tossing both buggy and donkey around manically.

---

[5] The idea for *Stupid Women* originated with Nigel Charnock who, just before he died, was directing a piece called *Stupid Men*. 'I had a desire to be as anarchic as Nigel, wanting a kind of kamikaze complete openness, voluntary participation in collision' (Houstoun interview with author 2018).

There were physical, verbal and group instructions such as: *Exit. Enter. Spin. Move the air. Jump on the spot. Drop dead slowly. Repeat an exercise until exhausted. Shake the body. Rearrange the space.* Streams of words. Some were slogans, or death endings such as: *Curtain at interval. Call it a day. Cut the cable. Drop off the twig.* Half the time I didn't know what performers were talking about. What the instructions do is make you do one thing at a time and not make judgements about what and where things happen, to keep out of the way of construction. The process relies on a commitment to nothing and to be willing to commit to it as long as that could endure. No one knew how long something might last. I could see that the more performers wanted to look cool, or in control, the more trouble they had; so, any attempts at control would end up backfiring on them. You are better off if you don't think.

HOUSTOUN interview with author 2018

Wendy shouts, 'OK'. Women stand still while Martin Luther King Jr's famous words 'I have a dream' ring out. Wendy dashes in and positions the clothes rack to frame the yellow donkey, which by now is precariously balanced on a stool centre stage. She runs out but then hurries back in with a black plastic bag, which she hands to TC, who swaddles the donkey so that only its face and ears are visible. Wendy runs out again to fetch a sombre black cloth adorned with skull and crossbones. Wrapping herself up, TC conceals her body, head and mouth – until only her eyes are showing – as though she is wearing a dishevelled burqa. TC sits on the ground next to the donkey propped on its stool and begins a patently fake ventriloquist act while the donkey improvises a gobbledygook text. Her voice muffled by the cloth, she vocalizes for the donkey in a high-pitched squeak: 'Gu've got a guture I've got a guture . . . gy gottom geally hurts? It's ruggish I gant it to stop I ghink gat we've all had enough now. What do you ghink agout d end of d gorld? what did you gay? I didn't gight gear you?'

When I talk to the performers on stage in *Stupid Women*, the blame always lies with me. If things fuck up, it's not their fault; it is clearly mine. Nine times out of ten my intervention fucks things up, which is how direction works. I was clearly giving contrasting, conflicting information to performers who were having to change their tack because 'The Director' has now come up with a better idea, or 'The Director' is full of herself. The joke was on me.

HOUSTOUN interview with author 2018

Stupid Women fell flat on its face. Following her two previous, successful solo shows, *50 Acts* (2011) and *Pact with Pointlessness* (2014), critics expected Ms. Houstoun to make a high-calibre, contemporary choreography, but what they witnessed failed to meet any expectations or satisfy conventional production values. The work received two negative reviews

FIGURE 4.1 *TC Howard in* Stupid Women *(Houstoun, 2015)*. Photo: Chris Nash.

(Watts 2015; Winship 2015a), both of one star – thus fulfilling its aims as a work of stupidity. 'They misunderstood the premise. People were waiting for the delivery of 'the thing', which was not the point' (Houstoun interview with author 2018).

Wendy received no funding for more shows (or for development). No presentable video documentation was recorded. By writing about *Stupid Women*, I am contradicting myself – purposefully: applauding the work for dropping into oblivion unnoticed and at the same time fixing it in written words. A dangerous undertaking, for the power of the work was its ad-hoc, improvised quality, its absurdity based in a failure to conform to the ideals of dance production. By writing about it, I am propping it up, reconstructing its bits, getting it remembered. Perhaps I am giving *Stupid Women* a gravestone in a cemetery of dance pieces that fell. As an aside, I am thinking of a cemetery such as Arundhati Roy's Jannat Guest House and Funeral Services in *The Ministry of Utmost Happiness* (Roy 2017), an imaginatively constructed graveyard in memory of inspirational poor, queer and unwanted misfits of Delhi.

Wendy's dissident instinct to create an aesthetic of stupid exposes her critical, experiential perception of dance and theatre. Skills she has honed over years of performing and making choreography, she now determinedly unravels with ironic wit and loads of political nuance. The resulting silliness is informed by an enduring love for artistic practice and a disillusion with institutional dance. Wendy *acts* stupid – and she does this in the moment of performance, objectively eyeing the performers while being herself observed. She astutely notices when a performer is failing an image she is portraying and teases that moment – in the moment. Yet the tease is on her, as her earnest, effortful interventions only disintegrate the scenes even further.

Performers enter her arena with professional commitment and trust, only to embark on ridiculous projects with absurd instructions, undoing through doing. In my conversation with TC, she tells me about her ventriloquist scene at the end of the show. 'It is a letting go, a giving in, a being part of the whole, an act of generosity. I knew as I was performing that I was experiencing the end of my career as a dancer. A great place to end, I was deeply happy in that moment. I felt I was dying with a great deal of joy' (Howard interview 2019).

> Putting a lot of effort into something that is not working is funny. And keeping on having a go despite it not working. There is a kind of amnesia built into it, I think. The skill is to mind your own business and not get wrapped up in success or failure, but to do actions as well as you can even though [you] do not know what [you] are doing. I am not sure I know either. It's more like an attempt well made – rather than a show well done.
>
> HOUSTOUN interview with author 2018

Stupid Women's humour is infused with Keaton-esque spirit, with an appetite for pratfalling – for the absurd, the surreal and anarchic. Physical pratfalls mean more than just demonstrations of failure performed for a laugh. In *Stupid Women*, falling, failing and laughing are metaphorical as well as physical; for both spectators and performers, they activate fissures and fractures; they collapse conventional expectations and the production values of contemporary choreography. The spectators' laughter is their physical undoing. *Stupid Women* is a cracking good laugh, a crack into which performers and spectators might just disappear. 'In my attempts I am sitting pretty close to the border of brilliant crap. I just might tip' (Houstoun interview 2018). Phew! Here's to falling about laughing.

PEN PALS

Psychotherapist Jan Roubal introduced the following experiment to participants at a Gestalt therapy conference.[6] We were sitting in rows, listening to Jan's seminar, when he invited us to turn to the person sitting next to us and balance a pen between us. With our eyes closed, each of us lightly touched one end of the pen with a single finger – cooperatively holding it – and let events unfold. My unspoken assumption was that as a couple, the task was to keep the pen aloft between our fingertips while following the movements we initiated together through the medium of the pen. As my partner moved, I automatically presumed I should maintain our connection, following her kinetic signals and keeping the pen from falling. Our pen soon dropped, accompanied by the clatter of pens dropping all around the room.

Discussion after the experiment focused on our different contact styles: who led, who followed, who initiated. I was trying hard not to fail my counterpart and had determined that the most important objective must be to hold the pen securely between us. Conversely, my partner was expecting me to lead and that she would follow. Inevitably, the pen dropped. In my attempt to hold the pen between us, I was straining to eliminate our differences and render us the same. I was in effect holding onto my partner through the pen, hoping we would stay together. In my effort to 'get it right', I had forgotten, first of all, to be myself, sense myself in my own breathing body, sitting on a chair with my feet on the floor. Therefore, while trying to be with her, I was depriving myself of the necessary support simply to be me. If I had been supporting myself, I might have realized the impossibility of the task.

---

[6]Sixteenth British Gestalt Journal Seminar at Study Society, Colet House, London (2017).

Try this experiment with a partner. First, focus on holding the pen between you. See how long you can keep it in place and then discuss. Try it again, and this time, before you begin, pay attention to your body in the chair and in contact with the ground, as self-support. Discuss the difference. The pen will fall – this is the valuable learning of the task. There is no efficient, seamless way to be different people together. Relationship is always a creative tension between separateness and togetherness (Jacobs and Hycner 1995) if we want to respect, rather than dominate, difference. The messiness of dropping the pen demonstrates that there is no predestined unison dance between us; seeking togetherness is not about establishing sameness, but about a meeting of singularities together, where tumbling into a space between is the name of the game. My partner and I tried it again, while maintaining interest in relations between our bodies, gravity and the ground; the pen continually dropped – much to our amusement.

FLATTENING THE CORPSE

Since the mid twentieth century artists across visual art disciplines have challenged the hierarchical privileging of uprightness, embracing the horizontal plane as a source of creativity. La Ribot, European interdisciplinary dance artist, consistently unravels this hierarchy in her performance work. Lepecki (2006), describing La Ribot's *Piezas Distinguidas* (1993–2003), notes the impact of witnessing her work in a gallery space where spectators, performers, objects and belongings are scattered on the same floor together. Lepecki senses La Ribot's '[y]ielding to gravity' that initiates 'a toppling, a debasing of whatever may be considered "well-built" – the well-organised, the directional, the teleological, the aimed, the representational, the perspectival, the architectural and the choreographic' (Lepecki 2006: 77). For Lepecki, her work 'levels us all as already falling' (Lepecki 2006: 77).

Another levelling work by La Ribot, *40 Espontáneos* (2004), brings forty performers onto a theatre stage primarily to laugh. In the process I watch them run and fall, putting on and taking off a variety of clothing, like shirts, T-shirts, trousers, skirts and brightly coloured everyday items; running in a single high-heel shoe with one foot bare, tripping, limping and falling; tumbling slowly out of embraces; weeping; holding up numbered cards; collapsing in chairs; staggering about and lying down prone while covering themselves with large panels of cardboard. Always laughing, all ways falling (Hargreaves 2004; Burt 2008).

When I have corpsed on stage (frequently in my youth as a ballet dancer), I can feel like I am dying, helpless, with 'nothing to fall back on, nothing to do, no one to be' (Ridout 2006: 134), and I experience a delirious sense of freedom yet also a loss of agency. Unplanned events on the stage provoke laughter that an actor tries to hide yet cannot; she is out of control, feels overtaken by an energy she struggles to hide. To corpse is to laugh without full release. 'Corpsing might seem to promise a line of flight, but it always chokes. It is a bursting out and a holding together at the same time' (Ridout 2006: 145). As I watch *40 Espontáneos* the internalized choking sensation of corpsing seems to be externalized, turned inside out, exposed, and agency is given to those who corpse.

La Ribot developed a laughing technique to support her performers in the process (Burt 2008). They are *doing* laughing as a continuity of action (Hargreaves 2004). They are not being funny, virtuosic or spectacular. Their laughter is contagious, I laugh, but there is no joke. The work is pedestrian, monotonous, relentless and non-spectacular. The laughter of this group of performers is a laughter that seems to echo with collaborative effortful pointlessness. Laughter that falls out of language evoking a flattening of bodies to a horizontal plane. There is something fatalistic yet honest about this performance of laughing and falling as a liminal act with no defined purpose other than as a leveller, a place of equality from which to consider life differently. Which brings to mind a quote by Hito Steyerl, a contemporary film-maker and visual artist. Although working through a different medium, Hito, similar to La Ribot, lays bare the relations between visual imagery, politics and power. Reflecting on artists' radical shifts away from conventions of perspective and fixed verticality in painting she writes that falling:

> [T]eaches us to consider a social and political dreamscape of radicalized class war from above, one that throws jaw-dropping social inequalities into sharp focus. But falling does not only mean falling apart, it can also mean a new certainty falling into place. Grappling with crumbling futures that propel us backwards onto an agonizing present, we may realize that the place we are falling toward is no longer rounded, nor is it stable. It promises no community, but a shifting formation.
>
> STEYERL 2011: 9

FEISTY DECAY

At the time of writing, the legendary dance artist Anna Halprin is ninety-eight years old. Anna is renowned for integrating dance with life and moving in response to the environment. She exerted a powerful influence on post-modern artists at Judson Church in New York in the 1960s and has continued making dance/art/life projects well into old age. In 2003, when

Anna was eighty-three, she collaborated with visual artist Eeo Stubblefield to create *Returning Home*, a film that extends Anna's project to integrate lived experience with artistic expression (Worth and Poyner 2004; Ross and Schechner 2007; Ross 2007).[7] For Anna, who rejects the notion of retirement, ageing is an artistic project entwined with dying, a process she confronts and works with creatively, transplanting herself into rural environments through movement and visual imagery, resolving herself with the inevitable disintegration of her body into the earth.

The film opens on a vast beach landscape where Anna – naked and swaddled in white gauze – is lying where the waves meet the shoreline. Her body drifts up the beach and rolls back out with the ebb and flow of the waves. Her filmy transparency blends with the sea froth – a sea that can neither give her up nor draw in close. Further into the film, I see Anna sitting naked in the mud, her body painted blue. As she smears mud and earth on her skin, she says, 'I felt a reverence for this aged body, beautiful old body, like all things around me'. She stretches and arches her torso, mud on her breasts and lips. She crouches down into a muddy puddle, a hole in the ground. She stretches inside a hollowed-out log; it is decaying and covered with bracken, twigs, compost, leaves, undergrowth and mud. Only her eyes are visible – opening and closing – and the swell of her breathing. 'I am rehearsing for my own return to nature.' She stands on a cliff top, leaning into the wind, wrapped again in white gauze. She resembles a ghostly figurehead on the bow of a ship – or a seagull hovering – stark against the sky with her head veiled and her arms spread like wings.

In a scene towards the end of the film, Anna is being fitted into a massive straw costume while standing in a field of wheat. She tells Eeo Stubblefield that she is exasperated with this regalia: 'I won't be able to move.' Frustrated with the fitting, she toddles off into the setting sun, stumbling down the path like the scarecrow from Oz, waving sheaves of straw still strapped to her arms. In a film infused with earnestness throughout, this moment is ironic and whacky. Although *Returning Home* is dedicated to Anna's 'physical return to dirt and death' (Ross 2017: 141), she vividly conveys here how funny, impatient and feisty she is – and continues to be – as an artist moving through dying.

Anna's attitude to dying adheres to that of another post-modern dance pioneer, Yvonne Rainer.

---

[7] *Returning Home Moving with the Earth Body: Learning Lessons in Life, Loss and Liberation* (Open Eye Pictures 2003): directed by Andy Abrahams, body art by Eeo Stubblefield, performed by Anna Halprin. *Returning Home* follows *Still Dance with Anna Halprin* (1998–2002), another collaboration with Stubblefield. *Still Dance* is a series of photographs of Halprin blending her body into landscapes across North America. Like the film, the photographs also engage with 'processes of ageing, death and dying' (Worth and Poyner 2004: 93).

[T]he evolution of the aging body in dance fulfils the earliest aspirations of my 1960s peers and colleagues who tore down the palace gates of high culture to admit a rabble of alternative visions and options. Silence, noise, walking, running, detritus – all undermined prevailing standards of monumentality, beauty, grace, professionalism, and the heroic. It is high time to admit the aging body of the dancer into this by now fully recognized and respected universe. Aging is the ultimate goal and hurdle, one that I myself must confront. So I tell myself, Yvonne, keep on reading your texts, but continue to dance, aches and all. Farewell to mewling 'I no longer dance.' Dance, girl, dance, and to all who observe me, I challenge you, 'Pity me not.'

RAINER 2014: 5–6

FLIP-FLOPS AND TUNICS

Laughing Hole (La Ribot, 2006) is a durational performance directed and performed by La Ribot, Marie-Caroline Hominal and Delphine Rosay. *Laughing Hole* happens in gallery spaces. On 1 April 2009, I observed the version performed at the Pompidou Centre in Paris.

The audience enters and sits around the outside of the space. The floor is littered with oblong cardboard placards lying face down; the visible sides are blank. The three women enter, dressed in plain tunics and flip-flops. They are laughing. For approximately six hours they laugh, fall, pick up placards and stick them to the gallery walls with brown masking tape. Each woman carries a roll of tape on her arm. Their journeys are arduous. They repeatedly fall before reaching a placard and again before reaching a wall. They hold up the signs while suspended – always laughing – in various half-falling positions. The performers wear small body mics. Their laughter is manipulated technically by sound engineer Clive Jenkins, seated in the space with a soundboard.

Eventually, over many hours, the walls become covered with handwritten statements such as: ALIEN BRUTALITY, IMPOTENT TERROR, ILLEGAL HOLE, MY GUANTANAMO, BRUTAL WAR, MASSIVE SHIT, ANOTHER OCCUPATION, IMPORTANT DETENTION, PLEASE LINE UP, DISTURBINGLY LOST. While there are some lighter statements such as LAUGH LINE and JUST FOR FUN, the overall mood is political and focuses on the plight of immigrants and vulnerable outcasts. Dance academic Ramsay Burt describes *Laughing Hole* as representing 'outsiders, including those who are forgotten and ignored but at the same time exploited for their cheap labour and those that are not accorded the same human rights as white Western citizens' (Burt 2017: 101).

While the women seemingly mock institutional patriarchy, they have – and yet do not have – agency in laughter. The references to themselves as fallen women are as powerful as the references to displaced outsiders. La Ribot, laughing, rolls on the ground with a placard saying JUST SALES. Another performer holds the sign BRUTAL POLITICIAN between her legs. She is also laughing. La Ribot stands laughing on a speaker, precariously balancing on one leg, while extending the other in a balletic arabesque. She is about to fall, but her placard reads STILL HERE. The performers evoke – in sinister terms – the fate of fallen women and prostitutes. As these women persist in laughing, often hysterically, a sense seeps through me that I have entered an asylum where I am incarcerated, together with these women. Their flip-flops and tunics now suggest the uniforms of inmates in an oppressively airless mental asylum.

The event becomes an ordeal of endurance – certainly for me – as I increasingly experience the hysteria of the three women as cries for help. The performance brings to mind Stevie Smith's poem *Not Waving but Drowning* (1957). I sense a desperate fight against the current, my fears of slowly drowning. The performers' laughter becomes a supreme effort, an attempt to wave to us on the shore, while the current is dragging them under. Bemused at first, I feel myself sinking, without breathing. I am unnerved by my helplessness, my worldly blind/deafness to the predicament of others who are shouting yet never heard. I am scrabbling at the sides of *Laughing Hole*, longing to escape, unnerved by what I have agreed to attend. The falling and laughing of the women rock my viscera, reach inside me to create formidably disagreeable effects, not of humour – but a sense of darkness, unease and tragedy.

> Nobody heard him, the dead man,
> But still he lay moaning:
> I was further out than you thought
> And not waving but drowning.
>
> SMITH ([1957] 1972)

GIBBERISH

I push back furniture, roll up the carpet and prop the laptop on a high chair to stream my 'Gaga' dance class on Zoom. During each forty-five minute session, I respond to instructions from agile young men dancing in their living rooms in Tel Aviv or New York. First, I am invited to cover all the mirrors in my front room so I cannot watch myself. I begin moving, following their flowing imagery, an account of which I write without punctuation to give an impression of my subjective experience: research the curves arcing through flesh free up joints loosen muscles spine made fluid explore its ripples through liquid flesh work joints in turn in isolation directions change arms stretch apart rotating shoulder sockets cushion heels and toes extending hips circling hop on hot stove lightly stretch imagine streams washing bones clean bones jump bones drop let bones fall down hold my flesh up dust my body off with hands free neck loose twist back turn around continue curving simultaneously flexing joints together stretch reach hip-blade far from fingers opposite side thrusting outwards faster faster smaller larger sensing skin giving skin be present receiving info feeling inside outside activate muscles squeeze juice from muscles explore thick texture protest gravity resist oppose push back gravity stand in first position balletic turnout pull up *pliés* stretch foot *tendues* leg up *developés* while continuing to curve with all parts of my body don't let gravity shape me never fix welcome chaos let go keep on move on through though not with gravity collapse my muscles grab my muscles defying gravity seeking burning sting sensations pain of effort melting pleasure glowing cells continue curving through my joints all one distinct and all directions shake now shake more my body all parts loosen all keep curving keep on lightly turn on music groove and boogie keep on go on keep on dancing ... After forty-five minutes I Zoom-wave goodbye and collapse to the ground, exhausted.

Gaga is a training technique developed by Israeli choreographer Ohan Naharin, who has followed a convoluted career path since the 1970s through a range of dance genres, influences and aesthetic eras. His layered experience resonates in Gaga – a practice capturing the attention of dancers around the globe – which relies on imagery interwoven with balletic vocabulary and tasks that enhance 'alertness of the senses and the use of imagination' (Rottenberg 2011: 295).[8] After experiencing this practice myself, I appreciate a touch of irony in Ohad naming it after childish gibberish. While I fling and flail, thrust and thrash, and juggle to catch all the imagery and instructions streaming through Zoom, I am flooded with a torrent of memories, of different dance vocabularies – tantalizingly familiar yet just out of reach like the sound of words spoken with no consonants. Yes, just as gibberish relates to language as meaningless nonsense, so my body now comprises a chaotic jumble of impulse and movement. I am both utterly present and entirely absent. As I let go with my bones yet deny gravity with my flesh, as my muscles burn and I increase my speed, I am certainly not falling. I am unravelling ballet's formal shapes and fixed fronts while maintaining ballet's technique and resistance to gravity. An experience, not like floating or flying, but like endlessly treading water with increasing urgency never to sink or drown. Slow ... down.

---

[8] Gaga is also popular with non-dancers. The class is similar but without the ballet vocabulary.

REPRESENTED REAL

Staging Ages (2015), a dance theatre production directed by Hanna Gillgren and Heidi Rustgaard of H2Dance, addresses stereotypes of ageing.[9] The work was made in collaboration with intergenerational performers, the youngest being eleven and the eldest – me – being sixty-seven. The directors' decision to bring together intergenerational performers was key, and the starting point was derived from the stereotypes we all brought to the studio about each other's ages. The choreographic structure and content were built on a series of gestures and poses that emerged from improvised interactions between the various performers. These choreographed group meetings were interspersed with individual enactments of memories and future projections relevant to our personal lives. The group scenes spread horizontally across the stage, while individual memories cut the stage space from back to front. Each of us walked to the front of the stage, announced a specific age and enacted a gesture remembered from that age. Central to the performance

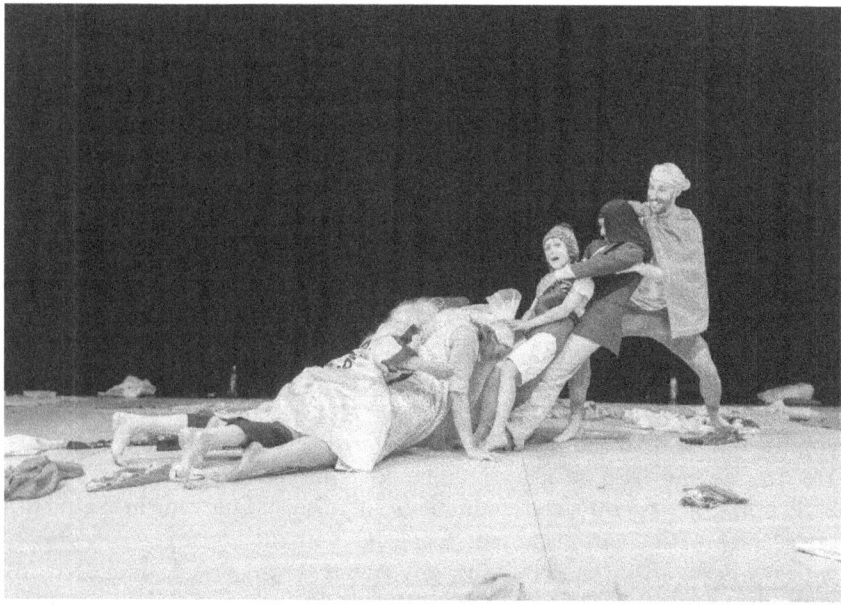

FIGURE 4.2 Staging Ages *(H2Dance, 2015). Performers: Emilyn Claid, Darren Anderson and Laura Doehler, alongside young dancers Honey Codrington-Makwana and Sandro Gillgren Bonfanti. Photo: Benedict Johnson.*

---

[9]Performers were Darren Anderson, Laura Doehler, Honey Codrington-Makwana, Sandro Gillgren Bonfanti, Sean Dodgson, Ella Sophoclides and myself. Music by Sylvia Hallett. http://h2dance.com/w-o-r-k-s/new-work/ (accessed January 2019).

was a chaotic playful dressing-up scene, that integrated our individual memories with the group choreography.

Towards the end of *Staging Ages*, I am improvising, on my own. While dancing, my co-performers project ageing stereotypes onto my body. Honey (thirteen years old) calls out, 'Seventy-two'. She comes forward and grabs my left foot, pressing it to the floor in a sickled position. I continue dancing, dragging my distorted foot along the floor. Darren (thirty years old) shouts 'Seventy-eight'. He comes forward and fixes my left arm and hand in arthritic tension, like a broken wing. I continue dancing. Laura (thirty-two years old) calls out 'Eighty-four', and curves my shoulders forward. Sean (eleven years old) shouts 'Ninety-two' and sets my legs shaking. Finally, Darren calling out 'Ninety-seven', tips my body over to one side. With these five restrictions, I continue dancing, gesturing with my right arm and hand that are free. Laura brings a chair and helps me to sit down. Sean twists my face towards the audience and takes away my spectacles. The performers stand around while I sit on the chair with my sickled foot, shaking legs, arthritic hand and arm, my collapsed spine and twisted face. My dancing partners then carry me, plus chair, and place me upstage left in the corner, looking towards the wings. Forgotten. From the spectators' perspective, this dance was challenging to witness, evoking feelings of loss while confirming their fears of falling old. 'I cried in that last dance' was a comment I received often after various shows (which I guess I was to take as a compliment).

When I first began performing these stereotypical ageing restrictions in *Staging Ages*, the scene was emotional for me, too, and I quickly realized I would need to establish a performing method whereby I was not overwhelming myself with the content. I absorbed myself with questions. How do I embody a gesture without its emotional content becoming overwhelming, yet remain fully present in the gesture? Can I find a fine line between performing gesture as a physical task and performing it as an emotive expression? I addressed these questions while moving, which became a play between real and represented ageing on my body. I began to sense when each ageing restriction began spilling into emotion and would then suspend that spill, hovering within the shape of the gesture with just enough awareness to evoke intention, but not enough to slip over the edge into emotion. I developed an ambiguity towards my narrative of ageing – playing between empty gesture and full expression – while sensing the uneasy balance, in life and performance, between external stereotype and sensed embodiment.

Falling old and dying entail continual negotiations between lived experience and culturally embedded stereotypical expectations, where the real and the represented are in constant play. There is always a temptation to succumb to external expectations. Each time I accept a seat from someone on the train, I am aware of this tension between how I appear to others and how I feel. The younger dancers' age projections were not mine, and I was not simply enacting an old person in *Staging Ages*. I was engaged in a two-fold task: working with a score of restriction while sensing a fine uncertainty between lived experience, and representations, of ageing.

CURIOSITY REFRESHED

I drop down into a squat while twisting my spine, corkscrew style, then stretch out an arm along the ground sliding out on my back into star position. I furl myself over to one side, then stretch out again on my back. I gather my limbs to the opposite side, spiral back up to standing position, then set off running, curving through space and banking through a crowd of bodies. Attuned now with others, I drop again. We rise, we run, we sing, we shoal, we flock, we rush and stream all around each other, our bodies twining, folding, coiling, orbiting the space and each other's mass. We are flowing at speed, buzzing through levels, swarming into the gaps opening up between us, crafting rhythms in collaboration and finding unison in ever-shifting patterns. Am I back in the 1970s at the X6 dance studio? No, it's 2010 and I am reliving the experience of Flying Low and Passing Through, dance forms created by David Zambrano.

David is a Venezuelan dancer who, in the mid 1980s, arrived in Manhattan and immersed himself in the dance improvisation scene flourishing at the time. He was energized by the innovations appearing in rapid succession – Skinner Release, Contact Improvisation, Westernized yoga, breakdance, non-hierarchical teaching and pedestrian action – all of which were revolutionizing politics and performance in the dance world by working, not against gravity, but with it. Following an injury, David set to work developing Flying Low and Passing Through, practices informed by this dynamic history. After many years of teaching internationally, David now works at his own studio in Brussels, a magnetic hub for young European dancers.

Flying Low is a practice emphasizing ways of getting into and out of the floor, as efficiently and economically as possible.[10] It does not consist of off-balance falling and the emphasis is not on the drop. The body instead is centred, and spirals down around a central axis. Dancers engage with gravity safely, economically and without resistance, moving in and out of the floor at speed and without extraneous effort. Passing Through is a practice of travelling rapidly through curved space, creating pathways, leading and following each other by turns, using hands, eyes and turning movements to narrowly avoid collision. Although students learn scores – basic movement scripts for getting in and out of the floor – these practices are for the most part non-hierarchical.

---

[10]Thanks to Scottish independent dancer Tess Letham, for sharing her knowledge of Flying Low.

There are no fixed points, no forward positions from which teachers hold court. Groups moves en masse, melding individual bodies in collective discovery of the timing and pattern of each improvisation. All assembled are as important as each other; the practice crosses boundaries, cultures and diverse physical abilities.

Until recently, dancers studied Flying Low and Passing Through as professional development, following their formal dance training. The work requires strength, stamina and co-ordination, along with keen anatomical awareness; it is particularly beneficial to dancers who, having achieved a high degree of proficiency and skill, are ready now to let it all go. Observing Flying Low workshops these days, I remember my youth at X6 Dance Space, my excitement about discovering these same movement patterns, spiralling toward and away from the ground around imaginary plumb lines, flocking through space in a group with no leader, improvising collectively in non-hierarchical space. Back then, we were curious, open to experimentation and eager to find new directions. Now, the forms are marketed, sleek and increasingly speedy, as befits the new generation of aspiring dancers in an accelerating, technological and media-driven age. Seeing the joy in dancers' faces as they practice Flying Low as a community of equals, as they collaboratively fall and rise around vertical axes, spreading and rolling along horizontal planes, I notice how the revolutionary impulses we explored in the 1970s continue to energize and refresh dancers' urge for change.

WHAT NOW

Exhaustion is not tiredness. Exhaustion is a consequence of persistent efforts to achieve set goals – and a state of successful productivity – and it follows the realization that success itself is always out of reach, there is nowhere to get to and achievement is but a delusion. This is a condition, not of tiredness, but of 'the dried up, the extenuated, and the dissipated' (Deleuze 1995: 12), where life's goals, needs, significations, plans and preferences lose their seductive appeal. 'That does not mean that you fall into indifferentiation . . . and you are not passive: you press on but towards nothing. You were tired by something, but exhausted by nothing' (Deleuze 1995: 12).

This exhaustion is existential. In *The Myth of Sisyphus* (1942), philosopher Albert Camus draws parallels with the figure from Greek mythology, Sisyphus, who every day, heaves a boulder up to the crest of a hill, only to see it roll down again. Exhaustion signals a moment of recognition, an awareness of life's effortful mundanity, a weariness, yet also an awakening.

> It happens that the stage-sets collapse. Rising, tram, four hours in the office or factory, meal, tram, four hours of work, meal, sleep and Monday,

Tuesday, Wednesday, Thursday, Friday and Saturday, according to the same rhythm – this path is easily followed most of the time. But one day the 'why' arises and everything begins in that weariness tinged with amazement ... Weariness comes at the end of the acts of a mechanical life, but at the same time it inaugurates the impulse of consciousness. It awakens consciousness and provokes what follows ... In itself weariness has something sickening about it. Here, I must conclude that it is good.

CAMUS [1942] 2005: 11

This notion of exhaustion, as a condition that signals potential for new directions, might describe the current state of the dance world from the perspective of European independent post-dance artists such as Mette Edvardsen, Jonathan Burrows and Mårten Spångberg.

The term 'post-dance' was first used as the title of a 2015 conference in Stockholm, which was not a conference in the conventional sense because it did away with all the usual protocols: no speakers, no papers, no organization, no evening performances. Rather, a group of people turned up to talk about what next. 'Post-dance gave us no solace ... peace was exchanged for a kind of productive anxiousness' (Spångberg 2017: 23). Following the conference, a collection of writings by attendees was published as *Post-Dance* (Andersson, Edvardsen and Spångberg 2017), the aim being to discharge problems, rather than harvest knowledge.[11]

Many post-dance artists, across Europe, have lived through institutional dance production of athletic bodies year after year for a market that feeds on spectacle. We are exhausted by neo-liberal demands for innovative performance products and by watching that product be swallowed up by capitalist consumerism. Dance faces 'a rather intricate dilemma being entangled in neoliberal governance, at the same time struggling with its autonomy ... knowing very well that neoliberal capitalism can and will instrumentalize everything, transform anything into a financial asset' (Spångberg 2017: 19). Post-dance artists emerge from dance's exhaustion asking 'what now?', and seeking means of expanding into the voids, gaps and overlooked interstices in the production of spectacle. One of those gaps is provided by academic research environments. 'Today it seems that the only places where there are still gaps and time (in a studio) which is not instrumental to production (product), is within artistic research and educational institutions. Let's take care of the gaps' (Edvardsen 2017: 221).

Exhaustion in the community of independent dance makers was also the underlying theme of *What Now*, a 2014 event held at Siobhan Davies

---

[11]Writers include Andre Lepecki, Mette Edvardsen, Mårten Spångberg, Bojanaa Cvejic and Jonathan Burrows.

Studios in London.¹² Twenty artists, including myself, were invited to take up residency at the studios for five days, with no goal other than to question how – without external influences and without a set agenda – we might interact with each other over an extended period of time. *What Now* 're-imagined itself as a public residency, taking as its starting point the suggestion that artists need to construct new conditions for the realization of community' (Independent Dance website). At *What Now* – we slowed down. Rather than identify ourselves through our attachments to artistic identities and products, we simply met to share time in the studios and over meals. We sat silently in circles, collectively pondering how to proceed through the day while resisting the pressure to make decisions, any of which could nudge us toward reverting to familiar conditions and practices. A frustratingly indecisive process, perhaps, somewhat reminiscent of the collective decision-making we undertook forty years previously at X6 Dance. Yet, as back then, this is how exhaustion with production can begin to uncover new pathways. As queer theorist Jack Halberstam suggests, valuing not doing is a political strategy, 'the maps of desire that render the subject incoherent, disorganized, and passive provide a better escape route than those that lead inexorably to fulfillment' (Halberstam 2011: 130).

At *What Now*, small acts of doing emerged out of nowhere, rather than being led by anyone with particular goals. One morning, I planned to do some writing in a space on the ground floor, then realized I had left my pen in the studio three floors up. It took the entire morning to retrieve my pen and return to the ground, thanks to the interactions I encountered on the way. My notes, written later that day, capture some of the experience:

> Work here seems to be about shedding individual identities, to see what emerges – or not – through collective waiting. Perhaps not making at all, but unmaking, failing to make. Each day we are being-in-relation with one another – to notice, to experience, to pause. Collaborative practice used to be about making something, however fractured it might be. Now I am simply experiencing a messy kind of being together. Recognisable frames are slipping away. I accept this messiness. What else is there now but to let go into nothing together? All has been done. All has been packaged up and sold. We meet with nothing, in calm urgency, because we have to, because only through slowing down the production of dance can we become attuned to potential growth. This challenge to let go of fixing things takes place during times of crisis, when change is sought.
>
> CLAID 2016: 270

---

¹² *What Now* was envisioned by Gill Clarke as an annual festival where speakers/artists would be invited to ask questions of dance and about dance. *What Now* 2014 was co-facilitated by Frank Bock, Hamish Macpherson and Efrosini Protopapa.

A VOID A DAY

The performance event WEST (Kinkaleri 2009) stares frankly at existential blanks of time and space as revealed through acts of falling. Kinkaleri is comprised of Italian artists from a range of disciplines – theatre, dance, video, radio plays, music composition, installation and print – who work together as a collective. WEST contains a compilation of videos of people falling in everyday locations in twelve cities around the world.[13]

The Paris sequence begins with a man and a woman in front of a carousel, against a background of blaring fairground noise. A number of people are standing nearby. A bicyclist crosses the foreground. The stillness of the couple catches my attention as conspicuous and strange in the context of the lively fairground. Abruptly, they fall – one backwards, one sideways – and land sprawling and spilling over pavement and road. They lie perfectly still while the bustle carries on around them. The scene in Rome depicts a young woman dressed in black, standing on the steps of an amphitheatre. In the background, statues of young, naked, white men on marble plinths are arrayed around the amphitheatre's curving lines. The woman falls suddenly. The camera maintains its steady view of a motionless body in black juxtaposed against upright white glory. In Amsterdam, a group of people drop to the ground beside a busy highway; the blur and din of traffic continue.

In making WEST, Kinkaleri approached complete strangers and asked them to undertake the experience of falling. Each participant was requested to maintain a steady gaze and – after the approximate amount of designated time had gone by – 'to fall to the ground ... in full awareness of it ... to leave a void, to operate autonomously as a body on the ground, without specific behaviour, without interpretation or melodrama' (Kinkaleri 2003). Participants were asked to lie still until informed that the filming had finished.

Prone and inactive, the performers' bodies present a stark contrast to events continuing around them; they expose the mundane, repetitive constancy of everyday time, an orientation that, in the context of falling, seems increasingly absurd. The simulated deaths in WEST bring existential perspectives to the way life is led with such pointless effort and speed. When these drops suddenly occur – with bodies falling out of everyday routines – everything else is subject to scrutiny and to questions into its existence and purpose. With this in mind, I clearly see how my own busy life – with consecutive days spent writing this book – could well represent an evasion of a void, my own avoidance of what in fact I'm exploring – the value of

---

[13] WEST was created over a five-year period, 2003–07, and premiered at Fabbrica Europa Festival in 2009.

falling as a creative resource. Kinkaleri's fallings expose that existential space; they spark the ever-pressing 'why?' of living, they trigger awakenings, they enliven quotidian lives.

OFF YOUR KNEES

The isolationist strategy in America in the 1930s, a belief that the more the country closed itself off from the world, the better off the country would be – was a protectionist policy that ultimately plunged the country into the Great Depression.[14] In dance history, the Great Depression is marked by the notorious dance marathons. Beginning in the 1920s as part of a craze to break world records in human feats, the marathons had become a popular form of entertainment by the mid 1930s (Martin 1994). As I gaze at the images on Mashable.com and read Martin's research, I imagine the following scenario.

It's 4 am and the gymnasium in Lanesboro, Minnesota, a provincial town in mid-west America, is hot and oppressive. A dance marathon began here twelve days ago with fifty couples; now only ten couples remain. Spatterings of spectators slouch in their seats, their attention drooping. Two dancers, Scooter and Madge, are locked in a bedraggled hug on the dance floor. Her arms are under his armpits, she is holding him up, hands clasped around his back. Scooter has locked his arms around her waist as he struggles against sleep, eyes closed, head lolling against her stomach, his feet dragging out behind him. Madge's back is on fire with pain in her effort to hold him from sliding further down. She is tottering in effort. She must keep them both dancing, she must prevent him from collapsing; yet the pull of gravity taunts them both. If his knees touch the floor, they will both be disqualified, back on the streets, cold and hungry. Their daily meals – sometimes ten snacks a day – and their dream of a cash prize will be gone. Madge must keep Scooter's knees from touching the ground. The woman of the couple next to them is moaning, her legs and feet are swollen, her dancing diminished to a slow stagger. Her partner punches her back and shouts at her to stay awake. Spectators nearby perk up, hoping for a fight or a disqualification. The music changes from waltz to rumba and the couples try to adjust to the new pace, shuffling and jigging up and down, faking dancing. The MC blows his whistle, a signal for the ten couples to stagger to one end of the gymnasium. The MC blows his whistle again and a race begins, dancers hobbling round

---

[14]The Great Depression was instigated to a certain extent by the signing of the Smoot-Hawley Tariff Act of 1930, which implemented a large increase in tariffs on imported goods, to protect American industry.

the space, round and round, attempting to run, while spectators cajole, cheer and jeer their favourite couple, alternating between pity and excitement. A spectator is standing and cheering, hoping to witness a spectacular collapse, a painful cry, blood or hysterics, or see a dancer hallucinate. One couple falls to their knees, another drops out. When the MC finally blows his whistle and turns on the dance music again, there are only three couples left. Madge and Scooter, dazed with exhaustion, are still standing, zombies walking.

Some dance marathons went on for weeks, contestants eating, drinking and shaving while dancing. They danced forty-five minutes of every hour, and when one partner took a break, the other kept dancing. Because the endless, sleepless dancing was not enough to engage spectators, marathons included sadistic events to entice bigger audiences, such as the run-around sprint race described above. Dancers willed themselves to stay standing, not for artistic reasons and not only for the possibility of a cash prize, but for the mundane reality of getting enough food for survival each day (Martin 1994).

The marathons were endurance tests for participants *and* constructed performances, seductive for their tension between reality and theatre. 'Survival was on display – but in quotation marks ... The theatrical aspect of marathons was always subverted by their brutish and cruel real-life qualities, just as the gruelling marathon life was constantly modulated into (painless, harmless) theatre' (Martin 1994: xx–xxi). The lack of sleep triggered strange behaviour that was real and performed. Performers' frequently had hallucinations, both performed for spectators and as lived experience. Where performance ended and real-life began was a fine line in the marathons. 'Picking daisies did in fact become a favourite way for performers to feign delirium' (Martin 1994: 61).

The real, excruciatingly slow falling of dancers, milked by managers of the marathons, allowed audiences to witness their own misery performed, to watch those worse off than themselves, to observe those who would shame, exhaust and humiliate themselves publicly – for a meal and promise of cash. Participants literally struggled to survive and performed this struggle at the same time, as a theatrical metaphor for economic failure, for America's shame. In my mind's eye I see Scooter slip through Madge's claw-like grip, his two knees grazing the well-worn floor. Their failure is complete. The spectators watch, some satisfied, some dismayed. Madge and Scooter's falling stood in for America's sense of shame during the Great Depression – theatricalized and made watchable. The seduction, creativity and drive of marathons were conjured by bodies of performers trapped in gravity's endless pull, while representing and expanding a cultural metaphorical space of economic, political and psychological falling.

In parallel, in New York, Martha Graham was reaching into her confidence as a choreographer and performer, developing codified, dramatic falls where each recovery represented idealized fulfilment of dreams for individual achievement. Across America, dance marathon couples were making a mockery of that dream. When performing a Graham fall, a dancer knows the precise timing of descent and recovery. There is no uncertainty, and by controlling time she has control over gravity. A marathon dancer has no control over time, which stretches out in front of her interminably, and the uncertainty provoked by endless time means gravity has power to dominate. The only certainty of time for a marathon dancer is the gradual exhaustion of her partner's body falling to the floor. His knees hit, time's up. In playing with time, dancers in both contexts were pitting weakness against strength to avoid the shame of failure that falling represented to Western ideals of success.

CAN I LET YOU GO?

Stand face-to-face with me. When I smile at you and you smile back we know we are holding things together – keeping each other up – supporting each other in this moment. Now I close my eyes and begin to fall. Intentionally and slowly, I release my smile, drop my head, allow its weight to curl me over to the ground. When I have fully dropped all my limbs into the floor, I stay there for a while, sensing gravity and ground, while you witness me. You remain standing throughout and notice what actions you would have liked to do and what emotions were evoked. I return to standing and we change roles.

When we have both taken a turn, we discuss the impact of watching each other's falls. What narratives, memories and emotions are evoked? When I was falling, did you want to reach out and bring me back up to standing? Did you want to make me feel better? Did you feel shame or embarrassment when you were falling yourself because I was watching? Were you embarrassed to witness *me* falling? Did you want to laugh? As we are relational, empathic beings, did you feel in some way you were losing me? Was there sadness? Witnessing someone surrender to the ground is freighted with culturally constructed notions of uncertainty, fear, loss and grief, which we often deny by joking or by stepping in to save the other. We experiment again. This time as I fall with my eyes closed, you follow me down and lie beside me on the ground. We stay there awhile, before exchanging roles. Again we discuss.

'Can I Let You Go?' is a safely controlled experiment in which we can examine our responses to each other falling, and therefore to our own falls. Observing someone falling like this can serve as a physical allegory for the wider cultural experience of loss and bereavement. Relational empathy is of course especially keen when someone we love falls or dies. Since we are empathic creatures, the fall of another can provoke our own memories and emotions of physical pain, loss and abandonment. In the field of Western medicine, doctors are trained to keep people alive. This objective is widely accepted and considered to be ethically correct, and the ethics are underscored by the relational distress we experience when we lose those we love. But when death is very close, recovery might not always be what those dying need or want; assuming so speaks more to our own experiences than to those of the dying. Rather than my need to upright the situation with exhaustive attempts to bring about her recovery, a dying person might prefer my relational ability *to be with* her dying. Rather than avoiding this darkly looming abyss, I have the option of entering that vacuum and understanding her presence there so that she is not alone. This is a far from straight-forward process; appreciating when and if to let someone go is neither easy nor comfortable. 'Can I Let You Go?' will always need a question mark. Yet if I sense falling somatically, I can begin to tender understanding of – and support for – my own and others' loss.

A client who came to work with me characterized her stressful life as 'walking a tightrope'. She felt terrified at the prospect of falling off and incapable of putting down her baggage for fear of losing balance. Somatic body work and engagement with gravity was key to our work together. She learnt through the process to fully exhale, to become aware of her weight in the chair and eventually to lower herself down and experience the gravitational support and comfort of the ground. Only then did she feel secure enough to unlock the grief she'd held frozen since her mother's death two years previously, to tell me of the agonizing decision to turn off her mother's life support and the feeling that she could never leave her dead mother's side. This was an event she had resisted revisiting by living her life high on a tightrope. Her story evoked memories of my own mother's death, and we cried together, there, on the floor. By acknowledging that I knew – in my own body – what she was experiencing as she fell, by knowing how she was supported by gravity and the ground, I could join her empathically in that experience, rather than reactively wanting to restore her to standing. Through this shared therapeutic exercise of witnessing each other falling, grief and fear are gently processed and rendered bearable.

NOTHING IN OUR WAY

I'm sitting in a small, south London studio theatre watching *No Title* (2014), a piece made and performed by Mette Edvardsen.[15] She walks on stage wearing a faded T-shirt, jeans, trainers and no make-up. She stands centre

---

[15]Performed as part of *Fest en Fest* 2020.

stage, removes her trainers and closes her eyes. Facing us, she begins a monologue she maintains throughout the piece.

> The beginning is gone. The space is empty and gone. The prompter has turned off his reading lamp and gone . . . Walls, other walls, a door opening and closing, gone. The ceiling gone. Lamps and speakers hanging, shadows moving in silence, gone. One leg and one arm, gone. One, two, and eight, gone. Hidden cables, power supply, black out, green emergency exit lights, gone. The corners of the room are gone. The foreground and background gone. Me not gone, not sleeping, not done, not gone. Layers of paint, holes in the wall and marks on the floor, what this space has told you already, gone. Fire extinguisher, people sitting in the dark, and the sound of rain, gone. Lipstick, chewing gum, wallets and mobile phone switched off, minute earlier, one year later, gone. Microphone stand, gone. The backdrop and the curtains are gone . . . tables, chairs, plants, gone.
> EDVARDSEN 2014

She walks slowly around the space several times with her eyes still closed, then returns to face her audience.

> Walking in circles, gone. Counting to one hundred gone . . . closeness gone. Things turning out exactly as planned, gone.
> EDVARDSEN 2014

She walks to the back of the stage, scrabbles for a piece of white chalk and – with her eyes still closed – draws a line from the back to the front of the stage. She then crawls back upstage, rubbing the line out as she goes, but missing much of it without the use of her eyes. 'Line gone,' she says, and walks back downstage.

> Distinction between thinking and doing has gone. Distinction has gone. Between has gone. Details are gone. The thing I wanted to say is gone. Things that do not speak are gone. Things we are unable to speak about are gone.
> EDVARDSEN 2014

She then takes stick-on representations of open eyes from her shoes and attaches them to her eyelids.

> Not looking, not not looking, not not wearing glasses, not not better like this, not not staring, not not looking back, not not looking another way, I was not here, I was not gone, the beginning of time is gone. The ice age is gone. The stone age is gone.
> EDVARDSEN 2014

At the end of the piece, she finds her shoes and puts them on. She walks to a side wall, takes off the fake eyes and sticks them on the wall. She walks back to centre stage, opens her eyes, and her final words are 'Darkness gone'.

Mette works within the context of European post-dance, a community of artists who share a disillusion with dance production and spectacle, a community united by the exhaustion of its members at meeting Western, neoliberal, production market demands. Dance need not be a primarily visual art form, she says, but can concern itself with 'how senses are working together' (Edvardsen 2017: 217). She does very little on stage; her curiosity is engaged by what else might be present beside her image, by what else might be imagined or shared between herself and her audience.

Mette's rejection of theatrical magic, spectacle, desires to please, dramatic expression and dancing or dance codes allows me to sense her presence in performance and a vulnerability that is both hers and mine. Her attention to the 'gone-ness' of material things means neither of us can hide behind anything, and I feel immersed in emptiness of affect. An existential nothingness pervades. Yet I do not feel despair. Exhilaration appears with the dawning sense that being alive is simply a clarity of perception, an affirmation of presence, a beginning, a relief. I am reminded of Mary Fulkerson's words on stillness, written almost thirty years previously. 'In my experience most of what is presented to me as believable, real and known is open to question. When faced with examination in stillness most ideas will show themselves to be irrelevant, unimportant, non-sequitors' (Fulkerson 1981: 6).

FIGURE 4.3 *Mette Edvardsen in* No Title *(2014). Photo: Bernhard Müller/ PNEU Festival 2020, SZENE Salzburg.*

Mette's text strips everything relentlessly away, while providing clarity on what remains. As she notes in the programme, '*No Title* is a writing in space, a writing that is both additive and subtractive. It is a writing that traces and erases, that moves and halts, that looks at things that are not there and recovers that which is instead'. She utters the final words 'darkness gone' when she opens her eyes and catches the light. The clutter of life, the detritus of assumptions, have been wiped away, which allows me to see her in sharp focus. Looking at her looking back at me brings a piercing sense of the fragility of human connection, vulnerably exposed. Nothing in our way.

BODY STORIES

The philosophy of ageing I seek to follow is one of paradox – to fully let go into dying, both physically and psychologically, yet be curious and adventurous while doing so. This contradiction parallels my experience in dance, of moving downwards in partnership with gravity to release a spread of movements and imagination. It is a paradox that manifests through my ageing body. As my body stills, physically stored memories, linked to movement, expand. As I sink into ageing, I become increasingly intrigued with how movement is recalled and how I acquired habitual dance movements. With careful attention, I can pick up on rich seams of stories unleashed by extending a limb; some are encoded in the sensation of movement, some in the image of the action. And, depending on how I execute the gesture, and the particular context, different kinds of memories emerge. I have only to stand in a studio – and look about – to be flooded with memories of other studios and of specific experiences of dancing. I can perhaps best describe this matrix of body, gesture, memory and space with notes I jotted down after performing in an improvisation session with *Staging Ages* (2015, dir. Hanna Gilgren and Heidi Rustgaard).

> A drop into a hip, a turned out foot, lifted wrist, shoulder curved forward, a slow turn of my head, drop to a knee, a ripple through spine and arms, clasp of my hands, an Achilles stretch and a circling pelvis with my body leaning forward. I want to slow this improvisation down to respect each gesture's memories. As I twist my torso with arms above my head, I remember a stage school performance of flamenco in childhood, composed in my bedroom with a group of classmates while drinking stolen sherry from my father's cabinet. Lunging into a kneel with my hands on my hips, I am 13 years old, performing a tarantella, taught by a teacher who knew nothing of tarantellas, except what had been appropriated by the Imperial Society of Teachers of Dancing. I am wearing a costume made by my mother with blue taffeta bows down my

bodice front. When I open my arms, I remember being a swan – and our supple, wing-like sweeping as a line of pale girls in bright white tutus run across the stage in the glare of footlights. With my right arm stretched out to the side, I remember the smelly green gym mats at X6 Dance Space and my attempts at mastering Aikido rolls where I am supposed to slide down the underside of my arm and lengthen myself out through my little finger. Turning my head over my left shoulder, I am performing in a small town in Northern England, looking to the wings for my dancing partner who has sprained his ankle and is frantically waving at me to improvise on my own. I slap my own wrist and am infused with seductive sensations. Did I learn that as a daughter, a sibling, an adolescent, a mother, or a lover? I clasp my hands behind by back, lower my head and draw my feet together, and I am engulfed by echoes of giggles and tears, being scolded for stealing plums from my godmother's garden.

CLAID 2017, unpublished notes

This is a practice of unlearning what has been implicitly remembered in order to take agency for what I have learnt. In philosophy, Merleau-Ponty's notion of the 'lived body' and of memory as embodied (1962) led the way for new phenomenological insights (Gendlin 1996; Sheets-Johnstone 1999; Parviainen 2002), including the distinction between explicit and implicit types of embodied memory (Fuchs 2012). Implicit memory includes knowledge acquired through repetition – to the point where it becomes habitual and involuntary – while explicit memory refers to the recollection of single incidents. As I turn older – and my gestures grow slower and more constrained – my body's continuing ability to re-enact movements from its store of implicit memories is interrupted by the *explicit* memories these movements evoke.

Learning to dance – training as a professional dancer – requires daily practice until movements become habit. Culturally defined movements of race, class and gender are also assigned to unconscious memory through habitual, repetitive process.[16] The constant repetition of kinetic patterns ingrains gestures into our flesh as implicit memories, in the same way we learn to stand and walk. These patterns are re*presented* whenever needed, implicitly remembered yet appearing in the present in a dancer's actions. 'Implicit memory does not represent the past, but re-enacts it through the body's present performance' (Fuchs 2012: 11).[17] Put simply, a sensed gesture

---

[16]Implicit cultural memory involves procedural body memory, situational, intercorporeal and incorporative memory (Koch and Harvey 2012; Panhofer 2017).

[17]Practitioners of Dance Movement Therapy integrate phenomenological knowledge of embodied memory into their work with trauma clients or others experiencing mental or physical health issues (Payne 1992). Dance provides therapeutic access to repressed or forgotten memories and can also bring pre-verbal memories stored in the body into present awareness. Somatic practitioners working in the fields of dance and therapy have long been familiar with the relationship between pain, memory and physical alignment (Ogden and Fisher 2015).

conjured into the present from implicit memory can evoke explicit recall of people, places, events and things, along with a gush of sensual details. Gestures themselves can release streams of stories. A parallel can be drawn with the iconic moment in Marcel Proust's *Remembrance of Things Past* (1913), where the fragrance of a madeleine floods the narrator with explicit recollections of implicit childhood memories. Fuchs labels this phenomenon a *'meaning core*. It is a nodal point of bodily recollection into which the lived past has condensed, as it were, and from which new meanings may unfold' (Fuchs 2012: 20, original emphasis). Kinesthesia is the sense of how limbs, joints, muscles and organs move in time and space, and much like the sense of smell, taste, hearing or sight, it too evokes memory. The performance of specific gestures can reveal complex histories associated with those actions.

> I take a step forward, look ahead down a long diagonal across the studio floor. I track the distance in my mind's eye and I am flooded with memories. Ballet class every Wednesday evening – aged eleven – I am standing in the corner waiting my turn to dance down to the corner diagonally opposite with a sequence of pirouettes. My legs are bruised from fighting with the boys outside and my stomach extended with white bread, butter and jam – all forbidden – I've scarfed for tea at a friend's house. I look down the diagonal again and I remember running and sliding into long lateral falls in Studio 6 at Dartington College – the Kurt Jooss studio – exhilarated by the view, the Devonshire hills stretching away through ceiling-to-floor windows. Or, I am in New York at the Graham studios queuing in line to perform: four jumps on the spot then four little prances bounding forward with my arms held stiffly at my sides. Or, in countless other contemporary dance studios – run-run-leap, run-run-leap – executed at speed while the pianist pounds keys in the corner. As I improvise – continuing to move forward along diagonal lines – stories appear and then slip away. I am writing them down now in an attempt to capture the fleeting colours and shapes. I pause – mid movement – to wonder why I ever do more, when such a small gesture evokes history and memories so rich. Why move at all, with imagination so alive?
>
> CLAID 2017, unpublished notes

These notes – which I wrote sitting on the floor of a dance studio – illustrate a practice of moving, remembering and writing, an interweaving process facilitating active conversation between all three components. The practice becomes livelier as I grow older. As a young person dancing, I was generally focused on getting better at it, on improving my technique, on increasing speed, extension and expansion. While I was aware of staying present to the physical sensations and external expression of any given action, my attention was more likely drawn to defining and perfecting particular movements, to ensuring their clearest articulation in time and space. Also, dancing used to be about using my skills to 'say something'. But not any more. I no longer have anything I need to say. As I turn my face towards the process of dying, an explosion of memories is taking place. Perhaps – because I am slowing down – there is more time to hear the echoes of gestures, the resonance of empty studios. I am ageing along with the memories of youth engraved in my body, patterned in my mind, memories I'm able to access anew by allowing my body to be old. Imagination and dying flourish hand in hand.

I enter a multi-dimensional haze in which a shed-load of memories dissolve into each other, tendering ways through, around and between, colliding, coalescing, catching. Depth and surface of body and recall are porously undefined, endlessly biddable.

A CRUEL SPRING

My sense of precarity intensifies. Invisible and air-borne, Covid-19 races round the globe, whipping through Europe, sweeping us from our feet, tossing us into whirlwinds of anxiety with no clear landings in sight. With over forty thousand people dead, the UK's death toll has exceeded that of any other European country. Medical science has no solution and no one yet knows just when or how this culling of nature's will end. The language used to describe the stages of living with the virus is increasingly nourished by orientational metaphors that are loaded with emotional and psychological intent. We are in lock*down* while numbers of deaths were *rising*, now they are *falling*. We were reaching the *peak*, now we are *flattening* the curve. April merges into May and the government suggests we begin to return to work – to get the economy moving – so now we are *coming down* the other side of the mountain while *ramping up* the economy. Metaphorically and psychologically, landing seems to be continuously deferred.

How presumptuous am I to suggest that falling – with body at the mercy of gravity and ground – could offer any kind of support? Yet I do know how panic and anxiety are calmed by gravity's pull, when we accept its power to hold us and draw us towards physical and psychological ground. As our most valuable support, the ground's not so far away. To land well, though, or to land at all, will require our consent to the reality of falling.

I look up from my laptop and gaze out at the garden. It's a splendid spring day. Poppies are shooting up, irises are in full flag glory and the Japanese maple is full of promise with carmine burgundy buds. A blackbird sings, perched on the swinging feeder under a high blue sky. I stand in the doorway, my flesh tingling in the fresh air while the afternoon sun warms the ground. The season is teasing me, engaging my senses with pleasures unavailable to others less privileged. Locked down, stuck at home, we stoically wait for a thinning of the herd and a world forever changed.

A fantasy of a future day floods into my thoughts. It's summer and I'm out with my son and his family. We're chatting and laughing. My grandson and I race up a hillside. At the top we find we're not alone. Grandmas and grandpas, co-parents and caregivers come over the brow from every direction to mingle and stroll, holding hands with the toddlers, nestling babies in their arms. Old and young together again, after months of separation, eyes shining with tears of grief and relief. Now we're shouting and running again, falling into the grass, tumbling and rolling down the slope of the hill, the aroma of damp earth infusing our senses. We clamber back up to fall down again on the lush green grass, again and again, tipping, toppling, slipping and sliding, more and more are joining us now, a supple cascade, continuous flow of youthful flesh and ancient bones, fearless, timeless companions.

DANCE WITH ME

We are at a nightclub. We are coming to the end of a long night and are both exhausted, thinking about sleep, but determined to continue dancing for a few more hours. The music drives on, echoing our mood of determination and exhaustion. Come in close to me to enact this score. Clasp your arms over and around my shoulders, while I embrace you by sliding my arms around your back. Let's snuggle in and dance as one, letting the music play on. Gradually, give your weight over to me. Rest your head on my shoulder, and let your knees sag while I hold you up from touching the floor with anything but your feet. Can you let me take your entire weight? Can I continue the dance while keeping you from falling? Let's try to maintain this dance for as long as possible – you yield to me while I hold you up. We stop, I am exhausted.

Dance with me again. This time, let me give my weight to you, rest on you – while you keep on dancing. When you are no longer able to hold me up, drop your arms and let me go. There is little chance I'll hurt myself as I will release when falling, and the ground is not so far away. It is such a simple movement to free your arms and let me drop. Yet can you do this? How do you feel when you let me go? Do you feel you are abandoning me?

Now switch and let me support you in a close embrace while we dance and allow me to let you go. How does it feel to be released from my grip? Actions and emotions are interwoven; whatever affects you also touches me. We are of each other, with love and care. Turn up the music and let's meet again. Let's hug, dance and let each other fall, commit each other to gravity and ground.

BIBLIOGRAPHY

Acocella, J. (2013), 'Bausch's Inferno', in R. Climenhaga (ed.), *The Pina Bausch Sourcebook: The Making of Tanztheatre*, 212–23, London and New York: Routledge.
Agis, G. and J. Moran (2002), 'In Its Purest Form: A Rare Insight into the Work of Joan Skinner', *Animated*, Winter: 20–22.
Albright, A.C. (2013), 'Falling', *Performance Research*, 18 (4): 36–41.
Albright, A.C. (2017), 'The Perverse Satisfaction of Gravity', in N. Nakajima and G. Brandstetter (eds), *The Aging Body in Dance: A Cross-Cultural Perspective*, 63–72, London: Routledge.
Albright, A.C. (2019), *How to Land: Finding Ground in an Unstable World*, New York: Oxford University Press.
Allegranti, B. (2017), '(Im)possible Performatives: A Feminist Corporeal Account of Loss', in V. Karkou, S. Oliver and S. Lycouris (eds), *The Oxford Handbook of Dance and Wellbeing*, 369–90, London: Oxford University Press.
Altman, N. (2004), 'Humiliation, Retaliation, and Violence', *Tikkan Magazine*, 20 (1): 16–59.
An Odd Couple (1965) [Film], dir. Alan Schneider and Samuel Beckett, UK: BFI.
Anderson, L. (1982), 'Walking and Falling', in *Big Science,* [Album].
Apter, M. (1992), *The Dangerous Edge: The Psychology of Excitement*, New York: Free Press.
Aramphongphan, P. (2015), 'Real Professionals? Andy Warhol, Fred Herko and Dance', *PAJ: A Journal of Performance and Art*, 37 (2): 1–12.
Arditti, M. (1993), 'At the Theatre of Blood and Bruises', *The Independent*, 6 November. Available online: https://www.independent.co.uk/arts-entertainment/dance-at-the-theatre-of-blood-and-bruises-dv8-tread-a-fine-line-between-athleticism-and-masochism-1502507.html (accessed April 2020).
Bailes, S. (2011), *Performance Theatre and the Poetics of Failure: Forced Entertainment, Goat Island, Elevator Repair Service*, London, New York: Routledge.
Bartlett, N. (2009), 'Plunge into Your shame', in D. Halperin and V. Traub (eds), *Gay Shame,* 339–56, Chicago: University of Chicago Press.
Beckett, S. (1983), *Worstward Ho,* New York: Grove Press.
Benayoun, R. (1982), *The Look of Buster Keaton,* New York: St. Martin's Press.
Benjamin, J. (1988), *Bonds of Love: Psychoanalysis, feminism & the problem of domination*, New York: Pantheon Books.
Benjamin, W. ([1935] 1998), *Understanding Brecht*, trans. A. Boslock, London: Verso.
Bergson, H. (1913), *Laughter: An Essay on the Meaning of the Comic*, London: Macmillan.

Berlant, L. (2011), *Cruel Optimism*, Durham, NC: Duke University Press.
Blake, W. (1790), *The Marriage of Heaven and Hell*. Available online: http://www.blakearchive.org/exist/blake/archive/work.xq?workid=mhh (accessed August 2013).
Born to Fly: Elizabeth Streb vs. Gravity (2014), [Film] dir. Catherine Gund, Aubin Pictures.
Brennan, M. (1997), 'Eurocrash – Jury's Verdict Awaited', *Dance Theatre Journal*, 13 (3): 4–5.
Brezavšček, P. (2013), 'Three Falls and the Event: Yves Klein, Bas Jan Ader and Tehching Hsieh', *Performance Research*, 18 (4): 56–62
Brown, B. (2012), 'Listening to Shame', *TED Talk*. Available online: https://www.ted.com/talks/brene_brown_listening_to_shame? (accessed July 2017).
Bourdieu, P. (1984), *Distinction: A Social Critique of the Judgement of Taste*, Cambridge, MA: Harvard University Press.
Buckwalter, M. (2012), 'Release – A "History"', in N. Topf (ed.), *CQ Chapbook 3: The Anatomy of Center*, 3–8, Northampton, MA: Contact Editions.
Burrows, J. (2017), 'Keynote Address', in D. Andersson, M. Edvardsen and M. Spångberg (eds), *Post-Dance*, 83–100, Stockholm: MDT.
Burt, R. (2006), *Judson Church Theater: Performative Traces*, New York: Routledge.
Burt, R. (2008), 'Preferring to Laugh', *Parallex*, 14 (1): 15–23.
Burt, R. (2017), 'Laughter from the Surround', in *Ungovering Dance: Contemporary European Theatre Dance and the Commons*, 99–116, Oxford: Oxford University Press.
Buta, B., D. Leder, R. Miller, N.L. Schoenborn, A.R. Green and R. Varadhan (2018), 'The Use of Figurative Language to Describe Frailty in Older Adults', *The Journal of Frailty & Aging*, 7 (2): 127–33.
Butler, J. (2004), *Precarious Life: The Powers of Mourning and Violence*, London: Verso.
Camus, A. ([1942] 2005), *The Myth of Sisyphus*, J. O'Brien (trans.), London: Penguin Books.
Carroll, L. (1865), *Alice's Adventures in Wonderland*. London: Macmillan. Available online: http://www.gutenberg.org/files/11/11-h/11-h.htm (accessed January 2020).
Chain Reaction (2012), Caitlin Moran talks to Jennifer Saunders, [Radio programme], BBC Radio 4, 24 August.
Chesterton. G.K. (1908), 'Spiritualism', in *All Things Considered*, London: Methuen.
Chrisafis, A. (2007), 'Down and Out in Paris', *The Guardian*, 24 March. Available online: https://www.theguardian.com/artanddesign/2007/mar/24/photography.features (accessed May 2020).
Claid, E. (2006), *Yes? No! Maybe. . . Seductive Ambiguity in Dance Theatre Performance*, London: Routledge.
Claid, E. (2016), 'Messy Bits', in N. Colin and S. Sachsenemaier (eds), *Collaborations in Performance Practice*, 259–79, London: Palgrave Macmillan.
Claid, E. (2018), 'Walking on Glass', *Emotion, Space and Society*, 28: 89–93.
Cohen, B.B. (2012), *Sensing, Feeling, and Action: The Experiential Anatomy of Body-Mind Centering*, Northampton, MA: Contact Editions.

Crafton, D. (1995), 'Pie and Chase: Gag, Spectacle and Narrative in Slapstick Comedy', in K. Karnick and H. Jenkins (eds), *Classical Hollywood Comedy*, 106–19, London: Routledge.

Cvetkovich, A. (2003), *An Archive of Feelings: Trauma, Sexuality, and Lesbian Public Cultures*, Durham, NC: Duke University Press.

Dance Without Steps (1978), [VHS documentary] made for *Arts & Environment*, producer N. Smith, published by BBC in collaboration with Open University.

Dancing Inside (1999), [Film] dir. Gillian Lacey, APT Film and Television Production. Available online: https://vimeo.com/174011040.

Davis, D. (2000), *Breaking (Up) at Totality: A Rhetoric of Laughter*, Carbondale, IL: Southern Illinois University Press.

Debord, G. (1967), *Society of the Spectacle*, trans. K. Knabb, London: Rebel Press.

de Frantz, T. (2017), 'I Am Black (You Have to be Willing Not to Know)', *Theatre*, 47 (2): 9–21.

de Frantz, T. (2018), 'Them. Recombinant Aesthetics of Restaging Experimental Performance', in B. Bissell and L.C. Haviland (eds), *The Sentient Archive: Bodies, Performance, and Memory*, 268–92, Middletown, CT: Wesleyan University Press.

de Lauretis, T. (1984), *Alice Doesn't: Feminism, Semiotic Cinema*, London: Macmillan.

Deleuze, G. (1995), 'The Exhausted', *Substance*, 24 (3): 3–28.

De Mille, A. (1991), *Martha: The Life and Work of Martha Graham*, New York: Random House.

Derrida, J. (1981), *Dissemination*, trans. B. Johnson, London: Athlone Press.

De Vos, L. (2015), 'Always Looking Back at the Voyeur: Jan Fabre's Extreme Acts on Stage', in G. Rodosthenous (ed.), *Theatre as Voyeurism: The Pleasure(s) of Watching*, 29–49, London: Palgrave Macmillan.

Diack, H. (2012), 'The Gravity of Levity: Humour as Conceptual Critique', *RACAR: Revue d'art Canadienne / Canadian Art Review*, 37 (1): 75–86.

Duggan, P. (2009), 'The Touch and the Cut: An Annotated Dialogue with Kira O'Reilly', *Studies in Theatre and Performance*, 29 (3): 307–25.

Dumbadze, A. (2013), *Bas Jan Ader: Death is Elsewhere*, Chicago: University of Chicago Press.

Dyer, R. (1992), *Only Entertainment*, London: Routledge.

Eddo-Lodge, R. (2017), *Why I'm No Longer Talking to White People About Race*, London: Bloomsbury.

Edvardsen, M. (2017), 'The Picture of a Stone', in D. Andersson, M. Edvardsen and M. Spångberg (eds), *Post-Dance*, 216–21, Stockholm: MDT.

Ekman, P. (2003), *Emotions Revealed*, New York: Owl Books.

Fanon, F. (1967) *Black Skin, White Masks*, New York: Grove Press.

Felsenburg, B. (1999), 'Wim Vandekeybus', in M. Bremser (ed.), *50 Contemporary Choreographers*, 357–63, London: Routledge.

Fensham, R. (2010), 'Not Walking Falling: Performing Intimate Immensity', in J. Rutherford and B. Holloway (eds), *Halfway House The Poetics of Australian Spaces*, 195–213, Melbourne: University of Western Australia Press.

Fox, C. (2013), 'An Avant-garde Falling', *Performance Research*, 18 (4): 63–8.

Frank, R. (2001), *Body of Awareness*, Cambridge and Santa Cruz, CA: Gestalt Press.

Frank, R. and F. La Barre (2011), *The First Year and the Rest of Your Life*, New York: Routledge.
Franko, M. (2014), *Martha Graham in Love and War: The Life In The Work*, Oxford: Oxford University Press.
Freedman, R. (1998), *Martha Graham: A Dancer's Life*, New York: Clarion Books.
Freud, S. (1925), 'Some Psychical Consequences of the Anatomical Distinction Between the Sexes', in J. Strachey (ed.), *The Standard Edition of the Complete Psychological Works of Sigmund Freud*. 19, 241–60, London: The Hogarth Press.
Friedman, N. (1993), 'Fritz Perls's "Layers" and the Empty Chair: A Reconsideration', *The Gestalt Journal*, 16 (2): 95–119.
Fulkerson, M. (1981), 'The Move to Stillness', *Theatre Papers*, The Fourth Series No. 10, Dartington: Dartington College of Arts.
Fuchs, C. (1996), '"I Wanna be Your Fantasy": Sex, Death, and The Artist Formerly Known as Prince', *Women & Performance: A Journal of Feminist Theory*, 8 (2): 137–51.
Fuchs, T. (2012), 'The Phenomenology of Body Memory', in S. Koch, T. Fuchs, M. Suma and C. Muller (eds), *Body Memory, Metaphor and Movement*, 9–22, Philadelphia: John Benjamins.
Gibson, E.J. and Walk, R.D. (1960), 'Visual Cliff', *Scientific American*, 202: 64–71.
Goffman E. ([1967] 2005), *Interaction Ritual: Essays in Face-to-Face Behavior*, New Brunswick, NJ: Transaction Publisher.
Gendlin, E. (1996), *Focusing-Oriented Psychotherapy*, New York: Guilford Press.
Gottschild, B. (1996), *Digging the Africanist Presence in American Performance Dance*, Westport, CT: Praeger Publishers.
Gottschild, B. (2003), *The Black Dancing Body: A Geography from Coon to Cool*, London: Palgrave Macmillan.
Graff, E. (1997), *Stepping Left: Dance and Politics in New York City, 1928–1942*, Durham, NC: Duke University Press.
Graff, E. (2004), 'When Your Heart Falls: The Drama of Descent in Martha Graham's Technique and Theater', *Women & Performance: A Journal of Feminist Theory*, 14 (1): 107–15.
Graham, M. (1991), *Blood Memory*, New York: Doubleday.
Greiner, C. (2007), 'Researching Dance in the Wild', *TDR: The Drama Review*, 51 (3): 140–55.
Grosz, E. (1989), *Sexual Subversions. Three French feminists.* Sydney: Allen & Unwin.
Grosz, E. (1995), *Space, Time and Perversion*, London: Routledge.
Gullette, M.M. (2004), *Aged by Culture*, Chicago: University of Chicago Press.
Hahnemann, S. ([1842]1996), *Organon of the Medical Art*, Berkeley, CA: Group West.
Halberstam, J. (2011), *The Queer Art of Failure,* Durham, NC: Duke University Press.
Hallett, A. and P. Smith (2017), *Walking Stumbling Limping Falling: A Conversation,* Charmouth: Triarchy Press.
Halperin, D. and V. Traub (2009), 'Beyond Gay Pride', in D. Halperin and V. Traub (eds), *Gay Shame*, 3–40, Chicago: University of Chicago Press.

Hanna, T. (1970), *Bodies in Revolt: A Primer in Somatic Thinking*, New York: Rinehart and Winston.
Hanna, T. (1988), *Somatics*, Boston: Addison-Wesley Publishing.
Hargreaves, M. (2004), 'Laughing, Crying, Contagion, Collapse', *Dance Theatre Journal*, 20 (2): 34–7.
Harvey, M. (2013), 'Promises Promises: Falling and the Best of Intentions and Falling in the Work of Three Live Artists', *Performance Research*, 18 (4): 83–90.
Heathfield, A. (2006), 'After the Fall: Dance Theatre and Dance Performance', in J. Kelleher and N. Ridout (eds), *Contemporary Theatres in Europe: A Critical Companion*, 188–98, New York: Routledge.
Hrab, O. (2016), 'Introduction', in M. Pawlouski, P. VerHelst and D. Byrne (eds), *Wim Vandekeybus: The Rage of Staging*, 5, Tielt: Lannoo Publishers.
Huxley, M. (2012), 'F. Matthias Alexander and Mabel Elsworth Todd: Proximities Practices and the Psychophysical', *Journal of Dance & Somatic Practices*, 3 (1–2): 25–42.
Innes, D. (2014), 'Why We Laugh: The Psychology of Humor and its Use in Film'. Available online: https://www.academia.edu/9728991/Why_We_Laugh_The_Psychology_of_Humor_and_its_Use_in_Film (accessed January 2020).
Irigaray, L. ([1977] 1985), *This Sex Which is not One*, Ithaca New York: Cornell University Press.
Irving, D. (2014), *Waking Up White, and Finding Myself in the Story of Race*, Cambridge, MA: Elephant Room Press.
Jacobs, L. (2009), 'Attunement and Optimal Responsiveness', in L. Jacobs and R. Hycner (eds), *Relational Approaches in Gestalt Therapy*, 131–69, New York: Gestalt Press.
Jacobs, L. (2014), 'Learning to Love White Shame and Guilt: Skills for Working as a White Therapist in a Racially Divided Country', *International Journal of Psychoanalytic Self Psychology*, 9 (4): 297–312.
Jacobs, L. and R. Hycner, eds (1995), *Relational Approaches in Gestalt Therapy*, Santa Cruz, CA: Gestalt Press.
Jeschke, C. and G. Vettermann (2000), 'Germany Between institutions and Aesthetics Choreographing Germanness?' in A. Grau and S. Jordan (eds), *Europe Dancing: Perspectives on Theatre Dance and Cultural Identity*, 55–78, London: Routledge.
Kaplan, E.A. (1983), *Women & Film*, London: Routledge.
Karkov, V., S. Oliver and S. Lycouris, eds (2017), *The Oxford Handbook of Dance and Wellbeing*, Oxford: Oxford University Press.
Keaton, B. (1960), *My Wonderful World of Slapstick*, New York: Doubleday.
King, J. (2004), 'Which Way is Down? Improvisations on Black Mobility', *Women & Performance: A Journal of Feminist Theory*, 14 (1): 25–47.
Kinkaleri (2009), *WEST*. Available online: https://www.kinkaleri.it/west.htm (accessed June 2017).
Kleinman, G. (2019), *Recreation and Significant Others: Seeking Post-work Possibilities in Contemporary Choreography*, PhD thesis, Dept. of Dance, University of Roehampton, London.
Knezevic, B. (2009), 'Amanda Coogan: The Fall, Kevin Kavanagh Gallery, Dublin, 25 June 2009', *Circa Art Magazine*, 15 July. Available online: http://circaartmagazine.website/reviews/amanda-coogan-the-fall-kevin-kavanagh-gallery-dublin-25-june-2009/ (accessed September 2019).

Knopf, R. (1999), *Theatre and Cinema of Buster Keaton*, Princeton, NJ: Princeton University Press.
Koch, S. and S. Harvey (2012), 'Dance/movement Therapy with Traumatized Dissociative Patients', in S. Kuch, T. Fuchs and M. Summa (eds), *Body Memory, Metaphor and Movement*, 269–386, Philadelphia: John Benjamins.
Koteen, D. and N.S. Smith (2008), *Caught Falling*, Northampton, MA: Contact Editions.
Kövecses, Z. (2000), *Metaphor and Emotion: Language, Culture and Body in Human Feeling*, Cambridge: Cambridge University Press.
Kristeva, J. (1980), *Desire in Language*, Oxford: Blackwell.
Laermans, R. and P. Gielen (2000), 'Flanders' Constructing identities: the Case of the Flemish Dance Wave', in A. Grau and S. Jordan (eds), *Europe Dancing: Perspectives on Theatre Dance and Cultural Identity*, 12–27, London: Routledge.
Lakoff, G. and M. Johnson (1980), *Metaphors We Live By*, Chicago: University of Chicago Press.
Leask, J. (2011), 'Lloyd Newson', in M. Bremser and L. Sanders (eds), *50 Contemporary Choreographers*, 2nd ed., 297–304, Routledge: London.
Lepecki, A. (2006), *Exhausting Dance: Performance and the Politics of Movement*, New York: Routledge.
Lepkoff, D. ([1976] 1997), 'Contact', *CQ/CI Sourcebook* 2: 16.
Levinas, E. (1989), 'Ethics as first philosophy', in S. Hand, (ed.), *The Levinas Reader*, 75–87, Oxford: Blackwell.
Levine, P. (1997), *Waking the Tiger: Healing Trauma*, Berkeley, CA: North Atlantic Books.
Low, S. (2016), 'The Speed of Queer: LaLaLa Human Steps and Queer Perceptions of the Body', *Theatre Research in Canada*, 37 (1): 62–78.
Lyall, S. (2020), 'For Prince Harry and his Wife Megan, a Tricky Balancing Act', *New York Times*, 8 January. Available online: https://www.nytimes.com/2020/01/08/world/europe/meghan-harry-united-kingdom.html (accessed May 2020).
Mackintosh, P. (2013), 'Falling About Research Lab'. Available online: https://roehamptondance.com/falling/writings/ (accessed July 2016).
Mackrell, J. (2015), 'Ultima Vez – What the Body Does Not Remember', *The Guardian*, 11 February. Available online: https://www.theguardian.com/stage/2015/feb/11/ultima-vez-what-the-body-does-not-remember-sadlers-wells-review (accessed June 2017).
Mackrell, J. (2016), 'Dancing up a Storm to Kate Tempest and Roller-skating for a Warhol Star', *The Guardian*, 23 May. Available online: https://www.theguardian.com/stage/dance-blog/2016/may/23/kate-tempest-and-roller-skating-for-andy-warhol-siobhan-davies (accessed May 2020).
Man On Wire (2008), [Film] dir. James Marsh, USA: Magnolia Pictures.
Martin, C. (1994), *Dance Marathons: Performing American Culture in the 1920s and 1930s*, Jackson, MS: University Press of Mississippi.
Martin, S. (2017), *Dancing Age(ing)*, New York: Columbia University Press.
Matt, P. (1993), *A Kinesthetic Legacy: The Life and Works of Barbara Clark*, Tempe, AZ: CMT Press.
McDonagh, D. ([1970] 1990), *The Rise and Fall and Rise of Modern Dance*, Princeton, NJ: A Cappella Books.

Merleau-Ponty, M. (1962), *Phenomenology of Perception,* London: Routledge and Kegan Paul.

Mercier, J. (2014), *Fucking with Ballet: Performing Queer Negativity*, PhD thesis, Royal Central School of Speech and Drama, London.

Mercier, J. (2019), 'Desperate Gestures', performance lecture, *Conservatoire for Dance and Drama Research Conference,* London School of Contemporary Dance.

Mr. Gaga (2016) [Film], dir. T. Heymann, Tel Aviv: Farbfilm, Heymann Brothers Films.

Mulvey, L. (1975), 'Visual Pleasure and Narrative Cinema', *Screen*, 16 (3): 6–18.

Muñoz, J.E. (2009), *Cruising Utopia: The Then and There of Queer Futurity,* New York: New York University Press.

Nakajima, N. (2017), 'Overview', in N. Nakajima and G. Brandstetter (eds), *The Aging Body in Dance: A Cross-Cultural Perspective*, 11–27, London: Routledge.

Nelson, L., S. Christiansen and S. Paxton (1981–2), 'Introduction to *Chute* Transcript', *CQ/CI Sourcebook,* 7: 86–7.

Nelson, R. (2006) 'Practice-as-research and the Problem of Knowledge', *Performance Research*, 11 (4): 105–116.

Novack, C. (1990), *Sharing the Dance: Contact Improvisation and American Culture*, Madison, WI: University of Wisconsin Press.

Ogden, P. and J. Fisher (2015), *Sensorimotor Psychotherapy Interventions for Trauma and Attachment*, New York: Norton.

Olsen, A. (2017), 'Reimagining the Dancing Body', in V. Karkou, S. Oliver and S. Lycouris (eds), *The Oxford Handbook of Dance and Wellbeing*, 179–93, Oxford: Oxford University Press.

Orange, D. (2008), 'Whose Shame Is It Anyway? Lifeworlds of Humiliation and Systems of Restoration', *Contemporary Psychoanalysis*, 44 (1): 83–100.

O'Gorman, R. and M. Werry, eds (2012), *On Failure*, special issue of *Performance Research*, 17 (1).

O'Reilly, K. (2017), *Kira O'Reilly: Untitled (Bodies),* H. Curtis and M. Hargreaves (eds), London: Intellect Books.

Osborne, L. and E. Claid (2015), 'Falling – A Creative Process', *GJANZ (Gestalt Journal of Australia and New Zealand)*, 12 (1): 17–29.

Panhofer, H. (2017), 'Body Memory and its Recuperation Through Movement', in V. Karkov, S. Oliver and S. Lycouris (eds), *The Oxford Handbook of Dance and Wellbeing*, 115–27, Oxford: Oxford University Press.

Parry, J. (1997), 'Defining the Cutting Edge', in L. Saunders (ed.), *At the Cutting Edge*, Proceedings of the 1996 NDTA/daCi Conference, 7, Finland.

Parviainen, J. (2002), 'Bodily Knowledge: Epistemological Reflections on Dance', *Dance Research Journal,* 34 (1): 112–13.

Pawlouski, M., P. VerHelst and D. Byrne (2016), *The Rage of Staging: Wim Vandekeybus*, Tielt: Lannou Publishers.

Paxton, S. (1975–6), 'Dartington March:', *CQ/CI Sourcebook*, 1: 4.

Paxton, S. (1977), 'Elizabeth Zimmer interview on CBC Radio', *CQ/CI Sourcebook*, 3: 23.

Paxton, S. (1979), 'A Definition', *Contact Quarterly*, Winter: 26.

Paxton, S. ([1986] 1997), 'The small dance', *Contact Quarterly's Contact Improvisation Sourcebook*, 1: 23–4. Available online: http://bodycartography.org/portfolio/smalldancestevepaxton/ (accessed May 2015).

Paxton, S. (2018), *Gravity*, Brussels: Contredanse Editions.

Payne, H. (1992), *Dance Movement Therapy: Theory and Practice*, London: Routledge.
Perls, F. (1969), *Gestalt Therapy Verbatim*, Moab, UT: Real People Press.
Petronio, S. (1979–80), 'Round Up', *CQ/CI Sourcebook* 5: 53.
Phelan, P. (1993), *Unmarked: The Politics of Performance*, New York: Routledge.
Phelan, P. (2010), 'Introduction', in E. Streb, *How to Become an Action Hero*, New York: Feminist Press.
Plevin, M. (2017), 'Portals of Conscious Transformation', in V. Karkov, S. Oliver and S. Lycouris (eds), *The Oxford Book of Dance and Wellbeing*, 231–54, Oxford: Oxford University Press.
Povinelli, D. and J. Cant (1995), 'Arboreal Clambering and the Evolution of Self-Conception', *The Quarterly Review of Biology*, 70 (4): 393–421.
Prickett, S. (1990), 'Dance and the Workers' Struggle', *Dance Research*, 8 (1): 47–61.
Probyn, E. (1995), 'Queer Belongings', in E. Grosz and E. Probyn (eds), *Sexy Bodies*, 1–18, London: Routledge.
Proust, M. (1913), *Swann's Way* [first volume of *Remembrance of Things Past*], Paris: Grasset.
Pozorski, A. (2014), *Falling After 9/11*, New York: Bloomsbury.
Quinlan, M. (2019), 'Mr. Gaga: Embodying the Exceptionalism of Ohad Naharin', *The International Journal of Screendance* 10: 74–93.
Rainer, Y. (1965), 'Some Retrospective Notes on a Dance for 10 People and 12 Mattresses called "Parts of Some Sextets"', *Tulane Drama Review*, 10: 168–78.
Rainer, Y. (2014), 'The Aching Body in Dance', *Performance Art Journal*, 106: 3–6.
Rajan, A. (2018), *The Decline of the West*, [Radio programme], BBC Radio 4, 18 July.
Ridout, N. (2006), *Stage Fright, Animals, and Other Theatrical Problems*, Cambridge: Cambridge University Press.
Ross, J. and Schechner R. (2007), *Anna Halprin: Experience as Dance*, Berkeley, CA: University of California Press.
Ross, J. (2007), 'Anna Halprin: Dancing Eros at the End of Life', in N. Nakajima and G. Brandstetter (eds), *The Aging Body in Dance: A Cross-Cultural Perspective*, 137–48, London: Routledge.
Rothschild, B. (2000), *The Body Remembers*, New York: W.W. Norton.
Rottenberg, H. (2011), 'Ohad Naharin', in M. Bremser and L. Saunders (eds), *50 Contemporary Choreographers*, 2nd ed., 291–7, London: Routledge.
Rubin, J. (1998), *A Psychoanalysis for Our Time*, New York: New York University Press.
Sacks, A. (1993), 'ARTS / Show People: Dance Rebel Without a Corps: 66. Emilyn Claid', *Independent*, 28 February. Available online: https://www.independent.co.uk/arts-entertainment/arts-show-people-dance-rebel-without-a-corps-66-emilyn-claid-1475907.html (accessed May 2020).
Schneider, R. (1997), *The Explicit Body in Performance*, London: Routledge.
Schweiger, E. (2012), *Ageing, Gender, Embodiment and Dance: Finding a Balance*, New York: Palgrave Macmillan.
Sedgwick, E.K. (2009), 'Shame, Theatricality, and Queer Performativity', in D. Halperin and V. Traub (eds), *Gay Shame*, 49–62, Chicago: University of Chicago Press.
Servos N. (2008), *Pina Bausch: Dance Theatre*, Munich: K. Kieser Verlag.
Siddall, C. (1976–7), 'Bodies in Contact', *CQ/CI Sourcebook*, 2: 12.

Siegel, D., (1999), *The Developing Mind*, New York: Guilford Press.
Sharrocks, A. (2013), 'An Anatomy of Falling', *Performance Research*, 18 (4): 48–55.
Sheets-Johnstone, M. (1999), *The Primacy of Movement*, Philadelphia: John Benjamins.
Smith, N.S. (1983–4), 'Editor's note', *CQ/CI Sourcebook*, 9: 91.
Smith, S. ([1957] 1972), 'Not Waving but Drowning', in *Collective Poems of Stevie Smith*, New York: New Directions Publishing Corporation.
Snæbjörnsdóttir, B. and M. Wilson (2010), 'Falling Asleep with a Pig' [interview with Kira O'Reilly], *Antennae: The Journal of Nature in Visual Culture*, 13: 38–48.
Soden, G. (2003), *Falling: How Our Greatest Fear Became Our Greatest Thrill*, New York: W.W. Norton.
Sousa Lobo, F. (2013), 'Theology After Bas Jan Ader', *Performance Research*, 18 (4): 69–72.
Spångberg, M. (2017), 'Introduction', in D. Andersson, M. Edvardsen and M. Spångberg (eds), *Post-Dance*, 18–28, Stockholm: MDT.
Spengler, O. (1922), *Decline of the West*, Munich: C.H. Beck.
Staemmler, F. (2012), *Empathy in Psychotherapy*, New York: Springer Publishing.
Stanley, S. (2012), *Failure Theatre: An Artist's Statement*, MA diss., Graduate Program in Cultural Studies, Queens University, Kingston, Ontario.
Stern, D. (1998), *The Interpersonal World of the Infant*, New York: Perseus Books.
Stern, D. (2010), *Forms of Vitality: Exploring Dynamic Experience in Psychology, the Arts, Psychotherapy, and Development*, Oxford: Oxford University Press.
Steyerl, H. (2011), 'In Free Fall: A Thought Experiment on Vertical Perspective', *e-Flux Journal*, April: 1–11.
Streb, E. (2010), *How to Become an Action Hero*, New York: Feminist Press.
Stolorow, R. and G.E. Atwood (1992), *Contexts of Being: The Intersubjective Foundations of Psychological Life*, Hillsdale, NJ: Analyatic Press.
Sufrin, M. (1987), 'The Silent World of Slapstick (1912–1916)', *The Threepenny Review*, 29: 21.
Taylor, M. (2014), *Trauma Therapy and Clinical Practice: Neuroscience, Gestalt and the Body*, Maidenhead: Open University Press.
Thomas, D. ([1947] 1971) 'Do Not Go Gentle into That Good Night', in *The Poems of Dylan Thomas*, New York: New Directions.
Todd, M.E. (1977a), *Early Writings 1920–1934*, New York: Dance Horizons.
Todd, M.E. ([1937] 1977b), *The Thinking Body*, New York: Dance Horizons.
Tufnell, M. (1978), *Dancing Without Steps*, [Documentary], dir. M. Tufnell and C. Crickmay, Arts & Environment, Open University.
van Deurzen, E. and Arnold-Baker, C. (2005), *Existential Perspectives on Human Issues*, Basingstoke: Palgrave.
Verwoert, J. (2006), *Bas Jan Ader: In Search of the Miraculous*, London: Afterall Books.
Walls, G. (2004), 'Toward a Critical Global Psychoanalysis' *Psychoanalytic Dialogues*, 14 (5): 605–34.
Watson, K. (1996), 'Aim for the Head. Go for the Gut', *Dance Now*, Summer: 24–26.
Watts, G. (2015), 'Wendy Houstoun and the Stupid Women', *DanceTabs.com*, 29 September. Available online: https://dancetabs.com/2015/09/wendy-houstoun-and-the-stupid-women-stupid-women-london/ (accessed May 2020).

Weeks, K. (2011), *The Problem with Work: Feminism, Marxism, Antiwork Politics, and Postwork Imaginaries*, Durham, NC: Duke University Press.

Weitz, E. (2012), 'Failure as Success: On Clowns and Laughing Bodies', *Performance Research*, 17 (1): 79–87.

Wheeler G. (1997), 'Self and Shame', in G. Wheeler and R. Lee (eds), *The Voice of Shame: Silence and Connection in Psychotherapy*, 23–57, Gouldsboro: Gestalt Press.

Williams, B. (1993), *Shame and Necessity*, Berkeley, CA: University of California Press.

Winship, L. (2015a), 'Wendy Houstoun, dance review: Houstoun, We Have a Problem', *Evening Standard*, 28 September. Available online: https://www.standard.co.uk/go/london/theatre/wendy-houstoun-dance-review-houstoun-we-have-a-problem-a2957031.html (accessed May 2020).

Winship, L. (2015b), 'Interview: Wim Vandekeybus – On What the Body Does Not Remember', *Londondance.com,* 29 January. Available online: http://londondance.com/articles/features.ultima-vez-wim-vandekeybus/ (accessed June 2018)

Wolfs, R. (2006), *Bas Jan Ader: Please Don't Leave Me*, Rotterdam: Museum Boijmans Van Beuningen.

Woodward, K. (2006), 'Performing Age, Performing Gender', *Feminist Formations,* 18 (1): 162–89.

Worth, L. and Poyner, H. (2004), *Anna Halprin,* London: Routledge.

Zaccarini, J. (2018), *Falling: The Thought of Circus,* Stockholm: Stockholm University of the Arts.

INDEX

A Separation (2014), 69–71
Absolutely Fabulous (1992), 150–1
accidental falling, 95–6, 111, 121, 132
   See also Celeste Dandeker; Kate Lawrence; Juku Sankai
Acocella, Joan, 149
Across Your Heart (1996), 144–6
Ader, Bas Jan, 7, 45–6, 150
aerial performance, 117–20, 134–5, 137
   ropes and equipment, 111–13, 119–20, 123, 133–5
   somatics and, 119–20
   vertical choreography, 135
   See also Trisha Brown; Lindsey Butcher; Kate Lawrence; Elizabeth Streb; thrills; John-Paul Zaccarini
ageing, 10–11
   being with, 11, 34–5, 183, 186
   and falling, 33, 35–6, 105–7, 127
   memory and, 183–6
   resisting, 108–10
   and somatic research, 33–5, 105–7
   stereotypes, 33–4, 170–2
   See also Jane Dudley; Anna Halprin; *Staging Ages*
ageism, 33
Agis, Gaby, 43, 44
Aikido, 16, 38–9
Airaudo, Malou, 49
Albright, Ann Cooper, 12, 15, 45 n.10, 115
Alexander, Frederick, 5 n.1, 25 n.3, 43
Allsopp, Ric, 15
Altman, Neil, 64
American Modern Dance, 3, 5, 30, 110
American Psycho (1991), 62
An Odd Couple (1965), 150

anatomical alignment, 5, 24, 43–4
   and Small Dance, 46–7
   See also Barbara Clark; Mabel Elsworth Todd
Anderson, Darren, 170–1
Anderson, Laurie, 142
apes, 122
Apter, Michael, 138
Aramphongphan, Paisid, 90–1
Arcade, Penny, 81
Arditti, Michael, 129 n.13
Arrangement (2014, 2019), 101–3
Art of Change: New Directions from China (2012), 113
Ashton, Frederick, 88
Audruckstanz, 48, 50

Baehr, Antonia, 54–5
Baggett, Helen, 144
Bailes, Sarah, 150
ballet, 66–7
   author's background, 14
   Graham technique, 22
   queer performers and, 84–7, 88–9, 90–2
   and shame, 14, 67–8
   somatics and, 44–5
barrel leap, 89
Bartlett, Neil, 82
basiphobia, 92–3, 116
Batsheva Dance Company, 35, 151
Bausch, Pina, 6, 48–9
BDSM (Bondage, Domination, Sadism, Masochism), 84, 86–7
Beckett, Samuel, 150
Béland, Marc, 89
Belgian Dance, 57–9
Benayoun, Robert, 149
Benjamin, Walter, 153

Bergson, Henri, 156
Berlant, Lauren, 13, 99
Bitch! Dyke! Faghag! Whore! (2012), 81
black identity, 10, 72, 76–7
    and falling, 82–3
    See also A Separation
Blake, William, 63
Blazing Saddles (1974), 70
Bloolips, 82
Blush (2002), 58
Bock, Frank, 35, 175
body mechanics, 5, 26, 27, 43–4
Body Mind Centring, 13, 31, 66 n.1
Born to Fly: Elizabeth Streb vs. Gravity (2014), 112
Bourne, Bette, 82
Bowery, Leigh, 91
Brennan, Mary, 68
Brexit, 11, 97
British Homeopathic Association, 18
British Royal Family, 73, 75
Broadway, Sue, 119
Broken Fall, Organic (1971), 46
Brown, Brené, 64
Brown, Trisha, 51, 111–12
Buckwalter, Elaine, 43–4, 47, 52
Burke, Alisdair, 52
Burrows, Jonathan, 7, 174
Burt, Ramsay, 167
Butcher, Lindsey, 12, 117–20
Butcher, Rosemary, 101
Butler, Judith, 13, 94

Café Müller (1978), 48–50
Camus, Albert, 173
Candoco Dance Company, 116, 120, 144
Cannonball Richards, 121
capitalism, 12, 28, 99, 174
    decline, 11–12, 99, 100
    markets, 7, 12
    productions values, 7, 12, 100
    See also cruel optimism; individualism
Carroll, Lewis, 127
Carver, Sonora, 121
Castle of Slow Death, The (1992), 120
Caught Falling (2008), 114

caught falling, 58, 129, 140, 141
    images, 16, 113, 114, 115–16
Cave of the Heart (1946), 30
Chaplin, Charlie, 149
Charmatz, Boris, 7
Charnock, Nigel, 13, 42, 52, 103–4, 127, 154–5, 158 n.5
    Newson, Lloyd and, 42, 127–31
    nihilism and, 155
    queer, 54, 104
Chesterton, Gilbert Keith, 156
Christianity, 20, 64, 156
Chute (1979) 41
Cinderella (1948), 87–9
    (1968), 88
circus, 12, 112, 123–4, 135, 139, 148–9
    See also pratfalls; thrills; John-Paul Zaccarini
Clark, Barbara, 5, 13, 25, 43, 126 n.11, 133
Clark, Michael, 91
Clarke, Gill, 45, 95, 119, 175 n.12
clause, 28, 128
Cohen, Bonnie Bainbridge, 13, 31
Contact Improvisation, 6, 38–41, 47, 130
    physical theatre and, 60–1
    race and, 77
    See also Steve Paxton; Nancy Stark Smith
Coogan, Amanda, 56
cool walk, 82–3
    See also Jason King
Coralli, Jean, 67
Covid-19, 11, 96–7, 186
Crafton, Donald, 149
Crickmay, Chris, 26
Croce, Arlene, 49
cruel optimism, 99
Cunningham, Merce, 38, 43
Cvetkovich, Ann, 81

dance marathons, 5, 177–8
dance spectacle, 7, 10, 68, 76, 92, 105
dance theatre, 6, 48–50, 58, 59–61, 68–9, 89–90, 127–30
Dance Umbrella, 91
Dance without Steps (1978), 26–7

Dancing Inside (1999), 11, 35
Dandeker, Celeste, 2, 116–17, 144–7
danger and falling, 1–2, 50, 69, 112–13, 121, 139
  See also circus; thrills
Darbyshire, Charlotte, 144
Darling Do You Love Me? (1968), 52–3
Dartington College of Arts, 26
Darzacq, Denis, 16, 114
Davis, Diane, 153
De Frantz, Thomas, 10, 70, 76–6, 103
De Mille, Agnes, 21, 22, 29, 109
De Vos, Joanna, 57
Dead dreams of Monochrome Men (1988, 1990), 42, 59–60
death, 59, 97, 180
  defying, 3, 13, 114, 122, 129–31
  drive, 13, 122, 124
  falling and, 1, 2, 58, 105
  Martha Graham, 108–9
  Wim Vandekeybus and, 57–9
  See also Bas Jan Ader; Nigel Charnock; Gill Clark; Covid-19; *Falling Man, The*; Yoshika Takada,
Death of a Loyalist Solder, The (1936), 115
Debord, Guy, 6
deep sea diving, 136–7
Deep Song (1937), 31
Deleuze, Gilles, 173
desire, 6, 49, 54, 124
  feminism and, 53–4
  queer, 13, 54, 86, 175
  shame and, 63, 81
developmental movements. 13, 37, 133
developmental psychology, 125
Diack, Heather, 150
Dilly, Barbara, 47
Dodgson, Sean, 171
Doehler, Laura, 171
drag, 55, 81, 87–9, 101
Drew, Richard, 115
Dudley, Jane, 11, 35–6
Dumbadze, Alexander, 45
DV8, 42, 59, 128
Dyer, Richard, 89
dying, 3, 4, 9, 15, 129, 180
  being with, 10–11, 33–5, 171, 183, 186
  for love, 54
  resistance to, 108–9
  with laughter, 164–5
  See also My Sex, Our Dance

Ellis, Bret Easton, 62
economic depression, 19, 178
Eddo-Lodge, Reni, 72
Edvardsen, Mette, 7, 174, 180–3
Ekman, Paul, 78 n.4
Ellis, Simon, 69–73, 79–80, 136–7
enlightenment, 28, 30, 122, 156
Eurocrash, 6, 68–9
Evel Knievel, 121
evoked companions, 126–7
exhaustion (with dance spectacle), 7, 12, 173, 175, 182
existentialism, 15, 32, 59, 176–7
  Samuel Beckett and, 150
  exhaustion, 155, 173–4
  nothingness, 32, 155, 182
  psychotherapy and, 1, 13, 32, 96
Extemporary Dance Theatre, 117, 119
extreme (X) sports, 12, 107, 121, 139

Fabre, Jan, 6, 57, 58
failure, 132, 150, 162–3
  being with, 15, 101, 132
  falling and, 15, 17, 19–20, 29, 57–8, 100–1, 124, 178–9
  queer, 13, 84, 88, 100, 103
  and shame, 14–15, 19–20, 29, 84, 88, 132, 178–9
falling, 1–187
  etymology, 20 n.1
  metaphor, 2, 4, 7, 15, 19–20, 56, 68, 149, 186
  and presence, 1, 3, 7, 11, 34, 69
  religion and, 19–20
  source of vitality, 1–2, 11, 34, 52, 148
  See also dying; laughter; shame
Falling About (2013), 16–17
falling tasks, 7–9
  practices, 31–2, 37–8, 51, 65–6, 78–9, 111, 140–1, 163–4, 179–80, 187

Falling Together, Falling About, Falling Apart (2014), 37
Fall (Christianity), 16, 20
fear of falling, 1, 2, 13
  conditional, 124–5
  and developmental psychology, 125
  instinctive, 124–5, 136
  neuroscience, 92
  as survival mechanism, 122
  and trauma, 2, 92, 106–7, 115–16, 123, 138–9
  See also basiphobia
feminism, 44, 53–4, 100, 127, 158
Fisher, Janine, 13, 138
Fisher, Jennifer, 15
Flying Low, 5, 8, 172–3
footwear, 141
  barefoot, 141
  high heels, 50, 141, 158
  See also Amy Sharrocks
Fox, Charlie, 15, 46
Frank, Ruella, 133
  and Frances La Barre, 13, 37

Gaga, 168–9
Gaye, Marvin, 82
Gendlin, Eugene, 184
Gibson, Eleanor and Richard Walk, 122 n.7
Gilfond, Henry, 31
Gillgren, Hanna, 170
Giselle (1841), 67, 84, 98
  falls, 67
Giselle, or I'm too Horny to be a Prince (2014), 84–7
Goat Island, 150
Goffman, Ervin, 79
Gottschild, Brenda Dixon, 73, 74, 77, 83
Graff, Ellen, 15, 22, 23, 30, 31
Graham falls, 15–16, 21–2, 29, 31, 36, 109, 179
Graham technique, 22, 31, 36
Graham, Martha, 21–2, 29–30, 108–10, 178
Gravity & Levity, 117, 119
Great Depression, 177–8
Great White Way, The (2009–9), 83

Greer, Germaine, 52–4
grief, 93–4, 179–80
Grosz, Elizabeth, 13, 29, 53, 54

H2Dance, 170
Hahnemann, Samuel, 18
Halberstam, Jack, 13, 100, 175
Hallett, Alyson, 20
Halperin, David and Valerie Traub, 13, 81
Halprin, Anna, 43, 165–6
Hamilton, Julyen, 34, 44
Hanna, Thomas, 5, 13, 33–4, 106–7
Hargreaves, Martin, 164, 165
Harvey, Mark, 37
Head (2018), 123
Heathfield, Adrian, 7
  dance theatre and, 48–50
Hell Bent (1994), 104
Heretic (1929), 31
Herko, Fred, 90–1
heroism undone, 152
  See also Bas Jan Ader; Joe Moran; Ohad Naharin
High Line, 62
Hinton, David, 42
HIV, 43, 128–9, 131
Hoff, Johanne, 16
Hollis, Frances, 16
homeopathy, 18
Hominal, Marie-Caroline, 167
Houdini, Harry, 121
Houston-Jones, Ishmael, 77, 103
Houstoun, Wendy, 10, 34, 157–63
How to Become an Action Hero (2010), 112
Howard, TC, 157–62
Hrab, Ondřej, 58
Human Being (1999), 104
Human Sex (1985), 89–90
Humphrey, Doris, 5 n.2, 30
Hunter, Cora Belle, 43
Huxley, Mike, 25 n.3

I'm Too Sad to Tell You (1971), 46
ideokinesis, 5, 23, 26
impasse, 100
In Just a Blink of an Eye (2005/2012), 113, 114

individualism, 12, 28, 29, 153
    and Martha Graham, 30–1
infants, 125–7, 133
    See also Falling Together, Falling About, Falling Apart (2014); Moro Reflex
Innes, David, 156
intentional falling, 2–3, 7–9, 16, 18, 100, 111, 179
    See also Falling About (2013); Falling Tasks
Irigaray, Luce, 29
Irving, Debbie, 10
Irwin, Bill, 148

Jacobs, Lynne, 75, 96
    and Richard Hycner, 164
James, Catherine, 15
Jenkins, Clive, 167
Jeschke, Claudia and Gabi Vettermann, 48
Jill and Freddie Dancing (1963), 91
Johnson, Kwesi, 144
Judson Church, 7, 90, 165

Karkov, Vicky, Sue Oliver and Sophia Lycouris, 13
Keaton, Buster, 149–50
King, Jason, 10, 82–4
Kinkaleri, 176–7
Klein, Yves, 56, 114
Kleinman, Gillie, 12
Knezevic, Barbara, 56
Koteen, David and Nancy Stark Smith, 30, 40, 47, 114
Kövecses, Zoltán, 9, 19
Kraanerg (1969), 14
Kristeva, Julia, 29, 153

La Chute (2006), 114
La Ribot, 101, 164–5, 167–8
Lacey, Gillian, 11, 35–6
Laermans, Rudi and Pascal Gielen, 6, 57
Lakoff, George and Mark Johnson, 7, 19
Lalitaraja, 16
Lansley, Jacky, 26 n.4, 158
Laughing Hole (2006), 167, 168

laughter, 3, 4, 17, 88, 103, 152–4
    as choreography, 54–6, 164–5, 167–8
    corpsing, 153, 165
    and shame, 155–7
    See also Antonia Baehr; La Ribot; pratfalls; *Stupid Women*
Lawrence, Kate, 12, 133–5
Le Corsaire (1856), 86
Leap into the Void (1960), 56, 114
Leask, Josephine, 131
Lecavalier, Louise, 89–90
Lee, Rosemary, 95
Lepecki, Andre, 6, 12, 15, 83, 164
Lepkoff, Danny, 40
Levine, Peter, 13
Lily, Peta, 16
limbic system, 92, 93, 138, 139
Limbrick, Simon, 16
Limón, José, 16
live art, 7, 45–6, 56–7, 113–14, 141, 150
Lloyd, Harold, 15, 149
Lobo, Francisco Sousa, 15, 45
Lock, Édouard, 89
loss
    and falling, 6, 49, 115, 171, 179–80
    being with, 94
Low, Stephen, 90
Lumley, Joanna, 150
Lyall, Sarah, 75

Mackintosh, Peri, 16, 78
Mackrell, Judith, 57, 91
MacMillan, Kenneth, 88
Malin, Victoria, 157–8
Maliphant, Russell, 42, 60
Man Walking Down the Side of a Building (1970), 111–13
Marina Abramovich presents . . . (2009), 56
Marini, Hari, 15
Markle, Meghan and Prince Harry, 74–5
Marley, Bob, 82
Martin, Carol, 177–8
Martin, Susanne, 11, 33, 34
Matt, Pamela, 25, 66, 75, 126 n.11
Meltdown (2011), 95
memory, 183–5
    loss of, 105–7

sensory-motor amnesia, 106
  See also RIG
Mercier, Joseph, 13, 84–7
Mercy, Dominique, 49
Mesmer, Annie, 157
metaphor, 2, 7, 9, 11, 19–20
  ageing, 10, 33–4
  falling, 4, 15, 19, 115, 143, 186
  laughter, 10
  shame, 9, 63
Minarik, Jan, 49
Ministry of Utmost Happiness, The (2017), 162
Moran, Caitlin, 151
Moran, Joe, 13, 43, 44, 101–3
Moro, Ernst, 133
Morrish, Andrew, 34
Move, Richard, 110 n.3
Mr. Gaga (2016), 151
Muñoz, José, 101, 103
Murphy, Eddie, 83
My Sex, Our Dance (1986), 127–31
Myth of Sisyphus, The (1942), 173

Naharin, Ohad, 151–2, 169
Nakajima, Nanako, 10
National Ballet of Canada, 88
Nauman, Bruce, 150
Nelson, Lisa, 41
Nelson, Robin, 11
neo-liberalism, 7, 12, 174
New York Poets Theatre, 92
Newson, Lloyd, 6, 42–3, 59–60, 127–9
'nigger', use of term, 69–71, 80
Night Journey (1947), 23 n.2, 30
nihilism, 43, 154–5
Nilsen, Dennis, 42–3
9/11, 92–4, 115–16
No Title (2014), 180–3
Not Waving but Drowning (1957), 168
nothingness, *see* existentialism
Novack, Cynthia, 39

O'Gormon, Roisin and Margaret Werry, 132
O'Reilly, Kira, 7, 56–7
Ogden, Pat, 13, 138
Olsen, Andrea, 31, 66, 75, 111

One Dixon Road (2010), 154–5
One Week (1920), 149
Orange, Donna, 64, 65, 93
Original Sin (1993), 103–4
Osborne, Lynda and Emilyn Claid, 9
Oxford Book of Dance and Wellbeing, The (2017), 13

Pact with Pointlessness (2014), 160
pain, of falling, 1, 2, 19, 68–9, 96, 106–7, 125, 179
Paludan, Marsha, 25, 43
Parkinson, Lea, 120
Parry, Jan, 68
Parviainen, Jaana, 184
Passing Through, 5, 172–3
Pawlouski, Mauro, Peter VerHelst and David Byrne, 58, 59
Paxton, Steve, 6, 16, 38, 47, 60, 114
Performance Research: On Failure (2012), 132 n.15
Performance Research: On Falling (2013), 15
Perls, Fritz, 13, 32
Petit, Philippe, 121
Petronio, Steve, 41
Phelan, Peggy, 112
physical theatre, 60–1
  See also Nigel Charnock; Dance Theatre; DV8
Piezas Distinguidas (1993–2003), 164
Pite, Crystal, 74
Plevin, Marcia, 75
plumb line, 65–6
Pook, Jocelyn, 35
Poole, Colin, 10, 69–72
Pope, L., 10, 83
Post-Dance (2017), 174
post-dance, 3, 7, 10, 182
potency, of falling, 7, 18, 51
  homeopathic, 18, 100
Povinelli, Daniel and John Cant, 122
Power of Theatrical Madness, The (1984), 57
Pozorski, Aimee, 115
pratfalls, 10, 148–51, 157, 163
  clowning, 148
  See also Absolutely Fabulous; Buster Keaton; Bruce Nauman

Prickett, Stacey, 30
Probyn, Elspeth, 13
prosperity, 99
Proust, Marcel, 185
Pryor, Richard, 83
psychoanalysis, 28–9, 53–4, 64, 122, 124
psychotherapy, 8, 96, 163
 and somatics, 13, 14, 75, 133
 See also shame; trauma

queer, 13, 80–2, 90, 100
 ballet and, 84–7, 87–9
 desire, 13, 54, 86, 175
 See also Nigel Charnock; Fred Herko; Joseph Mercier, Joe Moran
Queer Art of Failure, The (2011), 100
queer shame, 13, 80–2, 84–7, 88–9, 91
 and ballet, 87–9
Quinlan, Megan, 152

Ra Ra Zoo, 119
racism, 72, 70–3, 79, 98
 and ballet, 74
 and somatics, 75–7
 See also white shame
Rage of Staging (2016), 59
Rainer, Yvonne, 92, 166–7
Rajan, Amol, 99
relational falling, 9, 14, 17, 78–9, 96, 179–80
release technique, 5, 6, 25, 43–4, 47
 dance fashion, 51–2
 See also Joan Skinner
Remembrance of Things Past (1913), 185
Resurrection (1991), 103
Returning Home (2003), 11, 166
Ridout, Nicholas, 55, 153, 165
RIG (representation of an interaction that has been internalized) 126–7
Riley, Bridget, 108
Rire/Laugh/Lachen (2008), 54
rock climbing, 133–5
Rolland, John, 25, 43
Rollerskate (1963), 91

rolling, 26–7, 39, 126
Rosay, Delphine, 167
Ross, Janice, 166
 and Richard Schechner, 166
Rothschild, Babette, 13, 116
Rottenberg, Henia, 169
Roubal, Jan, 163
Roy, Arundhati, 162
Royal Ballet, 73, 74, 88
Rubin, Jeffrey, 28, 29
Rustgaard, Heidi, 170

Sachsenmaier, Stefanie, 16
Sacks, Anne, 34
Sambé, Marcelino, 74
Sankai Juku, 105
Sarab, 135
Saunders, Jennifer, 150
Schweiger, Elizabeth, 34
Scott, Caroline, 119
Sedgwick, Eve, 81, 82
Sentler, Susan, 16
Servos, Norbert, 6, 48
shame, 3–4, 63–4, 93–4
 ballet, 67
 failure, 14–15, 29, 106, 132, 178–9
 metaphor, 9, 11, 19–20
 racism, 10, 72, 73, 83
 relational, 64–5, 127, 132, 157
 See also white shame
Sharp, Martin and Martin Whitaker, 52
Sharrocks, Amy, 15, 16, 56, 141
Sheets-Johnstone, Maxine, 184
Shipwreck Kelly, 121
Sholiba (1979), 105
Shunk, Harry and Janos Kender, 114
Siddall, Curt, 41
Siegel, Dan, 138
Simson, Kirstie, 34, 44
Singh-Barmi, Kuldip, 144, 146
Siobhan Davis Dance Studios, 16, 157 n.4, 174–5
skateboard riders, 107–8
Skinner, Joan, 25, 43
sky diving, 117, 119
SLAM (Streb lab for Action Mechanics), 112

Small Dance, 16, 41, 46–8
smile, 78–9
Smith, Phil, 20
Smith, Stevie, 168
Smith, Sue, 144
Social Darwinism, 28
Soden, Garrett, 93, 107, 120, 121–3
somatic movement, 5, 13, 23–6, 27, 47
   ageing and, 106–7
   psychotherapy and, 75, 137
   racism and, 75–7
   See also plumb line; release technique
Spångberg, Mårten, 7, 174
Spengler, Oswald, 99
Square Dances (2011), 95
Staemmler, Frank, 78
Stages (1973), 116
Staging Ages (2015), 170–1, 183
standing, 24, 26, 37–8, 51, 140
   Dandeker, Celeste, 144–6
   See also Small Dance
Stanton, Erica, 16
Stark Smith, Nancy, 40, 47, 60, 114
Stern, Daniel, 79
Steyerl, Hito, 165
Still Angela (2002, 2004), 143
stillness, 47, 48, 51, 76–7, 182
Stolorow, Robert and George Atwood, 29
Stonewall riots, 81
Streb, Elizabeth, 12, 112–13
Stubblefield, Eeo, 166
Stupid Women (2015), 157–63
Sufrin, Mark, 149
suicide, 120
   See also Fred Herko; Lea Parkinson
supremacy, white, 29, 72–7, 95
surrender, to gravity, 2, 16, 18, 41, 68–9, 111, 114, 179
swivel walker, 144–6

Takada, Yoshiyuki, 105
Tamir, Maya, 151–2
Tankard, Meryl, 50
Tanztheatre, 48
Taylor, Miriam, 92, 93, 116, 137, 138
Them (1985), 77, 103
Thinking Body, The (1937), 24

Thomas, Dylan, 108, 110
thrill, 12, 13, 121, 139
Time to Fall (2013), 141
Times Square Crawl (1978), 83
Todd, Mabel Elsworth, 5, 23–6, 44, 75–6
Tompkins Square (1991), 83
Topf, Nancy, 25, 43, 47, 52
trauma, 8, 92–3, 106, 115–16, 123, 137–9
   See also fear of falling
Trump, Donald, 62
Tufnell, Miranda, 26–7, 44

uncertainty, economic, 7, 12–13
   being with, 2, 52, 100–1
Ultima Vez, 57, 193

V-Tol Dance Company, 120
Van Deurzen, Emmy and Claire Arnold-Baker, 32, 96
Vandekeybus, Wim, 6, 57–9, 68
vertical choreography, 134–5
verticality, 17, 19–20, 75–6, 83
   in ballet, 45, 59, 60, 66–7, 73–4
   individualism, 28–9
   stiff upper lip, 73
   transcendence, 34, 73
Verwoert, Jan, 45
Virginia Minx at Play (1992), 34
voguing drop, 84
void, 32, 92, 155, 174
   See also existentialism; WEST

walking, barefoot, 141
   on sand, 142–4
Walls, Gary, 28
Warhol, Andy, 91
Watson, Keith, 69
Weeks, Kathi, 12
Weitz, Eric, 148
WEST (2009), 176
Western decline, 11, 12, 99, 100
What Now (2014), 174–5
What the Body Does Not Remember (1987), 58
Wheeler, Gordon, 29, 64
When the Moon Rises (1988), 119
white privilege, 9, 12, 63, 73–4, 80

white shame, 9, 10, 64, 72–3, 75, 76–7, 80
  somatics and, 75–6
  See also Lynne Jacobs
Wigman, Mary, 48
Williams, Bernard, 63
window of tolerance, 138–40
Winship, Lindsey, 58, 162
Wolfs, Rein, 45
Women in Performance: A Journal of Feminist Theory (2004), 15

Woodward, Kathleen, 33
Worth, Libby and Helen Pyner, 166
Wright, Douglas, 42

X6 Dance Space, 26, 27, 44, 45, 175, 184
Xu Zhen, 113–14

Zaccarini, John-Paul, 12, 123–4, 139
Zambrano, David, 5, 172

www.ingramcontent.com/pod-product-compliance
Lightning Source LLC
Chambersburg PA
CBHW072235290426
44111CB00012B/2103